Katie Hickman

is the author of the highly acclaimed and best-selling *Daughters of Britannia: The Lives and Times of Diplomatic Wives*, first published in 1999. She is also the author of *The Quetzal Summer*, a novel set in the Andes, for which she was short-listed for the 1993 *Sunday Times* Young Writer of the Year Award, and *Dreams of the Peaceful Dragon* (1987), a travel book about a two-month journey on horseback across the forbidden Himalayan Kingdom of Bhutan. *Travels with a Circus*, her third book, was originally published as *A Trip to the Light Fantastic: Travels with a Mexican Circus*. It was one of the *Independent on Sunday*'s 1993 Books of the Year, and was short-listed for the 1994 Thomas Cook Travel Book Award.

Katie Hickman is featured in the Oxford University Press guide to women travellers, *Wayward Women*. She has one son from her previous marriage to Tom Owen Edmunds, and one daughter by her partner, the philosopher A. C. Grayling.

KATIE HICKMAN

Travels with a Circus

Flamingo
An Imprint of HarperCollins*Publishers*

Flamingo
An Imprint of HarperCollins*Publishers*
77–85 Fulham Palace Road,
Hammersmith, London W6 8JB

www.fireandwater.com

Published by Flamingo 2001

9 8 7 6 5 4 3 2 1

First published in Great Britain by
HarperCollins*Publishers* 1993 under the title
A Trip to the Light Fantastic: Travels with a Mexican Circus

Author photograph by Tom Owen Edmunds

All photographs in this book © Tom Owen Edmunds 1993

ISBN 0 00 710899 0

Set in Linotron Sabon

Printed and bound in Great Britain by
Omnia Books Ltd

This book is for my parents,
who first taught me the
humility of travel

ACKNOWLEDGEMENTS

In Mexico, we received great kindness and hospitality from many people all over the country. In Mexico City I would particularly like to thank Gonzalo and Lolita Robles, for all their advice and general cosseting (and several kilos of anchovy-stuffed olives); and also Victor Flores Olea at the Arts Ministry and Gabriela Chavez Morales at the Ministry of Tourism. Elsewhere in Mexico my thanks go to Edelmiro Ponce de León, Tte Hugo Navarro and David Spilsbury in Chihuahua, Temo and Chayito Perez in Jalisco, Padre Miguel and Antonio Chankin in Chiapas, and to Juan Andrade Nieves, and Pedro and Victor, for helping us get to Jesús María for the Cora's Easter.

In the UK I am indebted to the Mexican Ambassador, H. E. Bernardo Sepulveda for his kind advice, and to Alicia Cazorla at the Mexican Ministry of Tourism. Thanks also to Michael Fishwick, Richard Wheaton, Andrew Evans and Laura Jennings at HarperCollins, to Sir John and Lady Morgan for passing on so much of their invaluable local knowledge, to my parents John and Jenny Hickman, to Conrad Bird and Sophie Cottrell, and to James Heneage of Ottakar's Books. This book was partly written in the houses of my extremely kind and long-suffering friends: a big thank you as always to Beatrice and James Hollond, Jeremy Drax, and special gold stars for William Sieghart and for Rose Baring and Barnaby Rogerson who were brave enough to lend us their flats for months at a time while they were abroad. I am also indebted to Chris Parrott at Journey Latin America for generously providing us with our flights to Mexico.

My greatest thank you of all, of course, must go to all my very dear *compadres* and friends at Circo Bell's, for kindnesses too numerous to mention, without whom this book would never have been written. And last but not least I would like to pay special tribute to my husband, Tom Owen Edmunds, best and bravest of companions, who in ten years of travelling has never once allowed the word 'impossible' to enter his vocabulary.

CIRCO BELL'S
THE CAST

Bell's Family

Doña Elena .... The matriarch, founder of the circus

Mundo (Doña Elena's eldest son) .... clown, trapeze artist, and circus's artistic director
Carmen (Mundo's wife)
Ricky (Mundo & Carmen's eldest son) .... trapeze artist and elephant trainer
Pamela (Mundo & Carmen's eldest daughter) .... dancer and *bastonera*
Augustin (Mundo & Carmen's youngest son) .... Tintin the clown
Lely (Mundo & Carmen's youngest daughter) .... clown

Rolando (Doña Elena's son) .... impresario
Vicky (Rolando's wife)
Mara (Rolando & Vicky's eldest daughter) .... contortionist and aerial ballet artist
Gordo (Rolando & Vicky's eldest son) .... trapeze artist and elephant trainer
Olinda (Rolando's second daughter) .... dancer and *bastonera*
Belén (Rolando's third daughter)

Jorge (Doña Elena's son)

Rosalinda (Doña Elena's daughter) .... the telepathic profesora
Juan (Rosalinda's husband) .... circus photographer
Brissel (Rosalinda & Juan's daughter) .... dancer and *bastonera*

Karina (daughter of Victor, Doña Elena's deceased son) .... dancer and *bastonera*
Vanessa (Karina's sister) .... dancer

The Performers

Antonino .... equilibrium (balancing act)
Olga .... dancing girl
Omar (Mara's boyfriend) .... mime artist
Ramón .... clown and monocycles
Gallo (Karino's boyfriend) .... ringmaster
Charlie (Vanessa's boyfriend) .... clown and monocycles
Yvonne .... tightrope walker
Susu and Taynari (Yvonne's children)

Martinelli .... juggler
Teresa (Martinelli's girlfriend)
Anna (Teresa's sister)

The Chamacos (stage hands)
Jovita .... wardrobe mistress
Luis .... elephant keeper
Maria Magdalena (Luis's wife)
Jacaira and Lupita (Luis and Maria Magdalena's children)
Chillón .... foreman
Güera (Chillón's wife) .... ticket seller
Alejandro and Gabriela (Chillón and Güera's children)
Sylvia (Chillón's sister) .... popcorn seller
Chino (Sylvia's boyfriend) .... circus hand
Ilish (Olga's boyfriend) .... circus hand
José Jaime .... circus hand
Veronica (José Jaime's girlfriend)
José Jaime Jnr (José Jaime and Veronica's child)
Gato .... soundman
Chivo .... driver

But what many forget, in disguising themselves
as cheap magicians, is that the marvellous becomes
unequivocally marvellous when it arises from an
unexpected alteration of reality (a miracle), a
privileged revelation of reality, an unaccustomed
or singularly favourable illumination of the
previously unremarked riches of reality, an
amplification of the measures and categories of
reality, perceived with peculiar intensity due to
an exaltation of the spirit which elevates it to
a kind of 'limit state' . . .

. . . what is the history of America, if not a
chronicle of the marvellous in the real?
ALEJO CARPENTIER, El Reino de este Mundo

ONE

'Mexico? You will see marvels,' she said with a
look of illumination.

SYBILLE BEDFORD, *A Visit to Don Otavio*

Karina's first memory is of Niña.

Niña was pink. Not a dull, fleshy hue, as you might have
expected, but a brilliant, quixotic pink, the colour of a fuchsia.
Her underbelly was grass blue, like the sea. I remember Karina
telling me how she used to wake up in the night to feel the solid
weight of Niña pressing down on her shoulders, her neck coiled
around Karina's neck, her little head tucked behind her hair where
it was warmest. When she was hungry she would hiss softly into
Karina's ear to wake her up.

Karina remembers the day her father brought Niña home. He
had been given her as a present by a friend in another circus and
brought her back wrapped in a paper bag. At first Karina and her
sister Vanessa thought it was a puppy and were surprised to find
in its place a fuchsia-pink boa constrictor curled up, small and
snug, at the bottom of the bag.

Despite having a boa constrictor as a pet, by circus standards
Karina's childhood was a normal one. Her mother the magician, a
flame-haired illusionist from Ecuador, spent most of her daughter's
childhood sawing her in half, cutting off her head, dematerializing
her in and out of a crystal box. She was only two the first time
she became part of the act. They made her a tiny bikini, no bigger
than a pocket handkerchief, and in December a red hat like Father
Christmas, trimmed with white fur.

Niña lived with them in their caravan, along with a cage of
ornamental doves, decorative but empty-headed, which Karina's

mother also used in her magic act. They fed her on live rats, chicks and baby ducks, and found her to be an elegant and considerate eater, never leaving so much as the tiniest of bones behind. Once when she was left alone in the trailer she broke into the dove cage, and the family came back to find no evidence of her gargantuan feast except, in a corner under the bed, a pile of soft damp feathers.

Niña was in the habit of changing her colours frequently and would also occasionally shed her skin, sliding it from her with composure, like an evening glove. Karina's mother kept the skins and hung them on the walls of their trailer as decoration.

But it was Karina's father who Niña always loved the most. Whenever she heard his voice she would climb up to the window and look out hopefully, her tongue flickering with anticipation. When she died the whole family cried and things were never quite the same again.

But all this was long ago. When I knew Karina she was an orphan, like so many of the circus children; her father dead, her mother remarried and emigrated to the States, having spirited herself away from the circus world as suddenly as she had entered it.

Karina was my first friend in the circus. Gawky, awkward, mercurial in her tempers, she got her long legs and her splendid rounded bottom from her mother. All the circus girls envied Karina her bottom and wished that they could have one too – Mexican men, it seemed, were partial to them, and why else would they go to the circus other than to see a pretty girl? She lived with her sister Vanessa in a caravan filled to overflowing with the detritus of circus and adolescent girlhood – drying knickers and spilt makeup, a *bastonera* outfit (always grubby with half the sequins hanging off), dirty saucepans, teddy bears, dolls and broken cassette boxes. Two sulky girls, always in love.

'The story of the circus is a tragic one,' my friend Rolando Bell's, the impresario, used to say to me. 'You must write about the sad things; it is important that you do. No one can understand the circus without them. But if you should ever write anything untrue about us,' he would smile, waving his perfumed hands at me, 'I will come to England myself and I will kill you.'

The circus. My circus. Circo Bell's. EL CIRCO MÁS FAMOSO EN TODO LAS AMÉRICAS.

In the old days, I can hear Doña Elena, the matriarch, tell me, there were no caravans and no trucks. The circus travelled everywhere by mule. In those days it was the priests who decided whether or not the villagers went to see the shows. *'No piensen que van a ir al circo a ver piernas,'* they would thunder from the pulpit at mass on Sunday. 'Don't any of you imagine you are going to the circus to see legs. The Virgin of the Carmen needs a new petticoat and so on your way out all of you are going to put the money which you were thinking of spending on circus tickets into her collection box instead.'

It was not easy to move between the villages. The circus moved slowly, dragging itself across the mountains like a Leviathan. They slept wherever they could, piecemeal, on the ground, in people's houses. But although Doña Elena and her sisters were circus girls, slept rough, and from an early age had often showed their legs, they were brought up like good Catholics. On Sundays they went to Mass, wearing their hats and gloves.

Once day, she remembers, when they heard the priest forbidding his congregation to go to the circus, they came home crying to their mother. 'Whatever shall we do? What are we going to eat? Where are we going to sleep', they wept, 'if the priests keep on forbidding the villagers to come and see us in this way?'

Their mother, who was a resourceful woman, took one look at them and went to pay the priest a visit.

'Do you remember those little girls sitting in the front row at Mass today, so respectable, all in their hats and gloves?' she asked him. The priest said he did. *'Padre,* do you know what you have done today? You have taken the very bread from their mouths, the poor babes.'

When she had finished, the priest went to the church and rang the bell so loudly that the whole village came running to the plaza in alarm. Glaring down at them from the top ⊾ he church steps, he told them about Doña Elena and her sisters.

'So the Virgin of the Carmen's petticoat will have to wait. You're to go to the circus tonight, all of you. And if I catch anybody skiving, they'll have me to reckon with. I'll be there myself, so mind you're all on time.'

In Mexico, nothing is set in stone. The absence of black or white at first alarms, but it can liberate, too.

Which is stranger: that a woman should saw her daughter in half for a living, or that a Catholic priest should change his mind?

When I was in Mexico I learnt many things. Magic is not tricks. Magic, most often, is to be found in ordinary things. It is landscape, and myth, and the telling of stories. Magic is what you believe.

Tom and I were living in Mexico City when we finally found our circus. It was September and the Mexicans were preparing for Independence Day. In the old part of town, near the *zócalo*[1], everything was red, white and green, even the food. In the *loncheria* around the corner where we ate breakfast every day our fried eggs came with a side order of bright green jelly; at lunchtime in the Café Tacuba we were served green rice garnished with scarlet pomegranate seeds.

The hotel we lived in, sandwiched between the lottery-ticket vendors and a shop selling ornamental doves, was in Calle Uruguay. Humboldt once lived in this street, in the days when it was still possible for him to call Mexico City the most beautiful city in the world. Even when we were there it was a street of old and beautiful palaces, if you had the eyes to see them, although their stucco had long since crumbled, their baroque stonework blackened and arthritic with age. In keeping with the flavour of the rest of the street, the Hotel Monte Carlo was at once very grand and very cheap. The only way to get to its parking lots was to drive your car right in through the front door, past the reception desk and across the marble-floored foyer. Soap operas – *La Fuerza de Amor* or *Mi Pequeña Soledad* – flickered day and night on a TV screen which was placed beneath a sweep of extravagant stairs like something from a Ginger Rogers film. Wild cats played skittishly in between the potted palms.

Mexico City smells of drains, unalleviated, as in eastern lands, by the aromas of blossom or of fruit. It is a city for which I have always had an unexpected affection.

[1] *zócalo*: plaza or main square.

4

In the old quarter, streets lead off from the *zócalo* in rings of concentric circles, so that at first it appears easy to find your way around. Our circle, the known world of the beggar on the corner selling individual safety pins, Humboldt's house, and the Zapotec Indian woman who each morning laid a square of pavement with a carpet of fresh herbs – rosemary and thyme and *hierba luisa* – was at first confined to the very smallest of rings, no more than a block or two from the *zócalo* itself.

In the old quarter you can buy everything known under the sun: Christmas decorations, car exhausts, calendars and party invitations; bridal shops with their wax orange blossom and rhinestone tiaras; shops selling nothing but rosaries and religious artifacts of the most arcane and grisly varieties. There were streets given over to the lottery-ticket sellers, to tailor shops, musical instruments, *piñatas*, party hats and fifteenth-birthday party mementos. Down side alleys you could find purveyors of priests' vestments, naughty knickers, herbs, spells and lucky charms; and on street stalls the juice of melons, the flesh of guayabas and strawberries; tacos *al pastor*, whole roast chickens and re-fried beans. And, even amongst the very poor, music is everywhere: mariachi bands and marimbas, mambos and merengue, cumbia, salsa, and cha-cha-cha.

And yet sometimes I would have the feeling that all this exuberance was just a front. Mexico City may wear its heart on its sleeve, but its soul is another matter. The houses behind the shop fronts are unexplained places. Some, like Humboldt's house, were palaces once. But who knows who lives there now? When I walk these streets I am aware that I see everything, and nothing. From the street I look up and see a light in a window. I see a bare bulb hanging from the ceiling; the walls, distempered to a flaking green, are naked. Perhaps I can just see the top half of some battered old wardrobe, but I can only guess at what is kept inside it, at the bed beneath, the sagging mattress, the damp and musty blankets; at the lovers, their limbs entwined, betrayed against the pillows.

Often in Mexico what I see most vividly are the things I cannot see. These are strange, dislocated images. A patio, half-glimpsed through a curtain, or a door left carelessly ajar. A flash of green. A flight of dark stairs. A saint's shrine, perhaps, lit gaudily with

5

coloured lights. And far away, at the end of some corridor, a column of sudden daylight.

It was the same with the circus. I did not know its name, I did not even know what part of Mexico they would be in, but I never doubted for a moment that I would find them. Long before I had ever set eyes on them, I had invented them in my own mind. They were a travelling circus, family owned and run, and specializing in all the traditional circus acts. They had clowns and acrobats and jugglers and dancing girls. They were also of a very specific size – the size was important – small enough to feel like a family, large enough to absorb us without upsetting the delicate equilibrium of their lives.

My only clue was a photograph, an old black and white photograph which I had found by chance in Belgrade, one summer before the civil war. I have this photograph beside me now as I write. It shows an ageing circus artiste, a woman, standing outside the shadowy backdrop of some kind of travelling tent. Although she is not dressed for the show, she is too old and fat for sequins these days, somehow the photographer has persuaded her to strike a pose. The woman raises one stout leg. She turns her throat, stretches out her arms. It is, in many ways, a cruel photograph, this varicosed old woman in her dusty widow's shift and cheap sandals (when she holds out her skirts, pinched with surprising delicacy between a finger and thumb, she exposes herself grotesquely, naked to the thigh). And yet, when you look again, you notice something about the way she holds herself: an arrogance in the tilt of her chin, an absolutely perfect control. For that split second she ignites. I can feel the tinny circus music running through her, through her every vein and sinew, right to the tips of her old woman's fingers – an extraordinary moment of fire and grace.

To this day I do not know who took the photograph. I do not know when it was taken, or where. It is, in every way, anonymous. The woman, for all I know, is dead. And yet there was a moment when I first looked at her picture, and I knew I knew her. For a fraction of an instant I saw behind the shadowy curtains of the travelling tent and I knew everything there was to know about her. I knew how many of her children were now married, how many had died; I knew which acts she had perfected, and the countries she had travelled through to perform them.

It was a vision not just of a woman, but of a whole world. It would not go away.

In the end it was a taxi driver who told us about Circo Bell's. We had already collected together the names of a number of circuses but for some reason, perhaps it was the English name, this one immediately drew my attention. According to the taxi driver it had originally been founded by a famous English clown, Dickie Bell, although this was some time ago, and these days, he said, it was run by Mexicans.

Mexico City is the biggest city in the world and, although it is full of circuses, finding any one of them, let alone one in particular, was a daunting prospect. From the beginning we were given plenty of suggestions for where to look for them, but each time we turned up only to find that it was either another circus altogether, or else a piece of sooty wasteland containing nothing but the swirling fragments of a few tattered posters.

One day we went to a location in the Colonia Agricola Oriental, a district right on the eastern outskirts of the city. This time we found a single caravan on a stretch of deserted scrub land. The caravan was coloured silver and had a clown's face painted on the door. Above it was not the Bell's logo, but the initials AFG. There was no one around. Although a busy four-lane highway ran alongside the strip, the place had a peaceful air to it.

We went to have a closer look. Behind the caravan we found another trailer. Even from several yards away, a powerful smell, raw and steaming, rose from inside it. Behind the caravan was a boy, about twelve years old. He was standing quite still at the centre of an imaginary circle while a very small pony ran in circles around him. In his hand he held a long, ringmaster's whip. From time to time he gave the smallest flick with his wrist, so that the whip cracked over his head like a pistol salute. The late-afternoon sun shone on the scrubby grass around him, illuminating it with a dense golden brilliance. As they worked, both the boy and the pony were haloed with fire.

The boy's name was Jorge Palafox. His circus belonged to a

man named Fuentes Gasca. We had just missed them, he told us. The rest of the circus had left the Colonia Agricola that morning; only he had been left behind to look after the extra trailer until a spare truck could be found to come back and tow it on to the new *terreno*.[1] From here we could see that the trailer was open on one side, railed off with some iron bars. Inside was a lion cub in a cage, a baby elephant, which stood swaying gently from side to side, and three leopards with blue eyes. The smell, close to, was awesome.

From Jorge Palafox we discovered that AFG, which was the circus's name, so called after the initials of Mr Fuentes Gasca, was not suitable for us. We were hoping to be able to travel all over the country with our circus, but AFG operated only within the confines of Mexico City. However, the same owner had another circus which might be a better bet.

'What's it called?'

'Circo Gasca.'

'Circo Gasca.'

I wrote it down in my notebook. The elephant, which had slipped its trunk between the bars, began tentatively to explore the boy's pocket.

'But if that's no good you could always try Circo Union.'

Without looking round he deflected the elephant's progress, pushing its trunk back through the bars.

'Circo Union.'

I wrote that down too.

'Or Circo de Renato.'

With the sun on his face, rather than backlit as before, I saw that despite his small stature Jorge was far older than I had first thought, more like fourteen or fifteen. He spoke softly, almost shyly, like a boy, but his hands, resting against the bars of the trailer, were calloused like an old man's.

'That's an awful lot of circuses. Are you sure there aren't any more?'

I was joking, of course, but the boy regarded me with a serious frown.

[1] *terreno*: a plot of land

'I'm not sure I can remember them all.' He screwed up his eyes. 'Let's see. There's Circo New York, Circo Chino Pekin, Circo Lido, Circo Modelo . . .' He counted them off on his fingers.

'Hang on, how many circuses has the man got?'

The boy turned to rub his pony's neck, thinking carefully.

'Twenty-two, I believe.'

'Twenty-two?'

Tom and I looked at one another.

'That's a great deal of circuses for one man, surely?'

'Of course they don't all belong to one person. The Fuentes Gasca are a big family. They have many sons,' he added with some pride.

'Twenty-two sons?'

'No, not twenty-two.' He looked at us solemnly. 'Thirteen only.'

'*Thirteen* sons?'

'Thirteen.'

From Jorge Palafox we compiled a list of addresses, if you could call them that, where we might find some of the other Fuentes Gasca circuses in town. He also told us of a *terreno* where we might still be able to catch Circo Bell's. For some reason I still had a lingering feeling for them and so, on the off chance, we decided to try this last location first.

It was not a particularly practical decision. The *terreno* turned out to be located right up in the north of the city and it took us a long time to get there. By the time we found it, it was nearly dark. There was no circus. A man in a taco shop nearby told us that they had left two weeks ago.

'We don't seem to be having much luck with Circo Bell's.' I was disappointed.

'Perhaps we should just forget about them and try one of the Fuentes Gasca ones instead,' Tom said. He looked at his watch. 'It's getting late. Maybe we should start again tomorrow. What do you say?'

We looked at the list.

'Let's see if we can find just one more.' I was reluctant to give up so soon. 'Look, this Circo Gasca seems to be quite close to here. Let's just have a look at it, if we can, and after that we'll

9

call it a day. You never know, maybe we'll catch one of their evening performances.'

According to our list, Circo Gasca was at a *terreno* just behind the Basilica of the Virgin of Guadalupe, a place known in Mexico City as La Villa. Long before we could see the circus, we knew that we had found it. From several streets away we could hear the announcements, relayed with a kind of triumphant ellipsis, to a background of rusty circus music: *Cirrr-co . . . más famoso . . . to-o-do las Américas. Elefantes . . . Taiii-wan. TINTIN . . . pay-aso . . . en el muuuun-do.*

Snatches of it reached us on the dingy evening air. Our taxi ground on through the choking traffic, past building sites and crumbling houses, concrete walls covered in crude political graffiti. We strained to hear more, but the announcements faded beneath the roar of buses and trucks. Then they were back again, stronger this time, like a wavering radio signal. *In-creíble . . . Trrr-iple . . . Salto Morrr-tal . . .*

We rounded the corner. And there was the Big Top at last, its canopy striped red and white. A dark mass of caravans behind; at the front, the box-office, the name of the circus relayed across it in brilliant flashing lights. Not Circo Kröne after all, but

CIRCO BELL'S

TWO

When I finally arrived in Mexico, I discovered that
my father's imaginary country was real, but more
fantastic than any imaginary land.

CARLOS FUENTES, *Myself with Others*

The first thing to get straight about the circus is the brothers. Of
course, as in all the most important stories, there were three of
them: Mundo, Rolando and Jorge Bell's[1]. We met them on three
successive nights, the first three times we went to see the circus,
and I remember thinking that they were like Russian dolls, each
one bigger and shinier than the last.

In their younger days the brothers had been trapeze artists, the
three most beautiful men in Mexico, with bodies like Greek gods
and appetites for the world to match. In their youth all Mexico
had flocked to see them and women swooned at their feet. They
were the nonpareils, the talk of the town. Now, in middle age,
only Mundo was a working artiste still. Rolando was the impresario and Jorge, the largest and shiniest doll of all ... well, no
one quite knew what Jorge did, although of the three he told the
best stories, and once, on my birthday, made me a flower out of
a piece of tissue paper which, when he handed it to me, had
become miraculously perfumed like a real rose.

The first brother, on that first night, was Mundo.

When we arrived the evening performance had already begun,
and so when we asked to see the *gerente*, the manager, instead of
going in through the box-office entrance, we were ushered around
to the back of the tent. We pushed past a row of elephant trunks

---

[1] I have stuck to the family's own spelling of Bell's, which is copied from the Bell's
whisky logo, and always includes an apostrophe.

and eventually found a slim crack in the red and white striped tarpaulin.

We emerged to find ourselves backstage. A crowd of people were standing around in costumes and make-up. There were girls in pink feather headdresses, and clowns with long, bubble-toed shoes and painted faces. A man in a scarlet spangled suit was juggling, first with a collection of broad-brimmed Mexican hats, and then with a stream of orange ping-pong balls which he caught deftly between his teeth. A group of children, also in costume, were turning somersaults on a trampoline. No one had noticed us. On the other side of the stage curtains I could hear rusty music playing, and then a burst of applause announcing the end of one of the acts. I went up to the man in the scarlet suit.

'*Por favor*, can you tell me where I might find the *gerente*?'

'Sure.' Between mouthfuls of ping-pong ball he indicated behind me. 'That's him coming now.'

In a puff of white chalk a man in a spangled body stocking and a floor-length silver cloak came bursting though the stage curtains. The man was short and barrel-chested, and had dark hair oiled down over his forehead. His arms hung down by his sides, at the ends of which dangled two huge, chalky hands the size of hams. For a few moments he stood there, quite still, framed against the light.

'Excuse me, Señor, but are you the *gerente*, the manager?'

'I am.' He came down the steps towards me. As he moved, tiny eddies of chalk came steaming from him like smoke. His cloak swept behind him, dragging over the ground like a wizard's robes. 'What can I do for you?'

'I am a writer, from England,' I explained. 'And this is my husband, Tom. He is a photographer.'

'Biénvenidos.' As he came closer I could see that beneath the gorgeous regalia his face and neck were running with sweat. With a corner of his cloak he reached up to mop a glistening brow. 'I am Ricardo Bell's, but everyone calls me Mundo.' I felt my hand disappear into the damp, calloused cave of his palm. 'I would be glad to help you, of course, in any way I can. But first, come, let me find you a chair. We'll go somewhere where we can talk.'

He held up a piece of dark curtain on the far side of the stage entrance and ushered us through into the main part of the Big Top. But the front of the tent was really no more conducive to talking than backstage had been, if anything less so. Even during the acts there was a continual background activity. Circus hands in white shirts and black bow-ties hired out cushions, while others sold photographs and plastic wands, red clown noses, marionettes and sweets. Children, feverish with popcorn and excitement, shrieked up and down the aisles. Visitors came and went, all wanting a word with Mundo now that he had reappeared: friends and relations, both from within the circus and without, artistes from other shows, stage hands with problems and queries. Circus music scratched and wheezed, while outside I could still hear, faintly now, the announcement tape: *TINTIN* ... *payaso* ... *en el muuuun-do* ... *Elefantes* ... *Taiii-wan* ... *Trrr-iple* ... *Salto Morrr-tal* ...

If our conversation was fragmentary, so too were my impressions of the circus performance itself. I remember three elephants and a man with a peaceful face who balanced a lighted candelabra on his forehead. I remember a small dark girl in sequins who spun herself in figures from the top of a rope, and did not smile once during her whole performance, but who was so beautiful that it hurt to look at her. I remember everything and nothing.

When the performance was over, Mundo took us into a little office at the back of the Big Top. About half of it was taken up by an immense Suzuki motorbike which belonged to the owner of the *terreno*, Guillermo, a gangster with gold medallions sprouting from an immense, hairy expanse of chest. The room was soon filled with people in circus costumes. Because of the space taken up by the motorbike, it was very cramped in the office. At least six of us sat on three chairs, drinking black coffee out of a thermos. Mundo sat opposite, perched on the edge of the desk. He had taken off his silver wizard's cloak and was now dressed like the others, in clogs and a greasy *bata* thrown over his costume. As well as Mundo and Guillermo, there was a tightrope walker, a Colombian with the ancient, broken body of an old jockey who was paying a call from another circus; one of the trapeze artists, a nephew or son of Mundo's; and a visiting sister, Myra, with her husband, who I later learnt was the boxer Pepino Cuevas.

So far I had told Mundo, in a vague way, that I was a writer from England and that I was interested in circuses, but as we sat there I realized that the time had come for me to put my vision more clearly into words, not only about the circus but about Mexico, too.

'The first time we came to Mexico was two years ago.' I filled up my cup from the thermos. 'We weren't here for very long, just a couple of weeks, but it was long enough for both of us to know that we wanted to come back here one day. I to write, and Tom to take photographs.' Mundo crossed his chalky Popeye arms massively over his chest. 'Mexico is such a very old country,' I went on, 'and yet in many ways it is so new, too. Some countries reveal themselves easily, but with Mexico . . .' I thought of the darkened palaces of Calle Uruguay, and of the secret labyrinths I felt sure they held within them. *Often what I see most clearly are the things I cannot see.* 'Well, Mexico was different. With Mexico there was always something hidden. I felt . . . how can I explain it? I felt that I might dig and dig and dig, but that, however long I stayed here, I might never be able to uncover everything there was to know.'

Mundo smiled brilliantly. 'Picante! That's what we call it.' He threw up his hands. 'Hot, like our chillies! That's Mexico for you.'

'Sabor!' Guillermo, the gangster, smacked his lips with a fruity sound. 'Tasty, right? That's what we call it in songs sometimes. You know, salsas and stuff.'

Pepino Cuevas and Myra murmured their assent.

'Yes, there's all that. But for us it's something more than that too . . . there's something larger than life about Mexico, something *marvellous*, in the true sense of the word. Your history, your literature, particularly your literature, all are full of marvels.' I was warming to my subject now, but no one seemed to be at all fazed by it. My audience – even macho Guillermo sitting astride his Suzuki – continued to listen with interest. 'There's a whole style of writing in Latin America which in Europe we call *realismo magico*. Magic realism. I've always loved those kind of books, but I've always wondered about them, too. What is it that inspires people to write in this way? What are they trying to express? Then I discovered something. The writers of these books hate this expression 'magic realism'. There's nothing *magical* about what

14

we write, they say – not because they do not believe in magic, but because they know that we in the West only use the word to describe what is not true. Your novelists write this way because this is their truest expression of what life is like. This is real. This is your reality.'

'So, it's magic you're after, then, is it?' Mundo asked, holding out his cup to the trapeze boy for more coffee. 'Well, there's plenty of that here. In the circus world there's a phrase we always use: *la magia del circo*,' he made an expansive, ringmaster's gesture, 'the magic of the circus.'

Through the half-open door I caught brief, dazzling glimpses of some of the other circus performers as they made their way back to the dark caravans behind the Big Top: the creamy-skinned dancing girls, still jewelled and feathered like firebirds; a knife-thrower and a mime artist with a little Charlie Chaplin brush moustache. In their greasepaint and their coloured motley they seemed unbearably exotic, beings from another age.

'In order to get to know Mexico, to be able to write about it, I have to get to know the people, preferably one group of people, a village or a *barrio*,' I went on carefully. 'But this takes time, and Mexico is a big country.'

'You are right,' the Colombian said approvingly. 'You have to *learn* people. With patience, the way you learn how to fish.'

When he spoke I saw that his mouth was full of crude metal crowns where his teeth had been knocked out in a fall, but his language was laced with images, like fleurs-de-lis, and as elegant as a courtier's.

'Well, the way I see it, the circus is like a travelling village, right? With you I can travel around Mexico and yet still be with one group of people all the time.' I was coming to the crux of my argument now. Did they understand me? Was I making any sense at all? I glanced round the room. 'As children the circus is our first experience of magic, a single tangible point at which fantasy and reality meet.' Mundo mopped at his sweaty neck with a fold of his *bata*, but I could see that he was still listening. 'If we can travel with you, then I will write the story of the circus – but I can do more than that. You will be my focus, the eyes through which I will learn to see the whole of Mexico. Even those hidden and secret parts – the magic places, if you like – which I cannot yet see.'

I stopped. Mundo looked at me. In repose, beneath the dark thatch of hair oiled down over his forehead, a little thinning now towards the crown, his face had the melancholy cast of a pierrot. Now, suddenly, he smiled. He threw up his hands, 'Why not?'

Why not? I looked around. There was Mundo nodding his approval; everyone else smiling. I waited for them to express their surprise, for their objections. For their questions even. None came. *Why not?* I felt dazed. Was that all? It was as if writers and photographers from England turned up every day asking to join their circus. It was a moment – almost – of deflation.

Back in the more sceptical climate of England I had assumed that there would be opposition to my plan. Why should any circus take us on? We had no skills, no acrobatic prowess, nothing to offer them in return. I had prepared many arguments, many pleas and entreaties accordingly. Now I realized that none of them had ever really been necessary.

In their experience, I realized as I listened to them talking, the spell which had fallen on me that day in Belgrade was an everyday occurrence. In one way or another the circus is full of the enchanted: many come here for love, both girls and men; others are orphans, runaways, or simply nomads, such as myself. Our presence occasions neither comment nor surprise: it is expected, because it has always been so.

Looking back, it is typical of the way things often happen in Mexico that events should arrange themselves so simply, and with such symbolism.

I had come to Mexico because I had recognized it as a complicated place, a place of strong magic. And I had come to the circus because I hoped that, somehow, it might provide me with some of the clues that I would need to unravel this country. Now I discovered that the hill of Tepeyac, at the foot of which the circus *terreno* lay, is well known to be a magical site. It was here in 1531, as every Mexican knows, that the Virgin Mary miraculously appeared to a simple Indian convert, Juan Diego, as he was walking on the hill one day. The Virgin told Juan Diego to take a message to the archbishop in which she commanded him to build a temple dedicated to her on that spot. Juan Diego did what he had been asked but, naturally, no one would believe a humble Indian. The next day Juan Diego again went to the archbishop, but the same thing happened and he was sent away. Eventually, after three unsuccessful attempts, the Virgin said she would give him a sign which would finally convince the archbishop. Before Juan Diego's astonished eyes he saw roses growing up around him on the barren hillside. Gathering them up in his cloak, he took them to the archbishop and threw them down at his feet. As he did so, the image of Our Lady herself appeared, miraculously implanted into the rough cloth of his mantle.

The Virgin of Guadalupe: dark Madonna and patroness of Mexico. After the Vatican, her shrine is visited by more pilgrims than any other site in Christendom. The faithful, who travel in bands sometimes a whole village strong, swarm to her Basilica by the millions, the most devout performing acts of pious masochism in her honour.

The miraculous apparition on the mountain is a tale of conventional Catholic folklore. Or so it at first appears. In fact there is a curious subtext to the story, a dark undercurrent which sucks beneath so much of Mexican life, an endlessly reflecting and refracting mirror left over from another, older world.

Juan Diego's visions occurred on ground already hallowed by another god. Before the Conquest the hill contained the shrine of the Aztec goddess Tonantzin, the goddess of earth, of spring and of maize. In Aztec, Tonantzin means 'the Mother of God'[1]. To this day it may be that the Virgin of Guadalupe is venerated by the Mexicans with extraordinary fervour because she has only ever been a partially Christian goddess. The colour of her skin, which is brown, is a reminder of her pagan past. Like the Mexicans themselves, her ancestry is full of ambiguities.

[1] The shrine of the Virgin of Guadalupe became so popular so quickly amongst the Indians that even the Spanish friars were suspicious. Father Bernardino de Sahagun noted dryly: 'And so they come to visit this Tonantzin from afar, as much as before, which devotion is suspicious, because everywhere there are many churches to Our Lady and they do not attend those, but they come great distances here.'

The second brother, on the second night, was Rolando. Rolando had come-to-bed eyes, a voice like silk over gravel, and the vocabulary of an East End hood. Small and barrel-chested like his brother, there was something at once exuberant and melancholy about Rolando, a combination reflected in the decoration of his caravan, which was hung about with violent black and white zebra stripes. Circus paraphernalia – sequined costumes, spilt powder, false eyelashes and paints – lay about on the table at one end. At the other, partitioned off with more zebra stripes, was a large double bed heaped with coverlets and eiderdowns. Looking like something out of the 'Princess and the Pea', a little girl of about eight, with dark hair hanging to her waist, was sitting cross-legged on top of the pile, watching television.

'So, you want to travel with a circus, then, do you?' With one sweep of his arm, Rolando cleared the debris off the table and into the crook of his arm. 'Oye, Belén,' he called over to the little girl, 'go and tell your mother to bring us some supper, quickly now. *Chinga*, this place is a mess.' He opened the fridge door and shoved an armful of papers inside. 'Well, if that's really what you want, you've certainly come to the right place. Mexico has more circuses than any other country in the world, did my brother tell you that? With the possible exception of Italy, that is.'

Another child came silently into the caravan and deposited three plates on the table.

'Ah good, here we are.' Rolando motioned us to sit down. 'Please. Eat, eat.'

'Isn't your wife going to eat with us?'

'She's eaten already.' Rolando stabbed at the fried chicken on the plate in front of him. 'Isn't that right, *mi amor*?' He addressed the little girl who had brought in the plates and who was now tidying up around us. Without turning round she nodded.

'Can we meet her?'

'Sure.' Rolando waved his fork thoughtfully in the air. 'This is her, right here.' The figure turned and I saw that it was not a child after all, but a tiny woman, barely taller than her eight-year-old daughter. She had huge downcast eyes, and dark hair which curled girlishly into a bob. 'Mi mujer. My wife, Vicky.'

'How do you do?' We got awkwardly to our feet.

A thin smile, aimed vaguely in our direction, passed over the woman's face. Then she was gone again.

'Don't worry about her, she never says much.' Rolando went on chewing. 'Now, to business. The first thing is, you must get yourselves fixed up with a caravan.'

Out of the window I watched the woman climb into a second caravan, a makeshift camper rather smaller than the caravan we were in. Perhaps that was where she did her cooking. Rolando was still talking, offering advice about where we should get our caravan from, how much we should pay, but I was barely concentrating, my thoughts drifting out towards the circus camp.

Vicky was joined by a teenage girl with curly hair, another daughter, I guessed; I recognized her from yesterday's performance as one of the dancing girls. Behind them I could see the lights of the Big Top, strung like a garland around a huge candy-striped bandbox. Faint sounds of music reached us on the violet evening air. The second evening performance (there were two performances nightly, I now knew, at six thirty and eight thirty) was about to begin. Shadowy figures, some in costumes, others with *batas* or old robes pulled over their finery, were making their way from the semi-circle of caravans over towards the Big Top. I saw an old woman in curlers step down from the caravan next to the camper, a pile of blue feather headdresses in her arm. She stopped and exchanged a few words with Vicky and the girl, and I saw them glancing curiously towards us.

Later on that night we went to watch the performance again. Rolando sat with us pointing out each of the performers in turn. His son and nephew, the stars of the trapeze, following in the brothers' own footsteps; another nephew, the six-year-old Tintin (*el payaso más chiquito en todo el mundo*, the smallest clown in the world); a daughter and three nieces, the feathered dancing girls and *bastoneras*.

Although I was able to watch the performance more closely this time, it remained a fragmentary thing. I remember a juggler, a low-wire walker, and an enigmatic lady, the 'Professora', who with her eyes blindfolded could see what was inside people's handbags and was able to tell a man's name, his age, profession and even the precise time that was on his watch by her amazing telepathic powers. The Professora was followed by an unusual clown act which we had missed the night before. The mime artist with the painted face appeared, followed by some of the circus hands carrying a tiny wooden box which they placed behind him in the centre of the ring.

From the box the painted man pulled out a leg, and then another leg. The legs dangled over the side of the box, hanging there quite still for a moment: two disembodied limbs clad in baggy clown's trousers. Fascinated, the painted man reached into the box again. This time he pulled out an arm, followed by another arm, and finally, the body and woolly head of a full-sized toy clown unfolded seamlessly from the box.

The painted man took hold of the clown with delight. He stood it up, sat it down, propped it up against the box in an effort to make it stay in one position, but each time the stuffed figure, with its silly, smiling face and red wool hair, flopped over jointlessly on to the floor. If he held the clown's legs down, its body sprang up like a Jack-in-the-box; when he pushed the torso back, the legs kicked up again with an unruly life of their own. The painted man became animated, determined to conquer this new-found treasure. He picked it up, swung it round, doubled it back upon itself until the toy was bent backwards into an impossible arc. He threw it over his shoulder, twisted it, buckled it, tied its legs around its neck, threaded its rubbery limbs into every improbable contortionist knot. But to no avail. With a shrug he carried the toy back, folding it gently limb by limb back into the box.

The music stopped, indicating that the act had ended. The painted man took a bow, but then he turned quickly back to the box again and opened the lid. Inside the clown was now unfolding of its own accord. As it sprang from the box, the painted man pulled sharply at the baggy suit, which fell away, leaving in its place not a clown at all, but the dark girl in silver sequins.

Rolando turned to us with a look of pride.

'My eldest daughter, Deyanira,' he said. 'We call her Mara. After Maracaibo, in Venezuela, where she was born.'

'She is very beautiful.'

I watched as the girl went tripping to the front of the ring. In her sequins and tiny silver shoes she looked as if she was made of glass. It seemed impossible that someone so small and fragile could have withstood such brutal handling in the ring. She stood for a moment to receive her applause, perfectly poised, with a small smile which did not reach her eyes. There was something utterly distant about her, a solitary Snow Queen quality which no one, neither her partner nor the audience, seemed to reach however much they clapped or cheered. The next moment she turned, expressionless again, to be escorted from the ring and I lost sight of her.

After that I always watched for the sequined girl's acts, but I never saw where she went afterwards. She was never around in the interval or after a performance when I went to talk to Karina and the other girls; never seemed to be warming up behind stage, hanging round the office, or chattering with the others in the converted lorry, the 'wings' of the circus theatre where the performers waited to make their entrances. In those first days with the circus all the performers were dazzling figures to me, but none more so than this girl, Mara. I wondered if I would ever know her.

Jorge, the third and last brother, wore designer shirts and a rather too-well-cut suit. He had heavy, smooth-shaven cheeks perfumed with lavender water. The first time I met him he embraced me with a tender *abrazo*, and invited me to punch him in the stomach. Obligingly, I did so.

'See!' He thumped himself like a gorilla. 'Pure muscle, even now. I trust you did not hurt yourself?'

'Not at all.' I smiled back at him, nursing my crushed fist in my lap.

'Now you, *Thomas*,' he commanded. Jorge stood up, flexing his chest like a bull. 'As hard as you like. Don't be frightened, now.'

Tom's punch, rather stronger than mine, landed as before against a wall of muscle-bound sinew. Jorge did not even flinch.

'There, see.' He looked at us, highly gratified. 'The body of a trapeze artist! Impressive, no?'

The six thirty performance had ended and once again we were

gathered in Guillermo's office. As usual the place was in chaos. A strange mêlée of performers came and went, a sweaty, painted throng, feathers and glittering leotards concealed beneath their old worn *batas*. Visitors and friends, different ones every night, filled the three chairs, the desk, and even perched on Guillermo's motorbike.

I was trying to find out when the circus would be leaving Mexico City so that we could make our plans to join up with them, but so far without much success. Whenever I asked this question the brothers would look vague and speak charmingly but evasively of how much we would enjoy being on the road with them.

'When did you say you would be leaving Mexico City?' I asked Mundo.

'Next week, next month, next year . . .' He smiled brilliantly. 'Who knows?'

'But the circus *is* leaving here at some point?' I was anxious to establish this.

'*Seguro que sí*, but of course.' He smoothed a lock of hair down over his forehead. 'Next week, most likely. To Monterrey, up in the north. You'll like it there, I feel sure.'

'Monterrey?' Rolando looked amazed when I mentioned this to him. 'Monterrey? What nonsense. Who would want to go there? I'll have you in Acapulco by Christmas, you see if I won't.'

Through the open door of Guillermo's office the juggler, Martinelli, was warming up before the next performance. I could just see the tips of his silver clubs spinning up over the top of the stage curtain. I thought I'd try another tack.

'Mundo says you're leaving next week.'

'Next week, hmm?' Rolando looked enigmatic. 'Is that what he said?'

'Yes, that's what he said.'

'Hmm.'

'Well, is he right?'

'Don't look so worried.'

'Me? I'm not worried.'

'Oh yes, you are, *Inglesa*.' Rolando's teeth were very white. 'Look, the circus is going *en gira*, on tour, just like I promised you. You should learn not to worry so much.'

After several attempts, I began to realize that it was no good. No one in the circus had any notion at all of *mañana*. Unlike the usual maxim, they lived entirely in the present. Not only was it going to be impossible to find out when they were leaving Mexico City, but, as I had discovered in my enquiries over Monterrey, there was no consensus at all as to where they were going.

As a last attempt I decided to try Jorge.

'Jorge, do *you* know where the circus is going from here?'

Jorge was sitting, a vast smiling Buddha, behind the same desk on which Mundo had perched, still in his greasepaint, the evening we had found the circus. He unscrewed the thermos of coffee and offered me another cup.

'Señorita' – as he leant across the desk fragrant traces of lavender water wafted towards us – 'permit me to ask you one thing.'

'Of course.'

'Permit me to ask: where would you like to go?'

'Where would *I* like to go?' I laughed, hoping he would not detect the note of despair in my voice.

Jorge looked at me consideringly.

'I tell you what. Let me tell you a story.'

I had learnt, in what seemed like a very short space of time, that of all the techniques for not answering a question, this was the most effective.

'It is the story about my great-grandfather who, as you know, was a famous clown, an Englishman, Richard Bell.

'Many years ago, back in the last century, my great-grandfather came to Mexico with his circus.' Jorge leant back comfortably in his chair. 'The circus was a big success and it stayed in Mexico City for a long time. One night my great-grandfather noticed a very beautiful woman in the audience. The next night she was there again, and the night after. This woman was my great-grandmother. They fell in love and had a great affair.

'But the circus, of course, did eventually move on, as circuses always do, and one day not long after they had gone, my great-grandmother discovered that she was going to have Richard Bell's child. Now this lady was from a very good family here in Mexico City, she knew that if her family ever found out, it was quite likely that her father would kill both her and her lover, if he could find him. She had to get away, to "disappear" without anyone knowing where she had gone. It was the only way.

'In the end she took just one servant and travelled far, far into the countryside. She did not rest until she had reached the remotest village she could find, and there she stayed, where no one would ever find her. Six months later she gave birth to a baby boy. For a long time she could not decide what to call it. Should she give him my great-grandfather's name, Bell, or her own? She could not make up her mind. But then one day it occurred to her that she would do neither: she would give her son a completely new start in life, and a name all of his own. In memory of how he had come into the world, she called the child Refugio Encarnación.[1]

'My grandfather, Refugio Encarnación, was never told of his circus blood. When he grew up he became a doctor of some repute. He used to grow his own herbs on a piece of land just outside the village, a kind of orchard with lots of trees in it which provided cover for his plants. One day when he went up to his orchard to pick some fresh herbs, he saw, overhead, an astonishing sight. A hot-air balloon. The balloon sailed closer and closer. As it approached the orchard he could see that across the side of the balloon was written "Circo Garcia" in big red lettering. A circus had recently arrived in the village and they were using the balloon to advertise their arrival.

'The balloon floated over the orchard until it was just skimming the tops of the trees. And then all of a sudden it was no longer moving. *Qué horror!* It had drifted down so low that the basket had become stuck in the topmost branches of one of his trees. My grandfather raced over and when he reached the spot, to his surprise, he heard a faint voice calling to him, a woman's voice. He looked up. A most beautiful girl was peering down at him from the top of the tree.

'"Buenos días." She smiled at him from the basket. "It's an awful nuisance, but I think I'm stuck."

'He watched as with perfect composure she adjusted her hat, which was tied under her chin with a large bow, until she had restored it to its most charming angle.

[1] *refugio*: refuge; *encarnación*: incarnation

'"I wonder . . . do you think . . . do you think that you could possibly . . . ?" The girl smiled down at him from her perch between the leaves. My grandfather noticed that her eyes were the sweetest, darkest eyes he had ever seen; and just hearing the softness in her voice made his knees tremble. "If it wouldn't be too much trouble, Señor?"

'". . . trouble?" My grandfather gazed at her, moonstruck. "What? No, no, of course not. Right away."

'As swiftly as he could, he climbed up and rescued her from the tree.

'A week later, when the Circo Garcia left the village, my grandfather was with them and there was nothing anyone could say or do to stop him.

'Such a story!' Jorge sighed with pleasure. 'But it has always been like this in the circus. Even in our own family. We are not really called Bell's at all, you know. That is just a stage name. Our family name is Encarnación, after my grandfather, Refugio Encarnación, who gave up everything for love and to follow his own destiny. So you see,' he looked at me seriously, 'if you really want to join the circus, the whys and wherefores and hows are not important. It is what is in your heart that will decide it.'

Senator Trueba . . . was convinced of the superiority of English over Spanish, which in his view was a second-rate language, appropriate for domestic matters and magic, for unbridled passions and useless undertakings, but thoroughly inadequate for the world of science and technology in which he hoped to see Alba triumph.

ISABEL ALLENDE, *The House of Spirits*

In Karina's caravan, her grandmother was holding court. Stout, black-stockinged feet propped up on a pile of old *bastonera* outfits, Doña Elena lay on the divan lamenting the state of her health.

'Dios mío,' I heard her groan as I came in. One brilliant, all-seeing, kohl-blackened eye flashed open into my direction, and then rolled back, histrionically white, up in its socket. 'Ah, La Katty,' she announced, eyes tightly closed, to no one in particular. By now, everyone in the circus called me Katty. 'La Inglesa. Am I right?' Before I had a chance to reply, another spasm crossed her face. 'Ay!' She put her hand to her spine. 'Here, come here and feel this,' she beckoned me over. Taking my hand, she thrust it to her back. 'See how I suffer!' Under her jersey I felt the metal edge of the orthopaedic corset which enveloped her strong, old woman's flesh. 'See what they have *done* to me, these doctors! It's a wonder I can move at all.' She moaned softly, removing a heap of feather boas and old dolls from behind her head, and rearranging herself still further back into the sequined jumble beneath her on the divan.

Doña Elena, *grande dame* and moving spirit of the circus, enjoyed her pain in the manner of one who has been a martyr to it all her life, but is too iron-willed ever to have allowed it to be a serious inconvenience. When the circus had first started out, it was she who had stitched the tent with her own hands, night after night, until her fingers bled. Now in her seventies, she no longer lived with the circus, but arrived on a state visit once a week, usually a Sunday. 'La abuela solamente viene a regañar,' Karina had once lamented, 'Grandmother only comes here so that she can tell us all off.' But, like a Roman empress, we all knew that she was the undisputed power behind the Bell's brothers' throne.

When we were still waiting for the circus to leave Mexico City, I used to speak to her nearly every day on the telephone. When I enquired how she was, her reply was always the same: 'Aquí, sufriendo como siempre' – still here, suffering as always. The tragedy queen tones – she had a particular way of saying su-*friendo*, and striking her breast with her fist, as though she were delivering a line from a Greek tragedy – belied the amazing energy with which they were delivered.

When I went in the caravan was surprisingly empty. Karina, whom Doña Elena (never temperate in her affections) famously disliked, and her sister Vanessa, who equally famously was her *consentida*, were nowhere to be seen, worn down, I suspected, by their grandmother's constant chatter.

With her instead was Olga, one of the circus dancing girls, towards whom Doña Elena was currently directing her conversation. Olga, always the tiniest, shyest slip of a girl, was sitting flattened against the opposite wall of the caravan and had made herself so small and insignificant that it was some time before I even noticed she was there. She was staring at Doña Elena with huge, frightened eyes; mesmerized, like a very small mouse in the path of a huge, black, and very probably carnivorous spider.

'Tell me something, *Inglesa*,' Doña Elena redirected the beam of her gimlet-like gaze towards me now, 'are you married?'

I said that I was.

'I was just telling . . . what's your name, dear . . . ? ah, yes, Olga, of course . . . I was just telling Olga here that, if she can possibly help it, she should not get married.' Although she was still only sixteen Olga had run away to the circus to be with her boyfriend, Ilish, and her heart's desire, it was well known, was to marry him. 'Well, not yet at any rate.'

When she spoke Doña Elena had a way of rolling her eyes,

which were immense and ringed with black like an Arab, so that the whites flashed.

'Never make the mistake that I did, and marry too young.' She lowered her voice. 'Now, my husband . . .' she lowered her voice still further and her eyes narrowed, '*Dios mío*, how I hated him!'

Next to me I felt Olga give a tiny shiver.

'I always hated him. From the very first day we were married, not a moment passed when I didn't wish that he was dead.' Doña Elena looked at Olga reflectively. 'Of course, things were different in those days. I was so young when they married me, even younger than you. Just fourteen. A little girl – what did I know about marriage?'

'Then why . . . why did you, then?' I heard Olga's tiny, butterfly voice beside me.

'Why? I'll tell you why. Cowardice. That's why.' Doña Elena's eyes flashed; her gold bracelets rose and fell on her arms. 'You see, my husband loved me.' She nodded to herself, remembering. 'Oh, how he loved me. I saw him weep, once, he loved me so much. He used to beg me to marry him, but I wouldn't. I wasn't interested.

'Once my family had their own circus, but after my sister died my father became ill and we were forced to sell up. We went to work for this other circus, Circo Garcia. My mother used to say, don't be so stupid, be nice to him, be sweet (the boss's son, a good match, I knew that is what she was thinking) but I never would.

'If he asked me to go and eat ice cream with him, I would lie and say that I didn't like ice cream. When he knew there was a pair of shoes I liked, he bought them for me, but I wouldn't accept them. No. Never. The truth is, I didn't dare do anything which might compromise me in people's eyes, or let them think I had accepted him. Once, when I was looking into a shop window I found him standing next to me. Without my knowing it, he had followed me into town. He said, choose anything you like, anything, and it shall be yours. I looked at him as coldly as I could. There is nothing I want from you, I said, and walked away down the road.

'A few moments later I heard his footsteps running up behind me. Before I could think, before I could move, I felt his hands on me—' she paused, her body tense. 'I felt his fingers clutching at my dress . . . In terror I turned around. There he was on his *knees* on the ground before me. Tears were pouring down his face. *Te quiero, te quiero*, he screamed at me, don't you understand, I lo-ve y-o-u . . .' She breathed out slowly. 'I did not say a word. I just snatched my dress back and walked on down the road.

'The next day, my brother-in-law — he was always fond of me — came to me. He said, it's no good, Elena, you'll have to marry him. I said, give me one good reason why I should. My brother-in-law said, if you don't he says he'll kill you first, and then himself.' Doña Elena shrugged. 'Like I told you. Cowardice. I married him because I was frightened. And because I knew that they were stronger than me.' She looked at us, unblinking. 'You see, in those days, in Mexico, things were like that. If a man could not have a woman with her consent, he took her without it. And if he could not do that, he made sure that no one else could either. And he knew I knew it, all too well. You see, the same thing had happened to my sister. When she refused the man who wanted to marry her, because she was in love with someone else, he came to the circus one day with a gun. He shot my sister, there and then, straight through the heart. I was there. I saw it happen.

'The judge and the notary were called. I was given just five minutes to make myself ready. The judge said it was unusual to marry a girl who had tears rolling down her cheeks, but I made no objection. How could I, when I could feel my husband's gun, hidden inside his jacket, pressed against my ribs?

'That night I was so frightened. Instead of going to sleep with my husband, I hid in my mother's bed, but as soon as I was asleep she got up and went to find him and made him get in beside me in her place. But whatever tricks they tried, I was determined not to let him touch me. And so it went on, night after night. For a whole week I managed to keep him away from me. After that, he got bored of my finer feelings.'

Beneath her jewels and her silks and her *grande dame* refinements, Doña Elena's conversation was salty and free. For me, unversed in circus vernacular, she re-invented language. Words fell from her lips like spices, shot through with fire — impossible to translate — slivers of burning chillies, red and green and gold.

For her husband alone, when she spoke of him, she reserved an icy politeness. Her body, I realized with a sense of shock, still rages against him. Although her voice was always calm, as she spoke her face and her hands contorted, her eyes flashed with venom. This was not just a story. She was telling us these things because she had to, because more than fifty years later, her hatred had yet to burn itself out.

'All my children cried when he died, but I promise you I didn't shed a tear. Within a month of our marriage he was beating me. Within three, he was parading with his fancy women, without a care whether I saw him with them or not. Sometimes he would lock me in our caravan so that I could not go out or even talk to my friends. But it was a relief when he wasn't there. He was so jealous. He was always there, always behind me wherever I went, even in the kitchen. He exhausted me with his presence. I used to beg him, leave me alone for once, leave me in peace, but he never would. You know, in all the years we were married he never even bought me a pair of stockings. I was his slave: good for cooking, washing, cleaning, and having his children, and that was all.

'His children. Yes, of course. Many children.' She put her hand to her back, thinking for a moment. 'Of course, none of them have ever believed that I could have hated him so much. They ask me, Mamá, if you hated him so much, how come you managed to have so many children? I had thirteen children by him, you know, although two are dead now. I tell them, in the Revolution, when the soldiers would pass through a village, many women, girls of good families, even nuns from the convents sometimes, were left carrying children. Do you think it was because they wanted to?

'When the end came, we all knew he was going to die. One day he called me to his bed. I want to ask you something, he said. Before he could put any question to me I said, I know what you are going to ask. You want to know if, all these years, I have really hated you as much as I have always said I did. The answer is, yes.' Her voice thickened. 'I can't stand the sight of you. I will be glad when you are dead, because only then will I find peace.'

'Ah, you see. So much suffering.' Doña Elena leant towards us, her black Scheherazade's eyes unblinking. 'Do you know what his last words to me were? Can you guess? He said, you are still an attractive woman, Elena, and a strong one. When I am gone, you will have offers. But, for your own sake, Elena, don't just chose the first man who comes along. Next time, he says to me, *entréga te por amor*. Next time, give yourself for love.'

For a moment I thought she was going to start laughing. 'Next time!' she said. 'As if there would ever be a "next time".'

The lessons of the circus are hard. Like Mexico itself, things here seemed polarized. And yet, despite this feeling, it is not always easy to tell which end of the pole you have swung towards. In Mexico sometimes it feels as if you are floating in space. One moment you might have the very clear impression that you are standing up, but the next you realize that the very idea of 'up' has lost its meaning. Up from where? Up is at once no way and every way. The word is an impossibility. To describe your position truly, a new language altogether is required.

Mexicans delight in their inability to 'explain' Mexico, and so make a virtue of their contradictions. In order to learn the circus, I realized that I had first to unlearn it. Like every seeker of magic, I had first to dispense with the illusions: to slough off, like one of Niña's fuchsia skins, the clouded coating of glamour and innocence with which I had painted them. I had to learn to look into the dark.

Few of the circus people, it was true, had the initial impact of Doña Elena. In fact in the daytime, behind the scenes, Circo Bell's was so ordinary a collection of people, I almost wondered if I had come to the right place after all. Without the lights and the numerous guises of darkness, I saw the glittering costumes become dirty, flimsy things, the sequins tarnished and moulting, the limp feather headdresses half bald, as if afflicted with some strange, scrofulous disease. Fishnet stockings, so alluring at night, became a tawdry patchwork of holes and darns; dinner jackets were creased beyond hope, their collars and cuffs shiny with an ancient and indelible patina of grease.

We finally joined Circo Bell's on 18 October, at San Juan de Aragón, Mexico City. In a few weeks, Rolando promised us, we would all be off on tour (Acapulco by Christmas was still his cry), but in the meantime he had been offered a great deal on this *terreno* which, as we could surely see, was an opportunity not to be missed.

Rolando described the site as a *feria*, or fair. This meant that, in addition to the Big Top, the usual piece of wasteland contained the sad remains of a few pieces of fairground machinery. Pushed to one side of the ground like two rusting dinosaurs slumped an ancient merry-go-round and a toboggan run. On the other side sprouted an avenue of curious metal growths, the skeletons of the clothing and trinket stalls which occasionally operated here at weekends.

By day, I now discovered, the circus encampment was anything but glamorous. Most of the caravans were so old they looked as if they were held together with string, and would fall apart completely if you so much as sneezed inside them. I wondered how it was going to be possible to move them even a few feet, let alone think of taking them on tour around the country. They seemed permanently rooted in the mud. Huge TV aerials, some almost bigger than the vehicles themselves, dangled from the roofs; while a rotting detritus of bicycles and plastic buckets, rusting prams, water butts, and washing machines so old anywhere else they would have been collectors' pieces, were strapped, like mad Christmas decorations, on to the outside walls and doors.

One caravan, a tiny little thing shaped like a bubble car in a cartoon, was parked like ours a little apart from the rest of the camp. Various cats and dogs roamed around it, and a milk-white goat chewed languidly at some bales of hay piled up at the back. The caravan belonged to Luis, the elephant-keeper, a huge bullock of a man from the north. Even though the caravan looked too small for him to even stand up in, he lived here with his wife and their two little girls. Luis was a man of few words, but he never liked to be too far from his animals. After the evening performance we would often see him sitting outside on one of the bales of straw, hunched against the cold in his big green coat and baseball cap, staring silently into the night. Behind him in their pen his elephants, three dark shadows, swayed together as if to some subliminal pachyderm song.

The day we arrived at the circus, as members at last, we found that it had tented in the usual way: all the caravans and trailers were wedged nose to nose in a tight semi-circle around the back of the Big Top. Because the site was a small one, once the tent had gone up there was no room for us to get in beside them. Instead Mundo instructed us to park our caravan at the front, just to one side of the box-office.

After a display of polite interest in the workings of our trailer, a wonderful, part-caravan/part-tent American contraption known as a Pop-up, the small crowd which had gathered at our arrival dispersed, leaving us, in solitary apartheid, on the wrong side of the Big Top. It had taken us over a year of planning to get to Mexico, and another two months to find the circus and equip ourselves to travel with them. Now that we were here at last I should have felt elated. I didn't. I felt like a fraud.

That evening, after the first performance was over, we went on a slow, investigative walk round to the back of the tent. The performers had congregated in groups, chatting amongst themselves, running in and out of each other's caravans. I saw the *equilibrista*,[1] the man with the tranquil face, smoking a cigarette with one of the stage hands; and little Olga hurrying past them, her green feather boa still entwined around her neck. I saw one of Rolando's daughters, the one with the curly hair, and another of the dancing girls still in their costumes hanging around the entrance of what looked like an old bus, arguing with the old woman in curlers.

They greeted us courteously, but with a certain distance, I thought.

'Go on,' Tom muttered at me, 'mingle.'

'Mingle!' I felt suddenly overcome with shyness. 'I can't.'

'Of course you can,' he commanded. 'Just strike up a conversation.'

'A conversation!' My mind was a blank. 'Who with?'

We hovered self-consciously on the fringes of the crowd. No one spoke to us. In the distance I saw Karina, but she merely waved her hand and vanished from sight into one of the caravans.

---

[1] One who performs a type of balancing act in the ring with swords, candelabra, and so on.

Whenever we had visited Circo Bell's previously, I realized, it had always been with something particular in mind. We had no formal role in the circus, but we had come to watch the performance, to talk over our plans with the brothers, or to discuss the circus tour. Now that finally the project had come to fruition, now that we were here, I felt curiously purposeless. A few minutes later our perambulations brought us back to our own caravan again.

'So,' Tom said, almost crossly for him, 'and what do you suggest we do now?'

The answer came from an unexpected quarter. We were sitting drinking coffee after the last evening performance had ended when there was a knock on the door. It was two of the trapeze artists, Rolando's son, also called Rolando but known to the family as Gordo, and his friend, Jorge Morales. They were off to visit another circus later that night and had come to invite us to go with them.

'It is your first night with us,' Gordo explained. 'And we want you to know that you will always have friends here at Circo Bell's.'

Although we knew them by sight from their act, we had only ever spoken to them briefly once before, when Karina had brought them round to meet us during one of the performances. Jorge was nineteen, a quiet, courteous boy with a quick smile and the thick, olive-coloured skin of a gypsy. Gordo was just seventeen, dark, wiry and very slight for his age. We sped smoothly through the half-lit wasteland of streets and alleyways in his brand-new American pick-up. He drove with the same qualities he brought to his trapeze act, with speed and a rare elegance. He had been driving for several years now, he told us with pride, but the police had never caught him. Since he was still technically a minor, he possessed neither papers nor a licence.

There was only room for three of us in the front of the pick-up, and so Jorge Morales, dressed only in a thin jacket, a spotted bandana tied around his head, was riding in the open back.

'Won't he be cold in there?' I asked. 'We can squeeze up.'

Gordo shook his head. 'Es Mexicano,' his tone was one of

careful nonchalance, 'y los Mexicanos aguantan.' He is Mexican, and a Mexican can endure anything.

There was something at once engaging and alarming about Gordo's bristling young machismo; he seemed so anxious to impress us with Mexico, the Mexicans, and Mexican circuses in particular. Of course, at the very pinnacle of the list was that most celestial being of all, the trapeze artist.

We got on to the subject almost at once. It was the best act in the circus, he said, and the most highly paid.

'The *trapecistas* are the stars of the show.' He spoke with authority. 'Always. In every circus.'

He swerved, dodging a pot-hole in the road by running the outside wheels neatly up on to the pavement. 'I am also a *domador*, with the elephants,' – why, I wondered, did *domador* sound so much more impressive than 'animal trainer'? – 'but it was always the trapeze which I wanted to do most.'

He had only been in the act a year, he told us, but already he was throwing the triple, the much-vaunted *salto mortal*, the death-defying somersault, which was indeed one of the star billings in the show. (We knew this only too well: the taped announcement, recorded rustily over the theme music from *Raiders of the Lost Ark*, and kept permanently on repeat, was relayed from just outside our caravan.)

If Gordo had wanted to impress us with Mexican circuses, he could not have done better than to take us with him that evening. The Circo Americano, it was immediately obvious, was in almost every way both bigger and better than Circo Bell's. They had their own orchestra, and an extensive collection of animals, displayed under a tarpaulin at the entrance of the tent. But there was something even more noticeable than either of these. Unlike Bell's, which night after night since we arrived at the new *terreno* was forced to play to ever-dwindling audiences, the Big Top was packed with people.

We had arrived during the interval and there was a noisy, carnival spirit in the air. Mexican families with their squads of children crammed into every available seat, spilling exuberantly up the slatted wooden tiers towards the back of the tent, filling the boxes at the front and even the aisles, where the older children chased each other, or milled hopefully around the stalls selling paper cones of popcorn, toffee apples and bags of crisps laced with chilli sauce.

Gordo and Jorge were obviously well known here, and we were immediately greeted by a number of people: Jesús Vasquez, the son of the owner of the circus, a dude in expensive American leathers, his sister, and a cousin, Bruno. All three spoke English, since they had lived for a time in the States. Compared to Gordo and Jorge they were oddly sophisticated.

The show, we discovered when the second half finally began, centred around the musical antics of a vast pantomime cat, a well-known figure from a television show. We watched Bruno perform his new tightwire act, and Jesús dressed incongruously as a clown. The next act was a woman who performed a series of elaborate handstands, using a dog as one of her props. For the finale she balanced on two pillars made from wooden blocks, gradually discarding the blocks from one of the pillars and substituting the little dog, who sat upright beneath her, begging obligingly. At the end of the act she pushed away the second pillar, and was left, to a roll of drums, balancing with only the dog's head for her support.

After the handstand lady and her dog came a troupe of boxing chimpanzees. Wearing shiny blue and red shorts, singlets and boxing gloves, two of the chimpanzees climbed into a miniature ring, while the other two, standing at opposite corners with towels around their necks, screeched and jumped and chattered with excitement as the punches flew. Their trainer, a woman in a spangled suit and too much make-up, darted between them, whispering strange mantras of encouragement into their ears, whipping them into a frenzy of new effort. After the boxing match, the chimps performed a number of other tricks, sometimes together, sometimes individually. In between, they sat on a row of chairs which had been specially set up for them towards the back of the ring.

In their chairs, the chimps sat hunched and cross-legged, chattering softly among themselves. Their faces, in repose, looked wizen and inscrutable: four tiny, eccentric old men. They did not appear to notice the rest of the act, or the gasping, roaring audience all around them. Instead they seemed to turn in on themselves, as though contemplating some mysterious internal landscape of their own. I watched as with Confucian detachment they stared into the middle distance. Occasionally, with strange, fastidious little gestures, they would examine their hands, abnormally extended and hirsute, as though mutated through some unknown instrument of torture.

It was then I noticed that under their boxing shorts the chimpanzees were all wearing nappies. In my mind, I realized, I had already anthropomorphized these animals into old men. Now they had become babies, too.

In the circus, it is true, things are seldom what they appear to be. As spectators, we desire it to be so. But there was something so grotesque about this inversion that for the rest of the act I could hardly bear to watch. Not for the first time I was extremely glad that, apart from the elephants, Circo Bell's had no acts which involved animals.

Looking back at my circus quest it is hard for me to pin-point exactly what it was that made me so sure I should return to Mexico. As I had tried to explain to Mundo the day we found Circo Bell's, I had always been sure of the effect that Mexico had had on me, but never, until now, of the cause. Now I wondered if it was not that the circus and Mexico shared to some extent this same illusory power; a certain ability to disconcert, to challenge old certainties.

History alone tells us that this has always been so. The Americas were presaged in the Old World by dreams and by poetry long before they were proved to be real.

'Ever since man began to leave a record of his dreams,' the Mexican essayist Alfonso Reyes wrote, 'the likelihood of a new world has appeared in the form of a presage. It was forecast by fantasy some 3,000 years before Christ, when somewhere in the mysterious West the mythical Anubis presided over the dead. The notion of an undiscovered region in the west, which at times was a happy kingdom, and at times a gloomy sea, dates from the earliest Egyptian documents. At times this region was concealed beneath the shimmering ocean. At times it was projected as far as the sun itself . . .'

In Columbus's day, sailors took to sea with books such as Cardinal d'Ailly's *Imago Mundi* as their discoverer's breviary, a list of all the paradises that man had ever thought of, conjectured or desired. D'Ailly wrote of basilisks and dragons, of giant pygmies, of unicorns, Amazons, griffins and cyclops, of men without heads or with eyes in the nape of their neck, of others who howled like dogs, or who hopped about on one foot, which served them as a parasol when they slept. It was in the Americas, philosophers believed, that the classical utopias and legends of antiquity would be re-discovered as earthly wonders: Plato's Atlantis, the Garden of Eden, El Dorado, the Fountain of Youth.

'Thus, America, before she became solid reality,' Reyes tells us, '. . . was the invention of poets, the charade of geographers, the gossip of adventurers, the cupidity of traders, and, in sum, a strange craving and a longing to burst bonds.'

What can it possibly have been like for the first men from the Old World, conquerors and priests, to have inhabited this semi-mythical new land? Sometimes, I think, the strangeness of it all must have sent them mad.

The Augustinian monastery of St Nicholas of Tolentino at Actopan in the state of Hidalgo was founded, in the local pinkish stone, on 8 July 1546, just twenty-four years, ten months and twenty-five days after the conquest of Mexico. Although it has long been deserted, the composition of the monastery is traditional, familiar even, to a European eye, with its cloisters and chapter house, sacristry, kitchens and cells, and its fine church façade in the plateresque style.

The place has the feel of all empty places which have done their time: pigeons murmur along the colonnades and there is a musty smell of old stone and bat droppings. Inside, the deserted monastery is far bigger than it at first appears. We stopped off there the day before we joined the circus at San Juan de Aragón (we were on our way back from the States, where we had been to buy our Pop-up and a truck) and I can remember the way our footsteps clattered through the empty spaces, framed with stone and unadorned except for some flaking murals on the walls. In one room, a monk's cell on the top floor, the walls were covered with graffiti. Schoolchildren had been up here, or young couples. Juan

✥ Margarita. Cecilia ✥ Pancho. Human love blossoming again, after all the centuries honouring a celibate God.

It was only then that I began to notice that there was something wrong. Drawn upwards by the graffiti, my eye caught sight of a frieze drawn all along the top of the walls. It was a strange, repetitive pattern of a man riding a horse. In one hand the man was wielding a club. When I looked more closely I saw that the horse was not in fact a horse at all, but a mythological beast, part dragon and part fish. And in the fish's tail, like a hallucination, appeared the image of a woman's face.

I traced the frieze all the way around the room, and out into the corridor. I traced it as it made its way along the colonnades, snaking its way into each of the monks' cells in turn, zig-zagging along the top of the walls like some exotic vine. In each figure the same woman's face appeared, sometimes bigger, sometimes smaller; sometimes, on a corner or a bend, eliding a little further into the beast's fishy body, but each time, unmistakably, the same face: laughing eyes and a smile as ambivalent as the Mona Lisa's.

By the time it reached the stairs the narrow frieze had grown, gaining momentum until it spilt downwards, covering the entire stairwell in one vast black and white mural. These paintings showed scenes from the history of the monastery, solemn portraits of the founding fathers. I had seen these as I came up, of course, but now I looked at them with different eyes. Sure enough, the portraits were divided into panels, defined by decorative borders of animals, plants and ornamental foliage. But when I examined them, I saw that these creatures were not animals and plants at all, but strange hybrids of each other, mutating right before my very eyes. Beasts grew and took shape from the foliage itself. Horses' legs ended in leaves instead of hooves, and their backs and tails were formed from vines. Cherubs and men with clubs were no longer entirely human in form, but had grown serpents' tails which sprouted voluptuously from banks of sinuous creepers. There were lions and bulls, and many mythological animals too; phoenixes and unicorns, and other stranger creatures which I cannot name, such as a beast with the head of a griffin, the beak of a parrot, and a great, slapping fishtail. Their expressions were uncannily human.

I stared at them. The longer I looked, the more fevered the patterns became as though, released by my gaze, they were growing, cross-breeding and transforming on the walls of their own accord.

The smaller the scale of the paintings, the more disturbing they became. Along the downstairs cloister I found a narrow band of fleur-de-lis and greenery. In a simple leaf design I found a pair of eyes staring down at me, then a grinning mouth. A tiny face appeared. Then another, and another, until the whole vine was alive with demons and imps and water sprites cavorting though the foliage.

What was it about this place, I have always wondered since, which could have produced this deranged vision? What could have been passing through the artist's mind, through his soul? Was it just plain loneliness, or some more violent apostasy?

I climbed up to the roof and looked down over the town. Outside it was just another ordinary day in an ordinary town. In the distance I could see a sports stadium and an advertisement for the local pharmacy, Super Farmacia María Magdalena. Some boys in red shorts were kicking a football around the pitch, passing it back and forth over the parched earth. Among the weeds and tangled branches in the monastery garden beneath me someone had planted a small plot of maize. Maize: the most potent and sacred symbol of old Mexico, at once a food and a god. Even from high up, there was something spectacular about its height and strength, its leaves yellowing slowly in the flaying midday heat.

FOUR

'Bread, circuses, and something to worship are all
they need,' the Senator concluded . . .
    ISABEL ALLENDE, *The House of Spirits*

The bikini was scarlet and decorated with silver beads. It came
with a red feather boa, silver gauntlet gloves, a scarlet and silver
choker, garters, and a matching headband. I looked at it dubiously.
It was small. Very small. But not as small as the blue or the green
costumes which had also been on offer.

'I liked the blue better,' said Brissel, 'it showed you off really
well.'

'She means your *chichis*,' said Olinda, opening her huge eyes
even wider and grinning. 'You know what *chichis* are, don't you?'

'Shut up,' Karina said, crossly. 'Let Katty decide on her own.'

'Just *try* the blue,' Brissel was coaxing. 'Think what Tom will
say!'

I could imagine exactly what Tom would say.

'I think the red will be fine.' I grabbed the costume hastily,
before it disappeared again for ever into the thick humus of costumes, cloaks, feathers and headdresses packed in all around us.

We were sitting in the wardrobe, me and the girls: Karina and
her cousins Olinda, Brissel and Pamela. Olga, quiet and small,
and of a more serious turn of mind than the others, sat a little
apart from us reading a book.

It was the day of the grand parade at the new *terreno*, and
Karina had decided that it was time I made myself useful. We had
started off dressing in her caravan but, being both impatient and
easily bored, she had soon decided that we would get along better
with the others.

The wardrobe consisted of one half of a bashed-up old military bus. For modesty's sake the windows had been painted over, and the clothes hung up, several layers deep, in racks along the walls. The only space which was left was a narrow aisle, scarcely wide enough to turn around in, where the girls changed and made themselves up each evening before the performances. The effect, as we sat huddled together on the floor – warm, womb-like and slightly claustrophobic – was exactly as its name suggested, like sitting inside a wardrobe. The place had a peculiar scent all of its own: the sweet smell of young girls' pussies, mixed with the musty, old-sweat odour of the clothes hanging all around us.

'Here, put these on first.' Karina handed me a pair of the brown fishnets which all the girls wore under their costumes. She showed me how to roll the tops in neatly under the bikini bottoms, which she pulled up as high as they would go over my hip bones. As we dressed the conversation was conspiratorial and mildly bawdy.

'So, what do you think of the circus, then, Katty?' Pamela asked, wriggling her long legs into her *mayas*. 'Do you still think, like some people do, that we never wash or clean our caravans?'

'And that we steal children,' Brissel added eagerly, 'like the gypsies?'

'I wish *I* could have *chichis* like that,' Olinda ogled, one hand waving her mascara brush. 'Look at us all, flat as pancakes,' she lamented, squeezing her bud-like breasts together. 'All of us except Jovita, that is,' she lowered her voice fractionally, 'but you'd have to be mad to want those.'

Jovita was the wardrobe mistress, an alarming old woman whose head bristled permanently with a helmet of curlers. A state of perpetual war raged between Jovita, who looked after the costumes, and the girls, who didn't, and were forever laddering tights, losing beads and sequins, and leaving their feather headdresses lying around to be crushed and dirtied behind the stage.

It was some time before I discovered that not only did Jovita work in the wardrobe but, like the old woman in the shoe, lived here too. Every evening while the girls sat squeezed up in the padded aisle doing their make-up, she would sit like a gaoler just inside the entrance of the bus, sniffing and watching *telenovelas*, to which she was much addicted, on her old black and white television. Jovita, the girls told me, was incredibly mean and lived in terror of being robbed. Apart from her treasured television her only other visible possession was a picture of the Virgin of Guadalupe; the rest were secreted away, only she knew where, amongst the layers of frowsty clothes. At night I would imagine her sleeping there amongst the racks, still in her curlers, wrapped up in her blanket like the chrysalis of some ancient moth.

'Now you need some make-up.' Karina looked at me and sighed. Her face, still only half made up, was streaked garishly with lines of colour. 'Ay, we'll never be ready in time.' She looked at her watch impatiently. '*Oye*, cousin, can't you help us? I'm late already.'

She spoke not to Brissel or Pamela, but over their heads to where Mara, already changed and fully made up, had just pushed her way in and was searching for something along the racks of clothing. Mara squeezed herself down on to the floor beside me.

'*Ay*, Katty,' she peered at my face critically, 'you really should arrange yourself better. I have been observing you and, look, sure enough,' she made a little, scandalized *tsk* sound with her tongue, 'you're not wearing any make-up *at all*.'

Briskly, she pulled her make-up box towards her and got to work.

For the first few weeks that we had been with the circus Mara had remained the glassy snow queen that I had first imagined her to be, beautiful and remote, spinning in her silver sequins from the top of the rope. She held herself apart from the other girls. I never saw her with her cousins, Karina, Brissel, Pamela and Olinda, who chattered and joked and feuded, and ran in and out of each other's caravans all day long. Only sometimes, when we went to Rolando's caravan, I would catch sight of her talking in whispers to Omar, the painted mime artist in the box act; but whenever she saw us coming, she would lower her eyes and turn shyly away.

Then, for no apparent reason, she suddenly changed. Rolando had arranged for the circus to move to a new site, a field opposite a new housing development in the north-west of Mexico City, but when we arrived – in the middle of the night – the field had proved to be a waterlogged bog, and the ground was so unstable and muddy that it had been impossible to get the trucks and caravans in. For several days the circus had been stranded, still in its travelling convoy formation, parked in a roaring four-lane highway. We were sitting around one afternoon with Karina and her *novio* Gallo, the young lad who acted as the circus ringmaster, when there was a knock on our caravan window. Smiling, Mara put her head through the door.

'Can I come in?' Without waiting for a reply, she stepped lightly inside and sat down on the bed. 'I've always wondered what it was like inside your caravan.'

Outside the traffic thundered past. Because the walls of our caravan were soft-sided, each time a car, a bus or a lorry passed by, its canvas cheeks would suck in sharply, and then blow out again like a pair of giant bellows. Mara looked around, black eyes glinting.

'It's noisy in here,' she remarked serenely, 'much noisier than in our caravan.' It was true. The noise in the Pop-up, day and night, was stupendous. 'Is this where you sleep?' She patted the mattress next to her with her hand to test its thickness.

Now that she was here, Mara wanted to know everything. I showed her the two little gas rings on which we cooked and heated our water; the sink with its pump-action water tank; the storage spaces under the banquette seats, and the neat way in which the table could be converted into an extra bed. The whole caravan, Tom and I had thought when we bought it, was a masterpiece of American ingenuity and design.

'And what about, you know, a bathroom?' she said. I showed her the chemical loo which we kept in one corner. 'Oh, one of those.' She looked at it with interest. 'Those are no good here, you know,' she added cheerfully. 'You can't get the chemicals.'

'Sí, es muy bonito,' she said politely when I had finished the tour. She sat down on the bed again and looked around at us. Her smile would have made an angel weep. 'It's very pretty, but do you know, I don't think it would suit me at all.' She put one tiny hand to the canvas walls. 'With these walls, *ay Chihuahua!* You're going to be cold in here, just you wait and see.'

It was not only cold in our caravan, as Mara had predicted.

44

On the grand parade[1] itself, dressed only in fishnets and a small spangled bikini, it was arctic. Outside the Big Top the circus trucks formed a raggedy convoy, while Mundo arranged us all into position along them. The girls, tiny, brightly coloured dragonflies in all their gauzy finery, perched on the cab roofs, two to a truck at the front of the procession, while the other acts, jugglers, clowns, trampolinists and elephants brought up the rear in the larger vehicles. With the *Raiders of the Lost Ark* announcement tape playing at full blast, the convoy shambled slowly off up the highway, tooting its rusty horns.

The parade took about two hours. I shared the roof of our truck with Karina. Omar, who I now discovered was not only Mara's partner but her *novio* too, had offered to drive us. As the convoy rumbled its way back and forth along the network of roads around the new *terreno*, I caught sight of Tom in one of the long vehicles behind us, unrecognizable in full clown greasepaint. He was wearing a strange and voluminous striped outfit with a piece of rubber tubing inserted around the middle. As the truck lurched along I watched him bowing and waving to the passers-by, every so often pushing out his costume from behind so that his stomach ballooned out in front of him, bigger and fatter than ever. 'Quick, look at Tom, look at Tom!' I shook her arm but Karina refused to be impressed. She sat hunched forward, scowling straight ahead of us, a tracksuit top draped over her shoulders.

'I hate my uncle.' She drummed her heels against the bonnet of the truck. 'I hate him, I hate him.' Karina, who had spent some time in the States with her mother and was more streetwise in the way that she dressed than the other cousins, had been ticked off by Mundo for another of her more outrageous experiments. This time it was for wearing bright orange eyeshadow. '"Don't make an exhibition of yourself" is what he said.' She turned to me, her eyes like two huge black and orange bruises. Close to, I had to admit, she did look quite strange. 'But what does he think we're all doing, dressed like this? We'll make an exhibition of ourselves

[1] The grand parade took place in the streets each time the circus changed *terrenos*; not to be confused with the ordinary parades at the beginning and end of each performance.

whatever eyeshadow we wear,' she said angrily. 'But that's all right, I suppose. That's allowed.'

Her head drooped and I could tell from her voice that she was close to tears. But I had learnt by now that Karina was quite often close to tears; her whole life, in fact, was an emotional tightrope, permanently teetering between calamity and laughter.

In fact, what Karina was saying was very true. Exposing oneself in the circus ring, to an audience which consisted predominantly of children, was very different to exposing oneself to a general viewing on a Mexican public highway. At first, despite Karina's glumness, I was buoyed along by the newness and the excitement of the parade, and had been quite happy to wave and smile at the passers-by. It was only after the novelty had worn off a little that I began to be aware of what a high proportion of our street audience were men. Every corner we stopped at housed either a garage or a workshop or a building site teeming with men in overalls who came out to line the street when they heard the procession approaching. In fact, when I came to look more carefully, there didn't seem to be a single woman or child in the whole district. It was not only the men on the street, either. Men driving along the highway in their cars invariably slowed down to have a closer look. Gradually the flavour of that afternoon was altered. Where I had seen smiles, I now saw only leering faces. An innocent wave of the hand became a strangely threatening gesture.

Two well-dressed boys in a brand-new American Chevrolet drew up alongside us and wound down their window. 'Get 'em off, darling,' they shouted, before speeding off, laughing and gesticulating obscenely as they went. In the back of the same car were two girls. As the car passed by, I saw them point at me and laugh.

It grew cold. I pulled my feather boa more closely around my shoulders, both for warmth and in a vain attempt to cover myself up a little; a respite, however short, from the prying eyes all around me. After another half an hour I was not just cold, but chilled to the bone. I saw an old woman with a shopping bag stop on the pavement to watch us go by. I saw her laugh as the clowns went by; but when it came to the dancing girls her mouth suddenly puckered, as if she had sucked on something sour. *No vayan a ir al circo a ver piernas*, Doña Elena's story came back to me. I had never dreamt that I might be on the receiving end of the priest's words. I looked around at the others. Mara, who was positioned on her own at the front of the procession, stared expressionlessly straight ahead of her, looking neither left nor right. Behind her came Olinda and Pamela of the long legs; next Vanessa, Karina's sister, paired with the tiny Olga. After us came Brissel, and last of all the tightrope walker, Yvonne. None of them appeared to notice the scandal going on in the street around them. Occasionally, if we passed a group of children, they might permit themselves a nod or a wave, but these were exotic, sleepy movements, at once languid and yet strangely exaggerated, as if they were moving underwater. Otherwise they avoided all contact with the people on the street, and appeared neither to see or hear them. Instead they chatted amongst themselves, picked at their nails, rearranged their feathers or stared in a bored way into the middle distance. The puzzling lassitude (or so I had interpreted it) which so often crept into their acts, served them here like a camouflage, a kind of protective covering. It was as if the more they felt themselves exposed to the outside world, the more they turned in towards each other, weaving their thoughts and girlish chatter around them like a dreamy carapace.

With each new *terreno* the circus had been moving steadily outwards, in a north-westerly direction; but even now, after our third move, we were still in Mexico City. The name of the new site, Lomas Verdes, suggested that the place had once been an expanse of rolling green hills, but what we found was an area of rapidly expanding middle-class suburbs, arranged along a busy six-lane highway, the Avenida Lomas Verdes. The avenue was fronted with commercial centres and expensive, condominium-style housing developments. They had smartly turned out security guards, azaleas in tubs, and wistful names like Avenida de la Soledad. The shops, too, were American and expensive: Sandbornes, Kentucky Fried Chicken, Baskin' Robbins. There was even an American school. Blonde girls in tracksuits hung around at the gates and were picked up by cars with foreign number plates.

The circus had been pitched just off the Avenida Lomas Verdes, in the car park of a curious modern development, part bazaar, part recreation centre, which called itself El Skate Mall. When it first opened the original developers had gone bankrupt almost immediately but now, in a fit of optimism, the Mall was to have a second opening under new management and the circus had been called in as one of the promotional attractions. On Mundo's tannoy system, mixed with the usual *Raiders of the Lost Ark* theme music, it came over with a newly dramatic flavouring:

Es-*KAAY* Te . . . *MAALL.*

Of course, as far as the circus was concerned, the comfortable middle-class world of the Avenida Lomas Verdes was soon revealed to be only one side of the equation. Concealed beyond the car park, the ground sloped sharply downwards into a piece of scrub land overlooking the valley and the hills beyond. At night, with the lights shining, the view was pretty enough; but daylight revealed an ignominious scrawl of slums and communistic-looking tower blocks. Although the circus hands, the *chamacos* as they were known, had cleared the site as best they could, at the far end of the car park, where the caravans were now parked, the ground was still littered with rubbish. On one side lay piles of old building-site materials – rolls of barbed wire, pieces of packing case, twisted and rusting metal girders; on the other a squalid human detritus of detergent bottles, rusting tin cans, old nappies and plastic milk cartons.

The circus, which was of both worlds, belonged to neither. On the ragged borderland, which would be our home for the next few weeks, I watched the women struggle to recreate their daily lives, with resourcefulness and wit. I was learning to look at them not with an outsider's eyes, seeing only the squalid surroundings in which they were frequently forced to make their camps, but from the inside, in new ways. I saw how, in the tiny spaces in which they lived, five or six to a caravan sometimes, even the simplest household chores were feats of marvels. Most of the trailers had no heating, no plumbing, and only the most elementary electrics. I saw the lengths they went to to bathe every day and wear clean clothes, even though there was no running water and every drop, both for bathing and for washing, had to be carried by hand in buckets from the nearest tap.

In Rolando's caravan, which was parked next to ours, heroic

quantities of laundering and scrubbing were carried out almost daily by Mara and her mother Vicky. In the mornings when we woke up we would hear their old open-top washing machine, which was strapped to the back of their caravan with string, rumbling away manfully. Froth and foam would slowly gather into a head, rising until it became just one vast, trembling sud. Mara and her mother, and sometimes old Jovita in her curlers, stood by at the ready with vats of clean water, laboriously rinsing off each piece of clothing by hand.

The illusory power of the circus, its ability to create a world in which everything was either exciting or beautiful or mysterious, was never entirely diminished for me, even by these drab glimpses behind the scenes. In fact if anything my admiration for them, for their tenacity in creating so much from so little, was only increased. The magic which I was hoping to find had nothing to do with tricks. What I was hoping to find was more like an alternative language, like music or mathematics; not so much to do with the visible world as with some deeper, internal landscape.

As I have said, in one way and another the circus is full of the enchanted. In those early days I would watch the comings and goings of the circus camp from my window and wonder if I would ever really know them. Where had they come from? Why were they here? 'You have to learn people,' I remembered the Colombian tightrope walker telling me, 'the way you learn how to fish.' If I was going to learn the language of the circus, it would surely be by learning the people first, by listening to them and hearing the stories they had to tell.

Next to us, on the other side of our caravan, was Yvonne, the tightrope walker. At thirty, Yvonne was the oldest of the women performers. She had joined Circo Bell's only recently, arriving mysteriously in the middle of the night in a tiny caravan and depositing herself with her two young children on Mundo's doorstep. The next day she had started her tightrope act the circus way, no questions asked.

Yvonne had high cheek-bones and a secretive, watchful look about her. Except for her performances each night, she kept herself to herself and was never much part of ordinary circus life. I had never exchanged more than a few words with her, until one night when I was sitting watching the show from my usual seat to one side of the stage curtains. The music for Yvonne's act had just begun when I saw her come darting out of the wings towards me. 'Please, look after him.' She thrust her youngest child, a baby of eight months, into my arms and was gone. Ten seconds later she emerged again, from the stage curtains this time, smiling and curtseying to the crowd, and began her act as usual. Afterwards I carried the baby back to her caravan.

'He wasn't too much trouble, I hope?'

'Not at all. He slept the whole way through.'

She looked down at him with her slow, secret smile. 'I am sorry I had to do that to you. I was desperate. There simply wasn't anyone else and I can't just leave him.'

'Please don't mention it, any time. What's his name?'

'Taynarí.'

Taynarí was a tiny dark shrimp of a baby, very small for his age. When he heard his mother's voice, he opened his eyes. From his throat came a strange *rrr-rr* sound like a bird calling.

'And this is my daughter Sujeyli.' Yvonne presented me to a slim little girl of about ten, very dark-eyed and delicate-boned. 'We call her Susu.'

Yvonne's caravan, which was barely big enough to stand up in, was taken up predominantly by her bed, over which was hung a hammock for the baby. At one end of the bed was an old cooker covered in pots and pans, and opposite it a beaten up old wardrobe, full of holes and cracks in the wood. Feather boas in carnival colours hung down in rows from the cupboard doors. Sitting there, it was like being inside a tiny, brightly coloured, feather-lined nest.

Yvonne described herself as being 'del circo', which meant that she too was from a circus family. When her grandmother had first married, she told me, her husband's family had despised the circus and made her give it up. But she missed the life so much that soon she left him and married another man, a Guatemalan, who was from the same world as her, and she had gone on to found her own circus in Costa Rica. It was here that Yvonne grew up. Like Circo Bell's, it had been filled with her brothers and sisters, cousins, aunts and uncles. Yvonne's grandmother's circus had six boxing dwarves, dogs who walked on their hind legs, and a dancing donkey.

'But we did not have any big animals, like elephants. All the circuses in Costa Rica are poor circuses, not *de lujo*, you know, expensive, like this one. We were a very young circus, even younger than Circo Bell's. At one point so many of us were children that my grandmother decided she would make a feature of it: we became known as the Circo Infantil Americano. I was just five when I first started to perform. My father trained me. I was a contortionist, like Mara, although I have to say that at the beginning I didn't enjoy it much; I would much rather have been allowed to go outside and play.'

As we talked and Yvonne prepared the beans and maize tortillas for their dinner, Taynarí, who had been sleeping in his hammock, woke up and began to cry. His screams, high-pitched and piercing, filled the tiny caravan and set my nerves jangling. Yvonne picked him up and held him to her. Her face, when she looked at him, was very tired, the delicate skin beneath her eyes pressed with shadows, but her voice was still serene.

'There were six of us in my family.' She rocked the baby in her arms. 'My father was much older than my mother, ten or twelve years older. He came one day to the Catholic convent where she was at school and stole her away with him. Robbed her, as we say here. She was only thirteen.

'My father was a very tough, domineering man. All his children were afraid of him. Except for me. In character I was the one who was most like him. Rebellious, strong; not liking to be put upon by anyone. I was his favourite because I was the only one who stood up to him. Even when he beat me, I never cried, and I never cared. My father always loved me the most.'

Yvonne gazed down at her baby, who was sleeping again now, a lock of her hair tightly caught in one tiny, grasping hand. She untangled herself and put him back in the hammock.

'He was very strict with us when we were children,' she went on. 'There were four of us girls, but we were treated just the same as the boys. He taught us how to stitch the canvas of the tent when it was torn. And no matter what the weather, or how late it was, we all had to help with the putting up and taking down of the tent, just like our brothers. It was very hard.

'My father was jealous of all of us, but especially of us girls. We were not allowed any friends outside the circus, not even girlfriends, because he was convinced that they would bring us messages from *novios* and get us into all kinds of trouble. And, of course, we were never allowed out. In this way we grew up to be like him, to be resourceful and tough.

'When we were young my mother was an *equilibrista*, with her own balancing act, but I remember my father as many things. He was a contortionist, and a trapeze artist, and sometimes the ring-master too. But his best performance, the thing he loved the most, was the only one which he never performed on stage. He performed his magic act only for us. He did not do it very often, only when he was not too busy – which was hardly ever – but that is how I still see him.' Yvonne put her hand up to rock the little hammock. In his sleep, the baby sighed. 'My father has not spoken to me for more than ten years, but that is how I still see him, back in Costa Rica. As a magician. With his scarves and his cards and his coloured doves.'

Yvonne climbed out of her leotard and pulled on a pair of jeans. The leotard was burgundy-coloured with a high Chinese collar decorated with silver leaves. She changed quickly and methodically, tidying away her costume and her feather boa into the sagging wardrobe. From the shelf above her bed she took a pot of cold cream, rubbing it into her face with a practised hand.

'I was seventeen when I ran away.' She scrubbed off her heavy stage make-up with a handful of tissues. 'My husband – although we weren't married then – was fifteen years older than me. We were going to catch a bus and go abroad some place, make a new life for ourselves, but one of my cousins had seen him hanging around the circus and warned my father that there was something going on. My father said nothing, just waited and watched. Without my knowing it, the day I left he followed me all the way to the bus station. And, of course, I never did get on that bus.

'After that, my husband left Costa Rica on his own and came up here, to Mexico, to find work. But before he left we were married secretly. We were more careful that time, no one found us out. Later, when my father learnt what I had done, he realized that there was nothing more he could do. He never spoke to me again.'

Yvonne's daughter, Susu, watched her from the bed where she was sitting, her feet tucked under her, a slender-necked, exotic little bird. For a time we sat in silence, but this did not seem to bother Yvonne, and after a while she continued with her story.

'This is the second time I have left my husband. He wants me back, so he says, but I say, no way. I'm going to make it on my own this time, no matter what people say. When you are young, as I was when I ran away, you think that when you marry you will find freedom. I wanted to escape from my father's rule, but of course as soon as I was married I found that, if anything, I had even less freedom than before.

'At first we went south, to Colombia, and joined a circus there. I soon found that as well as performing in the evenings a whole new set of responsibilities fell to me. Every day I had to cook and clean, do the shopping and the washing for my husband. At first I didn't mind, I could manage. But later, when I had Susu, it was much harder. Two weeks after I had her I was performing again, but it wasn't the same. I was so tired all the time, and I had no one to help me, no family except my husband.

'But whenever I asked him to help me, I would begin to have problems with him. If I was late getting ready for the performance and the baby started to cry, I would say to him, please, you go to her, can't you see I'm busy right now. I can't do two things at once. But . . . well, you know how no man likes his friends to see that his wife is bossing him around.'

Yvonne smiled slowly.

'He used to knock me around a bit, you know the kind of thing,' she shrugged, but there was no bitterness in her voice. 'The first time I left him, he swore to me that if I came back things would be different, but I know better now.

'When I left him, people said to me, you'll be sorry. With two small children, you think you can survive on your own in this world? Even if you do, they said, no one will respect you. A woman on her own, you know, she goes with anyone, with lots of different men. She's bound to, anyone can tell you that.'

'And you believed that?'

Yvonne laughed. 'The moment they told me it was impossible, that I would never survive on my own, I decided that I would do it. I had to, if only to prove that they were all wrong. I took it as a personal challenge that I would *salir en adelante*, go forward on my own. And here I am.'

'Aren't you lonely sometimes?'

'No.' She shook her head. 'It is peaceful on my own. I like it.'

She seemed so self-contained, aloof almost – even from her own children.

I rarely saw her touch or caress her daughter. Instead, I would sometimes catch her regarding Susu thoughtfully, as though she were hardly flesh and blood at all, but some luminous puzzle of her own making. Yvonne must have guessed what I was thinking.

'My husband used to berate me, saying that I did not love my daughter, but he's wrong. It's true that I have never been very domesticated. I was never cut out to be the *típica mujer abnegada*, as they say here in Mexico, born only to suffer and to produce children. My husband used to say this because I am stricter with her than other mothers. Instead of letting her play all day like the other children, I make her do her lessons. Exercises to get her body into shape, so that when the time comes she'll be able to do any act she likes in the circus.'

There was a tap on the door and then a voice, 'Can Susu come out and play?' Susu looked at her mother, who nodded, and without a word the girl skipped lightly from the room. Yvonne watched her go and for the first time I thought I saw a flutter of anxiety behind the serene façade. When the door was closed again she turned to me.

'You see, I have tried to bring her up not to make the same mistakes that I did,' she said quickly. 'I say to her, don't marry young, the way that I did, for you will live to regret it all your life. You must think of yourself, give yourself the chance to enjoy life before you give yourself into the hands of a man. I warn her never to go alone with any of the *chamacos*, never to trust them, never to let them touch her . . .' She trailed off, as though startled by her own outburst.

A sinister thought occurred to me.

'Have you had trouble with them, the *chamacos*, I mean?'

'No, never.' Yvonne shook her head. 'The boys here have always treated me with respect. They call me Señora Yvonne and carry my water for me sometimes and help me hammer in the pegs for my tarpaulin outside . . . but you can never be too careful.' She looked at me with meaning. 'You can never let them get too close.'

She reached over and drew an object out from underneath her pillow. It was a knife. She held it up so I could see, turning it delicately in her hands.

'When I am on my own, I sleep with this knife under my pillow.' She drew one finger down its blade as if she were stroking it. 'Sometimes I wake up in the night and I am so afraid. I take the knife out and I call out, *Quién es?* Who's there? Usually it's just the wind, or one of the dogs sniffing at my door. But one day,' she slipped the knife gently back under her pillow, 'one day, I know it won't be either of those things.'

As I was leaving we stood together at the door of her caravan. It was dark and below us in the valley the lights glimmered and winked. Some of the performers had already started gathering for the second performance. I saw Karina, an old coat over her costume, slip by into the tent to find Gallo. Some of the circus children, Susu, Tintin and his younger sister, Lely, ran shrieking and laughing, chasing each other round the caravans at the entrance to the Big Top. Beyond them Luis, the keeper, was feeding his elephants and I could hear the breathy *hu-ppppph* of pleasure as they lifted up the whiskery bales of grass in their trunks. A new thought occurred to me.

'Have you ever thought of leaving?' I asked Yvonne. 'The circus, I mean.'

'Believe me, I've thought about it and thought about it. But then I always imagine how I will feel at this time,' she nodded towards the Big Top, 'at the *hora de la función.* When there would be no music and no lights; and no crowd queuing up at the *taquilla*, and I realize that it is impossible for me to leave. I would miss it too much.

'When you are *del circo*, the circus is more important than anything. It is more important than your country – circuses can tour abroad for years at a time. More important than your family even – I haven't seen mine more than twice in the last thirteen years.' She smiled at me, her inimitable secret smile. 'You see, the circus is not just a way of life, it *is* your life. It gets to everyone sooner or later.'

> But what many forget, in disguising themselves as
> cheap magicians, is that the marvellous becomes
> unequivocally marvellous when it arises
> from . . . a privileged revelation of reality . . .
> ALEJO CARPENTIER, *El Reino de Este Mundo*

As Doña Elena had first taught me, the lessons of the circus are hard.

We had been in Lomas Verdes nearly a week before I discovered the real reason that we had not stayed at the previous *terreno*, the field which was so waterlogged that our entire convoy had been forced to park in the road next to it for several days. It was not because of the conditions at all. We had been moved on by pressure from the local inhabitants.

'When they saw our caravans parked there, some of the women came to see Mundo and told him that we couldn't stay there,' Yvonne told me. 'They said that it gave them *pena* to see us there, especially the women and children. *Pobres creaturas*, they called us, poor creatures, without water or any place to wash. And the children playing around in the mud, so close to the road, too. It was bad for us to live like that.'

'Who asked them to feel sorry for us?' I was indignant.

Yvonne shrugged. 'No one, of course. We don't feel sorry for ourselves, so why should they? But I know women like that. That wasn't the real reason they wanted us to go. The real reasons are always the same: they are afraid that their children might play with our children, who will teach them bad habits and bad language, might even give them a disease of some kind, who knows? They are afraid that our boys will steal from them and insult their daughters. They are afraid that we will go begging to them, for food, or even for money.' She gave me her slow, lop-sided smile.

'I have known *barrios* where they have refused to give our people so much as a glass of water once they knew they were circus folk. So, that's how things are. What can you do?'

In Mexico the circus is a marginalized world; a caste of untouchables, as some would still see them, existing only on the fringes of society; abused, and sometimes even persecuted, by a people still profoundly ill at ease with their own conception.

In 1546, when the monastery at Actopán was built, the two worlds, Indian and Spanish, were still exactly that – two worlds apart. Even then, nearly quarter of a century after the Conquest, for those who came to Mexico from the Old World, the strangeness of the New, the hallucinogenic power of the land and its people, seemed almost to derange the senses. What would be the outcome, did they ever stop to wonder, should the two worlds really meet, become flesh and blood together?

More so than any other Latin American nation, the Mexicans are a hybrid people. A race of mestizos, half Indian, half Spanish: tough, melancholic, difficult to get close to.

'What is a true Mexican like?' I was on the night train going north one time, when I met some men drinking tequila in the bar. They thought for a moment.

'The true Mexican is *macho*,' one said.

'He is *triste*,' said another.

'*Enamorado*,' said the third.

Macho. Sad. Always in love.

We ordered some more drinks. Tequila is an unusual substance, made not from grain or grape but from the maguey cactus. Like most forms of raw alcohol it has practically no taste, but instead 'an underwhiff of festering sweetness', as Sybille Bedford once described it, 'as though chrysanthemums had rotted in gin'. In small amounts it induces unusual truthfulness, in slightly larger ones, a philosophical turn of mind, and in only marginally greater quantities, something approaching *ekstasis*.

'Macho, yes. And in love, that too. But sad, why sad?'

We were approaching the philosophical phase.

'Sad because of our Indian blood,' they replied, 'for the Indian is always sad.'

One of my companions was a municipal accountant; his friend

had just finished training as a vet. They wore laundered white shirts, stretched a little too tightly over their spilling bellies. The third man was returning to Texas, where he now lived, after a visit to his family in Mexico City. He sported the careful badges of the émigré: a Stetson, checked shirt and crocodile boots, each a little too large, a little too cracklingly new, to be wholly convincing. All three had the clipped black moustache of middle-class, mestizo Mexicans.

'But as Mexicans surely you must consider your true nature to be both Indian *and* Spanish?' I went on.

The accountant sprinkled more salt on his lime. Before replying he squeezed a few drops of the juice meditatively into his mouth.

'It's like this,' he explained. 'All that Spanish part, it's not something we're proud of.'

'The Spanish only came here to oppress us,' the vet said, 'they were no better than common vandals.'

'They tore down our temples and burnt our manuscripts and books. They desecrated all our sacred treasures, stole our precious stones. All our gold and our silver was melted down, sent back to Spain, to a foreign king . . .'

'They killed our great emperor, Moctezuma, and reduced all our chiefs and priests to common slaves.'

'Our great and ancient culture was destroyed because of the Spanish. If it wasn't for them, think what Mexico might be today.' They looked out of the window at the burning, cactus-stabbed plain. 'Not a dust bowl, not like this. We could have been like the United States, who knows . . .'

The Spanish Conquest devastated the power of the indigenous Mexicans, first through the well-known triptych of warfare, disease and forced conversion to Christianity, and then later through interbreeding, but it did not destroy them altogether. Although Mexico is now an overwhelmingly mestizo country, anthropologists still list more than fifty separate Indian groups, each speaking their own language, who remain pure-blooded descendants of the pre-Hispanic peoples. But although the mestizo Mexicans believe passionately in the splendour and greatness of their Indian past, frequently at the expense of their Spanish roots, it is rare for them to invest their Indian present with this dignity. Like the circus, the

Mexican *indígenas* are a marginalized people, amongst the most dispossessed and underprivileged in the land. And yet it is in these small groups, some of them no more than a few families strong, that the steely flavour of old Mexico, in all its anarchy and magic, can still be found.

In the Lacandón rainforest the night was like a hallucination, a negative of the day. The outline of the bushes, of the turkey huts, of each individual blade of grass glowed in the intense white light of the moon. Beyond them the trees were bound in milky vapour, fine as spirit matter. From my hammock I could hear the spectral voices of the roosters calling.

We had come to Betél, a remote settlement close to the Guatemalan border in the deep south of Mexico, and one of only two remaining settlements of the Lacandón Indians, because we had heard that we might be able to find a guide here, a man named Antonio Chankin, who would take us to Bonampak, a ruined Maya site in the jungle nearby. We had driven to Betél from the town of Palenque, many jolting hours to the very end of a dirt track which frequently becomes impassable in the rainy season. For much of the way the landscape, once virgin rainforest, was denuded; cattle grazed around the sad charcoaled remains of a few trees, their splintered trunks pointing heavenwards like leprous limbs. But towards the end of the track, as the trail dwindles, the rainforest closes in again and it is as if you have entered a different element, like diving into water or walking on the moon. In the rainforest, it has always seemed to me, everything, even the quality of your breathing, is transformed.

Until the latter part of this century the Lacandón Indians, marooned in their jungle, had only the most cursory contact with the outside world. Anthropologists believed them to be a distant branch of the Maya. They were thought to hunt with bows and feathered arrows, and to worship a sun god, even though the canopy beneath which they lived was so impenetrable that their pools of water gave off no reflections. According to one source, the old ceremonial centres of the ancient Maya – nearby Bonampak and Yaxchilán on the Usumacinta river – were still places of special veneration. But, on the whole, the little information that we could glean about them was largely contradictory.

The photographs we had seen were more telling. The best of these, and one of the earliest, taken by the French explorer Désiré Charnay in the mid-nineteenth century, shows a charming group of jungle wraiths with pudding-basin haircuts and simple flowing white smocks, their necks fettered gorgeously with ropes of jungle beads, seeds and pips and coloured pods. Their expressions are humorous and intelligent, if a little bemused; a far cry from the feral ennui of their more modern portraits.

It is the familiar, heart-breaking story. *Estos imbéciles*, those imbeciles, as an otherwise civilized friend in Mexico City once described them to us, now number only a few hundred beleaguered souls. Through laziness and ignorance, you are likely to be told, they have recklessly squandered the two things which might have redeemed them. First, their ancient culture, to the American missionary groups; and second, the very jungle itself, vast tracts of which were conceded to them, only to be sold off to foreign companies in the form of lumbering concessions.

We found Antonio Chankin without difficulty. Antonio was a Seventh Day Adventist and, like so many of the modern Lacandón, he had the long buttery-yellow locks and bleached, white rabbit eye-lashes of an albino. He lived in a hut close to the roadside, an open-sided thatched shelter with a few rotting hammocks strung from the rafters at one end, and a primitive hearth – a fire surrounded by three flat stones – at the other. The floor, which was of beaten earth, rich in insect life and half-eaten vegetable matter, was picked over by various forms of livestock, chickens and a ferocious, sixteen-pound turkey which strutted around displaying itself promiscuously, quivering and rattling its tail like a porcupine's quills.

Antonio had a wife, Juanita, a sour-faced, pot-bellied little woman, who wore a dress printed over with bunches of violent orange flowers, and a clutch of children with sonorous Old Testament names, Isaac, Noah and Israel. It was too late to attempt the walk to Bonampak that day, but Antonio said that we could stay with him that night and we would set out early the next morning. As we hung up our own hammocks from the rafters, the family clustered round. The children, piled into one of the hammocks, watched breathlessly as we sorted through our things. They hung so close over us, that from time to time I could feel their breath against my cheek. Juanita sat down opposite.

'What's that?' She jerked her head towards Tom's sleeping bag.

'It's like a blanket,' he explained. 'For sleeping in.'

'Oh.' Juanita's mouth drooped. She put her hand out and slowly patted the roll. 'We don't have anything like that,' she said dully. 'How much did it cost?' Her fingers hovered over the material.

Tom was caught off guard. He thought for a moment. 'I can't remember exactly,' he shrugged. 'Not much, it's only an old one.'

'Can I buy it from you?' There was an emptiness about her question, even as she asked it, as though she already knew the answer. Her gaze was fixed steadily on the object of her desire.

'Well, I . . . I'm not . . .' He looked at her and then down at the sleeping bag again. 'I'm afraid I need it. I wasn't really thinking of selling.'

'Oh.' Juanita's mouth drooped again. For a while she said nothing, but her eyes flickered, with the hopeless avarice of the very poor, over each of our possessions in turn.

I had thought us circumspect in the amount of luggage we travelled with – we had come to Betél with only the minimal amount necessary, or so we thought, for a few days walking in the rainforest – but as the evening wore on, under Juanita's scrutiny, our few travel-tattered possessions became transformed into a hoard of such reckless profligacy I felt almost sick.

Juanita set up an impromptu commentary.

'And that's your toothbrush,' she intoned.

'And that's Tom's toothbrush,' Antonio, swinging dreamily beside her in his hammock, chipped in. 'Look, they *both* have a toothbrush, Juanita.'

'And so how much might a toothbrush cost?' Juanita mumbled on gloomily to herself. 'Five *thousand* pesos!'[1] There was a shocked pause, before she would be off again. 'And that's your hairbrush.'

'But look, Juanita, he doesn't use the hairbrush, he uses a comb . . .'

[1] About £1.

'Gracious.' Juanita's lips pursed. 'A hairbrush *and* a comb.' In the quickening dusk I could no longer see her face, but her orange dress glowed darkly, an avenging imp on the other side of the hut. 'How much for the hairbrush? The comb?'

At this point, her children joined in, swinging in their hammock and chanting, *Cuánto cuesta, cuánto cuesta*? How much, how much? like a mantra. In the light of our torches (there was no electricity in their hut) their bright eyes shone through the netting of the old hammock like a shoal of small but flesh-eating fish. As the evening wore on our embarrassment turned to dismay. Although the hut was open-sided, I felt hot and claustrophobic. They would suck the very breath out of me, I thought, if only they could.

'Let's go,' I said to Tom. 'This isn't going to work, I can tell.'

'Where to?' he replied. 'Look, it's only for one night. Perhaps things will get better in the morning.'

We did our best. We gave them all the rations we had brought with us. We gave them aspirin for Antonio's rheumatism, and cold cream for Juanita's wrinkled cheeks; we gave the eldest son, Pedro, a cassette tape and, against all our principles, bought the younger children *refrescos*, crisps and pots of mayonnaise (a great delicacy) from the stores in the next-door village. But somehow it wasn't enough. I have never felt so rich, so foreign, or so completely besieged.

The track to Bonampak, once you were on it, was quite straightforward, a muddy jungle trail, impassable in a vehicle but easy to follow on foot. Antonio, wearing a pair of ancient corduroys and a strange wicker hat not unlike a solar topee, strode on ahead of us. Over one shoulder he carried a string bag with a bunch of bananas in it which made him look, disconcertingly, as if he was just strolling off to the local supermarket. All around us the rainforest hummed. Even though it soon became obvious that we could quite easily have followed the track on our own, as Tom pointed out it was more fun to go with a proper guide. 'Someone who can tell us about the plants and the birds and animal trails. These guys know this jungle better than anyone,' he said. 'Their knowledge is amazing.'

Sure enough. Before long we saw Antonio crouch down and

examine the ground beneath him intently. He beckoned us over. 'Look,' he pointed to some tracks in the mud at the side of the path. 'Combi!'

'Combi?' Tom and I looked at one another.

'A kind of deer perhaps?' I hazarded a guess. 'Or a wild pig?'

We looked at the tracks again. Although it was hard to tell in the soft mud, they did not look much like either of these.

'Combi!' Excitably, Antonio stabbed at the markings with his finger again, trying to make us understand.

'What kind of combi?' We huddled round him, fascinated.

'*Combi.*' Antonio looked up at us with exasperation. '*Volks-wagen* Combi!' He let out a mad cackle. Then he looked at his watch. 'Nine thirty-*seven* already.' He blinked his sandy eye-lashes, serious again suddenly. 'We must get going, or we'll be *late*,' he said accusingly. He strode off in front of us into the jungle again, rubber boots belching softly in the mud.

All morning we followed Antonio's thin figure through the forest. With his long yellow hair and his wide-brimmed hat, string bag over one shoulder, he looked like some weird jungle wizard striding jerkily ahead of us beneath the dripping canopy. Every so often he would stop and point things out. Sometimes this was certain types of fruit – bananas or wild mamey which he was planning to come back and pick when they were ripe – but in Antonio's world these were of only the most workaday interest. What caught his attention far more was the trail of human detritus which was slowly building up along the path. We did not see any more Combi tracks. Instead we found two old cushions, a shirt and, best of all, a pair of men's trousers which someone had recklessly jettisoned in a ditch at the side of the road.

'Look at this!' Antonio would regard the latest treasure with wonder. 'And this!' He subjected each new item to an intense, almost obsessive scrutiny, like a lepidopterist with a particularly rare and fascinating new specimen. 'Here, you take them,' he said generously to Tom after he had finished examining the trousers. 'You could do with a new pair.' He erupted into another of his mad cackles. 'Well, he could do with a new pair, couldn't he?' He turned to me, wheezing, and pointed at Tom's tattered clothes. '*He* can have them,' he whooped, clutching his sides. '*He* can have the trousers in the *ditch!*' Then, pulling himself together, he consulted his watch again with a serious expression. 'Goodness me. Eleven thirteen. Already!' His brow puckered. Forgetting the trousers completely, he struck off along the path again with new vigour.

'Must hurry . . .' I could hear him muttering to himself, '. . . late . . . we'll be *late*. . . wouldn't do at all . . .'

We came to Bonampak at noon, emerging on to its shimmering, grassy esplanades with something like shock. Before we explored the site, we sat down to rest in the shade of some trees, spreading out the picnic we had brought with us at the foot of the ruined pyramid. The turf beneath us was smooth and manicured, oddly formal like an English vicarage lawn. Apart from the caretaker, we were utterly alone at the site that day. There was something eerie about the silence, a man-made silence of abandoned court-yards and cool grey stone.

As a Maya ceremonial centre, the site of Bonampak is a rela-tively unimportant one, a Late Classic[1] structure which would almost certainly have been under the suzerainty, both political and cultural, of nearby Yaxchilán. The startling discovery which was made at Bonampak, when it was 'discovered' in 1946, was a sequence of wall paintings, miraculously preserved in their lime-stone vaults for over a thousand years.

Unlike the Aztecs, by the time of the Spanish Conquest in 1519 the golden age of the Maya was long past. The Classic art of the Maya, and their post-Classic codices, suggest that they perceived the earth as being like the back of a monstrous crocodile resting in a pool filled with water lilies. We know that they performed human sacrifices and ritual blood-lettings; we know that they drank hot chocolate (which they invented), and developed an enig-matic hieroglyphic script of such intricacy that it has yet to be fully deciphered. We know, too, that a flattened head and crossed eyes were considered signs of beauty; and that they inlaid their teeth with jade.

In artistic and intellectual terms, at their greatest florescence no

[1] Archaeologists refer to the apogee of the Maya civilization as the Classic period, usually dividing this into Early Classic (AD 300–600) and Late Classic (AD 600–900).

other contemporary civilization in the New World, and few in the Old, could touch them. Under the Maya mathematics and astronomy reached a level comparable to that of the Babylonians, and unsurpassed by any other ancient people. They discovered the concept of zero and, although they used only two other symbols (one and five), both their numerical system and the calendars they evolved were of such complexity that they were able to calculate and record the cycles of the sun and moon, their eclipses, and the movements of certain planets, with extraordinary accuracy.[1] The dates which archaeologists have deciphered on Maya stelae and in their three surviving codices cover vast periods, sometimes millions of years back into a mythological past. Indeed, the calculation of time was of such importance to the Maya that until recently it was believed that their religion was the worship of time itself.

So, who were these brilliant, savage, chocolate-drinking astrologers? Possibly more study has been made of the Maya than of any other ancient people in the New World, and yet, a more complete picture eludes us. We are left with seemingly unconnected facts; with whimsical details and glittering oddity.

The murals at Bonampak contain the date 2 August AD 792. The paintings, spread out over three rooms, represent the Maya at the height of their powers. They are scenes of extraordinary beauty and cruelty. In the first room nobles in white robes attend the presentation of a child, thought to be the last great dynastic accession at Bonampak. The second room is dated a year later, and shows that a battle has been waged in which the warriors of Bonampak have emerged victorious. According to their astrological auguries, on 2 August AD 792 Venus rose as the Morning Star demanding human sacrifices. On one wall captives from the battle, naked and humiliated, are ranged on the steps in front of their captors. Every last detail of their plight is lovingly rendered. One prisoner is having his nails torn out; two others already bend, lamenting, over their tortured fingers which sprinkle droplets of blood. Above them, on the top steps, a naked figure pleads for his

---

[1] The Maya calculated the moon's cycle to average 29.53020 days. Modern calculations put it at 29.53059 (see *The Maya*, Michael D. Coe (Pelican, 1971)).

life from the conquering lords who stand proudly around their chief, Chaan-muan, richly tunicked and fetlocked in jaguar skins. In their hands they carry fans and parasols and batons; their noble profiles almost disappear beneath the weight of their headdresses, decked with flowing quetzal feathers and fantastic animal masks. The third room shows the captives being sacrificed on a pyramid, while the royal family perform a ritual blood-letting. Seated on thrones, the women pass rope and sting-ray spines through their tongues, as a group of lords in towering quetzal plume headdresses dance in their honour to an orchestra of rattles, trumpets and turtle carapaces.

Blood-letting rituals, such as the one so graphically shown at Bonampak, are one of the most curious aspects of Maya ceremonial life. Historians believe that blood-letting was more than just an arcane rite, but was an obligatory part of the institution of kingship, and that every important astrological and religious event required sanctifying through this means. Like the later Aztecs of central Mexico, the Maya believed that blood was the food of the gods, and that to maintain order in the cosmos it was vital to propitiate them in this way. But this was not all. By sacrificing their own blood, the rulers sought visions of their gods and ancestors, giving them a temporary, but real, existence in the world of the men who worshipped them. Those rulers who succeeded in summoning the 'vision serpent' successfully, became the link between the human and the divine, and thus the focus of enormous power amongst their own people. Indeed, for the duration of the ritual they might even have been considered to become the very god they had summoned.

That day, standing in the empty little room at the top of the pyramid, their world seemed unbearably strange, bound by visions and masochistic etiquette. Perhaps it was to one of these tiny vaults, their walls stained with scenes as dark as blood itself, that the ruler and his family retired to prepare themselves for the ceremony. Their preparations were rituals in themselves, ascetic marathons involving days of fasting, sexual abstinence, and purifying steam baths.

I tried to imagine what it must have been like when they emerged from the room at last, with hundreds, perhaps even thousands of their people congregated at the foot of the great pyramid, waiting in holy dread for the gods to show themselves once more. With horrible suffering the women would have pierced their tongues, and the ruler his penis, with sting-ray spines or needles specially sharpened with obsidian or flint.[1] The blood from their wounds was allowed to flow down paper strips, which were then burnt as offerings. How would it have felt to have gazed down on the crowd from that great height, dazzled with pain and hunger, with the smoke of censers and their own massive blood loss. Surrounded by their priests and lords, masked in feathers and animal skins, with their fabulous anklets and pendants, their necks hung with shells and precious jade, they must have gazed into the clouds of perfumed smoke; and who knows by what act of hallucinatory will-power might the vision serpents have been summoned after all?

The Bonampak murals were never completed, and we will never know if the child presented there ever reached his majority. Around AD 900 the Classic Maya civilization collapsed. 'The only fact about this mysterious downfall which is known with any certainty,' wrote the archaeologist Michael Coe, 'is that it happened. The rest, like so much about the Maya, is pure conjecture.' Further north, in the Yucatán, their intellectual elites were replaced by cruder leaderships, the Toltec and other Mexican tribes. But in the rainforests of the central lowlands, with the exception of a few isolated groups such as the Lacandón, the population appears to have dispersed completely, their great ceremonial centres abandoned for ever to the soft green rotting of the jungle.

Somehow we had no desire to stay very long at Bonampak. As we walked the weary three hours back through the jungle, Antonio Chankin, with his greasy yellow locks and his string bag over one

---

[1] Shortly after the Conquest, the Spanish Archbishop Diego de Landa recorded: 'They offered sacrifices of their own blood, sometimes cutting themselves around in pieces, and they left them this way as a sign. Other times they pierced their cheeks, at others their lower lips. Sometimes they scarify certain parts of their bodies, at others they pierced their tongues in a slanting direction from side to side and passed bits of straw through the holes with horrible suffering; others split the superfluous part of their virile member leaving it as they did their ears.' (See *The Blood of Kings: Dynasty and Ritual in Maya Art*, Mary Ellen Miller and Linda Schele (Kimbell Art Museum, 1986).)

shoulder, seemed a scrawny substitute for the reeking and bloody marvels of his ancestors. Inside the forest, in the hot pall of afternoon, the heat was enervating. With several hours still to go I felt two blisters coming up on each of my heels. I walked slower and slower. Antonio kept looking at his watch.

'I can do this walk in two hours when I'm on my own,' he grumbled. 'If we go on like this, we won't be back until five or six. We'll be *late*.'

But even his White Rabbit chivvying had lost its charm. We passed the ragged trousers and the Combi tracks without comment.

Back at Antonio's hut, both his mood and ours began to soften. Our walk to Bonampak, and the things we had seen there, had expiated something in us. My feet were in shreds, we were hot and tired and dirty, and yet curiously – perhaps because of it – something in all of us had relaxed.

Tom and I went down to the river with Israel. He sat on the bank and watched us as we floated in the water. The water was brown and peaty. After the rainforest, the feel of it against my skin was like slipping between cool, sweet-smelling sheets. We floated on our backs, looking up through the trees at the tropical sky and feeling the little fishes nibbling at our feet. 'Es porque no te conocen,' Israel said. 'It's because they don't know you. They never do that to us.'

That night Juanita cooked maize tortillas, greyish, leaden discs the size and consistency of Wellington boots. Afterwards, when it was dark, we lay in our hammocks and listened to their radio. Even among the Lacandón, the Iraq war was the hot news item. *Iraq!* and *Bush!* the younger children, Isaac and Noah and the little girl Elisabetta chanted at us. Antonio and his eldest son Pedro, a gentle, solemn-eyed youth of seventeen, swore that on still evenings sometimes they could hear the bombs themselves, although they sounded very far away, they said, far beyond the outer limits of their forest.

Little by little we were adjusting to each other. As we became more familiar to them we ceased to be objects of merely material curiosity; and we, in turn, began to uncover new and thoughtful layers beneath their skinflint squalor. Tempted by the cool river, at Antonio's invitation we stayed on in Betél. We went walking in the village with Pedro and were allowed to test out their bows and arrows, exquisitely tuned working instruments, although they are largely made to be sold to tourists these days. We visited their *milpas*, the plots of land in which they grow their staples of maize and beans, and saw the wild fruit and honeycombs which they gathered from the forest. Israel showed us how to lay traps for the doves, making circles on the ground with handfuls of scarlet seeds. We swam and played with their children, were savaged by mosquitoes, and lay awake through the languid silver nights watching the rainforest recede in spirals of ghostly vapour.

The traditional beliefs of the Lacandón are remembered dimly, if at all, long since tempted away by the evangelical serpent of Seventh Day Adventism. At the temple-hut in Betél Christian hymns replace the old sun and ancestor worship. Both men and women dress plainly, many still in the white homespun shifts of their forebears (although gone are the beautiful ropes of jungle seeds and pods: for personal adornment encourages the sins of pride and licentiousness). All public spectacles and gatherings, other than those held for religious reasons, are frowned on. Alcohol is forbidden.

Although this new spiritual asceticism is perhaps not as far removed from that of their distant ancestors as we might think, compared to the beauty and the horror of the Maya it does seem fatally dull. Antonio was, however, a man of unexpected resourcefulness.

We had first noticed his preoccupation with time on our walk through the jungle to Bonampak. First with amusement, for with his unusual pale skin and hair, and slightly red-rimmed eyes (albinos are congenitally sensitive to light), he was almost ludicrously like the White Rabbit from *Alice in Wonderland*, looking at his watch and urging us on to some unknown appointment at the far end of the forest. Later on, though, on our way back when we were tired and our feet were sore, our amusement had faded to irritation. What was he in such a hurry *for*? We could not work it out. He had nothing particular to get back to; and it was not, I don't think, that he was just bored and wanting to get home.

Our slowness upset him deeply, as if by straying beyond the time limits which he had set himself, we were offending against some unfathomable natural order or taboo.

If we had thought his behaviour was strange in the forest, back in Betél it began to take on almost obsessional qualities. At first I noticed this only when the subject of time came into our conversations. One afternoon I was lying in my hammock talking to his little daughter, who had brought along her school books to show me.

'So, what time do you get to school, Elisabetta?' I flicked through the pages of one of her textbooks.

'A las nueve,' she said. 'At nine o'clock.'

'Sí, a las nueve.' I had thought that Antonio was asleep, but he now echoed her from his hammock, adding with gravitas. 'A las nueve en punto.' At nine o'clock *on the dot.*

The times of their temple services, I noticed, carried this same precision. They went in 'a las tres *en punto*', and came out again, 'a las cuatro *en punto.*' Soon, the great question became not 'how much?' – although Juanita still showed a lingering fondness for it – but 'at what time?' *A qué hora?* If we said that we were going for a swim in the river, or for a walk in the village, or to look at the school, Antonio would want to know at what time we were going to do it. 'Later' or 'in half an hour' were not good enough. 'What do you mean "later"?' His old face would pucker crossly. 'Do you mean at ten o'clock or eleven o'clock?' Then, when we had been lured into giving a more precise time, he would give us laborious time-checks, counting us down until he thought it was time for us to go. 'It's two minutes to eleven,' he would announce. 'You'd better get along or you'll be late for your swim,' and so on.

This insistence was very mysterious to us. These days it is rare to find a group of people who live so completely beyond the constraints of a modern timetable. The Lacandón had no offices or jobs to go to, no buses to catch, no shops, no bars, no cinemas with opening hours, not even a television set between them with favourite programmes showing at certain times of the day. In the absence of electricity or any kind of artificial light apart from their torches, even their waking and sleeping hours were determined by

71

the natural cycle of the day: they went to sleep when it got dark, woke up shortly before dawn.

Once I was watching Antonio lying in his hammock, as he did for a large part of each day, staring up at the ceiling of his hut when, *apropos* of nothing, he suddenly looked at his watch. 'Ah,' he said, to no one in particular. 'Three thirty-seven.' Then he went back to looking at the ceiling again. I realized then that there was something about the measuring of time for its own sake, quite unconnected with the normal activities associated with it, which was a peculiar source of satisfaction to him; something quite abstract and outside my own experience. Compared with my thinking – logical, English, strictly two-dimensional – Antonio's was pure poetry.

Antonio told the time on any timepiece he could find (Tom's collapsible travelling alarm clock was a particular source of envy), savouring the combination of hours and minutes as if, like fine wine, each one carried a subtle flavour of its own: thin, ethereal minutes, scented like river water and mist and rising sap, for the early dawn; deepening through the morning into hours which dropped like mellow fruits, apricot and wild mamey. Perhaps the midday shifts were slower moments, hot, languorous seconds reeking of desire, of earth and the pulsing forest. I imagined the afternoon hours quickening again, each segment still tasting sweet, but with tangier, citrus flavours, until dusk came, a short but delicate span whose each individual minute could be savoured thoughtfully, ticking with herbs from the *milpa* and a smoky *arrière-goût*.

It is possible that part of his pleasure was no more than simple pride in owning a timepiece, and in being able to tell the time at all. It is tempting, too, to see in it some deep atavism: a last, dusty thread linking him to his distant ancestors, the time-obsessed Maya. I believe that the truth is somewhere in between. For Antonio, the contemplation of time was like reciting poetry. It was as though he saw in its very abstractions a beauty and an order; a powerful if only dimly understood magic, illuminating the last days of an ever-diminishing world. For magic, as the circus had first taught me, is not tricks. Magic is many things. It is, to borrow Carpentier's phrase, 'a privileged revelation of reality': a way of thinking, poetic rather than logical, which makes the world anew.

Although both Antonio and Pedro had been to Bonampak many times, they had never been to its neighbour, the great ceremonial centre, Yaxchilán. So, when we finally left Betél to go there, Tom suggested that as a way of saying 'thank you' we should invite the two of them to come with us, not as our guides, but as our guests this time.

Even today there are no roads to Yaxchilán, not even a track through the jungle. Poised on a great bend in the Usumacinta river, the ruins remain largely unexcavated, their crumbling stone pyramids, palaces and ball courts laced tightly into the nape of the forest. In Frontera, a flea-bitten Chol settlement an hour downriver, we set about hiring a boat, a long canoe with an outboard motor on the back. As we bargained with the boatman a large crowd gathered round us, staring and pointing at Pedro and Antonio. Less than an hour's drive from their home our roles had already been brutally reversed: now it was they who were, in no uncertain terms, the freaks in our travelling show. The men's faces were hard and there were many of them. I could feel them looking at me too. Instinctively the four of us drew together.

(In fact, the only thing of real note which happened in Frontera was in the *comedor* on the waterfront where we had a dingy lunch of fried eggs and tortillas before setting off. On the wall above us, incorporated into a framed commercial photograph of the dazzling Alpine meadow variety, was a huge clock-calendar. Both Pedro and Antonio were speechless with admiration.)

Motoring downriver, the men in Frontera were soon forgotten. Perhaps it was the liberating power of travelling a road together, perhaps merely the discovery of the Alpine clock, I don't know, but we arrived at Yaxchilán in a state of intoxication. There is a surreal quality to this part of the rainforest, and to the visionary architecture which it inspired, which affects everything around it. As we climbed up through the tangle of stones and vines and fallen masonry, it was hard to distinguish where the forest ended and the ruins began. I felt completely exhilarated, drunk with all the green growing around me, breathing in the air as though it were some kind of drug. We were enmeshed, like tiny insects, in a vast web of leaves, bark and lichens, but I did not care. For the first time, I felt, we were really entering Pedro and Antonio's world.

Antonio, like a bony yellow mountain goat, leapt ahead. 'Look at this!' he called us over. 'This is a ceiba tree: good for making canoes.' 'And this,' Pedro followed him. 'This bamboo we use for our arrows.' Gleefully they urged us on, frogmarching us between them, faster and faster. 'See this plant?' Antonio pointed to a leafy creeper on the ground. 'This one is good for newborn babies *cuando les sale sus chiles*, when their chillies come out.' (Presumably some kind of nappy rash or prickly heat.) 'And that one is the *zapote chico*, we use it for making our bows.'

Above and below us were massive creepers grown to the thickness of tree trunks, and the sinister *mata palos* which throttles the trees it grows on, pushing them right up out of the ground so that their roots take on a whole terranean existence, like enormous cages or strange vegetable polypods. They showed us which fruits were good for eating – weird gourds and seeds with arcane names, Osh and *huevos de burro* (donkey's balls) – and where to procure such useful items as glue and incense and soft fibres for making clothes.

All day we climbed and scrambled through the ruins. Once we came to the top of a pyramid, surfacing just above the canopy of the forest. Beyond the sweep of the river we could look down over the whole steaming jungle, ringing with insects and the call of howler monkeys. Another time we came across a triumphal staircase, carpeted with moss, teetering like a cliff-face down to the bank of the river. We found forgotten labyrinths haunted by baby-faced bats; grassy courtyards and underground passages; roof-combs ornamented with thousand-year-old stucco; stone lintels perfectly carved with battle scenes and vision serpents. Magnificent birds, toucans and emerald-green parrots, watched us from the trees.

Antonio and Pedro, as drugged as we were, raced through the forest like two men possessed. In the plaza at the base of the great stairwell they flitted like jungle wraiths from building to building, wild hair streaming behind them, whooping and exclaiming over each new find.

'Look, this is a tomb,' one would say to the other.

'And this is where the king lived,' the other would counter.

'See here; what's inside?' Examining a passageway.

'Look! This is where they buried treasure.'

Don Manuel, the keeper of the ruins, a sluggish-looking *mestizo* wearing a string vest, knew Antonio and Pedro from Bonampak. From time to time he made a vain attempt to explain some archaeological points to them.

'That is where the food stores were kept,' he said when they emerged from the hidden passageway again. 'Yaxchilán was a great merchant centre. They used to trade things up and down the river.'

He treated them with the slow, slightly patronizing jocularity of all lower-class mestizos towards the *indígenas*, but Antonio, impervious to his tone, wasn't having any of it.

'No, no,' he turned to me earnestly. 'It's where they kept their *treasure*. Can't you tell?'

'And look, what's up there?' Pedro pointed to a tuft of masonry sticking out from one of the terraces.

'Up there? Oh, there's nothing there,' Don Manuel said.

Pedro and Antonio did not care. They looked at one another. 'Well, we're going to look anyway.' They raced off, beckoning to us, 'Come on, come on.'

Don Manuel stared after them, smiling faintly.

'These Lacandónes . . .' he sighed. 'Well, I'll leave you to it.'

Above us, the two of them were squatted, wide-eyed, over a nest of fallen stones. What did they see there? I wondered. And would I be able to see it too? Don Manuel looked up at them as he walked past and shook his head.

'Antonio Chankin, who would have thought it . . .' I heard him say to himself. '*Loco . . . totalmente loco.*' Mad. Quite mad.

SIX

> Magic is not tricks; it is a way of discovering
> reality.
>
> ANON

One night, standing around backstage waiting for the performance
to begin, I had a rare moment of revelation in which I seemed to
be standing outside my own body, looking down on myself and
my surroundings as though from some far height. I saw myself,
an exotic figure in an old denim shirt, beneath which a pair of
darned brown fishnets, a scarlet spangled bikini and feather boa
were just visible. Like the other girls, my face was caked in heavy
stage make-up; and when I blinked, I felt the scratch of Mara's
false eye-lashes against my lids.

I seemed so at ease, waiting here with the other performers. In
the background, beyond the blue and silver curtains, the parade
music hiccoughed rustily.

I looked down at myself with surprise. What had felt so normal
only a second ago, now seemed like an eccentric joke. What was
I doing here? As a little girl surely I had always hated circuses?
Hadn't there always been something about their twilight world,
that sinister borderland between our child's world and the real
world, which had been too disturbing, even then?

But I no longer cared. Yvonne was right; this was not a lifestyle,
this was a whole new life. Since the grand parade around the
streets of Lomas Verdes I had been persuaded by Karina and Mara
that I should also have a go at taking part in the nightly processions
in the circus ring itself. I had not entirely forgotten my previous
experience, the stares in the street, lascivious and disapproving by
turns, and the uncomfortable feelings they inspired, but in the

ring, they assured me, in the safety of the circus itself, things were quite different. Besides, in the ring I was to ride Hannibal, one of the elephants, and no one messed with her.

And so I found myself in the wardrobe again, getting dressed for my first real circus parade. As before, Karina and the other girls advised on my costume, and Mara made me up. Circus make-up is like stage make-up, with a heavy base and exaggerated lines and colours designed to show up under the lights. Under Mara's ministrations I felt my skin become curiously rigid, as if she had covered my face in a thick clay mask.

'And last of all,' Mara fiddled about in her make-up box, '. . . *las pestañas*.' With a flourish she brought out a pair of false eyelashes. 'I knew something was missing last time. Watch this, now we can make you into a real circus girl.'

I looked at them doubtfully. Still in their box they looked old and dusty, like dead insects.

'You sure?' Speaking through clenched teeth, so as not to crack the mask, I was reduced to a kind of ventriloquist's shorthand.

'No-o, Katty,' Mara laughed, pushing my hands away. She settled herself more comfortably on the floor, leaning back against the racks of fusty costumes. 'Now, where's it got to . . .' There was never much light inside the wardrobe – Jovita only ever bought bulbs with the lowest possible wattage – and inside Mara's make-up box layers of eyeshadows and lipsticks glowed in the dim orange light like trays of dirty jewels. 'Ah, aquí está.' Holding up a small tube, she smiled at me. 'The glue.'

Just then, over the sighs and violins of Jovita's *telenovela* I heard the first notes of music coming from the Big Top. In the pit of my stomach, I felt a terrible lurch.

'Music . . . !' I started up in panic. 'We'll be late.'

'No-o, Katty.' Still smiling serenely, Mara pulled me back. She tossed back a lock of hair from her exquisitely painted face. 'When that music begins it means we still have a good five minutes before the parade. Look, Brissel hasn't even started getting ready yet.'

Brissel came spinning through the curtain which separated the clothes racks from Jovita's tiny den. With little jumps and squeals she started to drag on her costume as if her life depended on it.

'*Guau!* Katty, look at you.' Brissel crammed her hair into her silver *bastonera*'s turban. '*Pestañas* and everything.' She shimmied into her costume. 'What will Tom say?'

Tom was waiting for me at the bottom of the wardrobe steps. 'What *have* they done to you?' I saw him gaze up at me, blinking.

My eyelids felt heavy, abnormally extended by the weight of the false lashes. Perhaps Brissel was right. I gave him what I hoped was a sultry look.

'Like it?'

'You look like a transvestite.'

'Thanks. You always did know how to flatter a girl.'

'Katty, Katty, *vamos*. Rapido.' There was no time to argue. Karina, lacking Mara's serenity on these matters, grabbed me by the hand, her pink *bastonera* feathers lurching. She hurried me through the back entrance of the Big Top and up into the old truck from where the stage curtains led out into the circus ring. We looked around for Luis and the elephants, but they were nowhere to be seen.

'Where are they? Oh, where are they.' Impatiently Karina tapped her foot. 'I'm on in a moment, why can't he hurry up?'

The overture was nearly finished. The *bastoneras'* dance came before the parade, I knew.

All around us the truck was filling up with people, the cramped space bulging with coloured plumes, spangles and fraying silver lamé. Chatting, stretching, doing warming-up exercises, adjusting costumes, headdresses, straightening the seams of tights – most of the performers were still in a state of semi-undress. I wondered how any of them would ever be ready on time. I could see Mara practising the splits and Jovita, her curlers just visible above an armful of swaying feather headdresses. Outside the Big Top, still in his trailer, I could see Mundo calmly putting the finishing touches to his clown's greasepaint. Brissel, who was always late, came dashing in past him, still grinning, her headdress awry, teetering up the gangplank on her high heels. Despite everyone's apparent nonchalance the air crackled with nervous energy.

The music ended.

'Look, I've got to go.' Karina tore off her *bata* and gave a last hitch to her costume. 'Just wait here for Luis. You'll be OK.'

'Karina, wait . . .' Her sense of panic was beginning to infect me too. 'You can't just *leave* me. I don't know what to do.'

'You don't have to *do* anything. Just ride the bloody elephant.' Her tone was brusque. 'And wave, like I showed you, remember?' She turned out her palm and moved it stiffly from side to side. 'And smile.' She bared her teeth. 'That's it. Now I really must go.' As Karina ran off I saw Gordo come racing in past her. 'Primo, primo!' I heard her call to him. 'Cousin!' She waved her hand in my direction. 'Ayudala. Help her, can't you?' Then, in a flurry of pink feathers, she was gone.

Luckily Gordo seemed to know exactly what was required. He waited with me in the wings, from where the elephants always made their entrance, while they were dressed. Luis did this with painful slowness, covering them methodically in their crimson and silver cloaks. By now the *bastonera* dance was nearly over. The parade was next, but still Luis fiddled about, adjusting their head-pieces, plaques with C and B, for Circo Bell's, entwined over their foreheads. We would never make it. My first parade and I was going to miss it. I was in a fever of nerves. Standing beside me, Gordo was his usual breezy self.

'You look very pretty,' he said, eying up my costume appreciatively.

'Thank you.' At least someone thought so. But I was too far gone to really care. My eyelids itched with the generous layer of glue which Mara had applied to keep the ill-fitting eye-lashes in place. All I wanted was for Luis to finish and to be able to climb up on to the elephant before it was . . .

Too late. With a tremendous fanfare, the parade music burst from the loudspeakers. Gordo pulled back the curtains a crack. Dimly, half blinded with false eye-lashes and nerves, I saw the other performers emerge from the stage curtains. I watched as they filed past, waving to the crowd. First Olinda, Brissel, Pamela and Karina in their *bastonera* costumes; then the clowns – Mundo and his six-year-old son, Tintin, and two other lads, Ramón and Charlie; Mara and Omar, hand in hand; the tiny Olga as an *estrella*, Yvonne the tightrope walker, Antonino the *equilibrista*, Martinelli the juggler . . .

At last the elephants were ready. Gordo gave Hannibal the signal to kneel down; then, with a quick leg-up, showed me how to climb up on to her back. I settled myself as far forward as I could with my feet tucked behind her ears and held on to the chain of her headdress as she heaved up on to her feet again. Outside the parade was coming to an end. I could hear Gallo announcing Ricky, Mundo's eldest son, and Jorge Morales, the trapeze artists. And finally, with only seconds to go . . .

'Rrr-olando Bell's Junior . . .' Gallo bellowed into the microphone, rolling his Rs. '*Los gigantes elefantes de Taiii-wan . . . y . . .*'

With a lurch I was out there, drenched in blinding white lights, smiling, waving, squinting over Hannibal's head into the dark, '. . . y . . . KA-TY . . . *la g-rr-inga est-rrr-ella*.'[1]

I had only intended to go out in the parade once or twice, just to see what it was like, but there was something so compelling about being part of the circus performance that I went out the next night, and then again the next. Soon no one bothered to ask me if I was going out in the parade that day. In fact the only questions that were asked were when, for some reason, I did not. Mundo even put me in his announcing tape: *La Gringa Estrella*, the Star Gringa. In the circus, I was beginning to realize, it is considered strange not to perform, in however humble a capacity. My willingness to take part – the dressing up, the make-up, even the false eye-lashes – had never been a laughing matter to the circus people. What had started out as mere whimsy on my part, soon became something rather more serious. Riding Hannibal had become my act.

Circo Bell's had pulled us into their world so quickly it seemed hardly possible. I had always thought of the circus as an image for Mexico. Now I began to see it as a mirror of our own lives, too. As travellers, the life of these itinerant artists was as familiar to us as our own faces reflected in the glass. My involvement was total. Everything that I once thought or believed, everything I once was before I came to Circo Bell's, was suspended; while in my new life, the circus life, each day I found myself uncovering new and finer layers of meaning. As my absorption grew, the world

[1] *gringa* means foreigner; *estrella* means star.

outside the circus receded. I saw no newspapers, watched no television (apart from *telenovelas* in the wardrobe) received no phone
calls, and only the odd, rare letter. On the very few occasions
when we went to visit other friends in Mexico City I found that
I had increasing difficulty focusing on them. Their conversation
and their concerns – including, to our amusement, an only thinly
veiled disapproval of our unseemly new careers – softened, blur-
ring around the edges, until one day, with a soft *pop!* they vanished
altogether.

With Tom, who was working hard on his collection of photographs of Mexico,[1] away from the circus more and more, sometimes for as much as a week at a time, and Karina increasingly
taken up by the daily dramas of her relationship with Gallo, at
Lomas Verdes I had much of the days to myself. Or at least that
was the theory.

The theory was that I should use the mornings in which to write
and spend the rest of the day talking to people in the circus,
perhaps interviewing them about certain aspects of Circo Bell's.
Then one day Mundo's eldest daughter, Pamela, came to me and
asked if I would teach her English. So after that I spent the mornings writing, with an hour's break in the middle when I gave
Pamela her English lesson. Our caravan was parked next to
Rolando and Vicky's on the furthest edge of the parking lot, and
their eight-year-old, Belén, often used to come and visit me. When
she saw Pamela's books, Belén was entranced. Before I knew it,
she had brought her pencil and papers along too, and so I had
her for half an hour or so each morning as well.

One morning Mara tapped on my door. I half wondered, in
some trepidation, if she was going to ask for an English lesson
too, but she said she had only come to collect her sister. Vicky
had discovered what was going on and did not want Belén to
disturb me any more.

'Don't be ridiculous,' I protested. 'Please tell her Belén is not
disturbing me in the least. I love to teach her.'

Ten minutes later Mara tapped on the door again. She was
holding a plate. 'From my mother: pollo en mole,' she explained,

[1] *Mexico: Feast and Ferment*, Tom Owen Edmunds (Hamish Hamilton, 1992).

(chicken in a kind of chocolate sauce, a great Mexican delicacy). 'She says she hopes you might like it for your lunch.'

Later in the afternoon I took the plate back and said how good it was. The next day, at exactly the same time, Mara tapped on my door again. 'Guacamole,' she said, handing me another plate. 'And tortillas.' She indicated the maize cakes, shaped like thin, round pancakes, on the side. 'You put some guacamole inside the tortilla, like so, see?' She rolled the tortilla up into a sausage shape. 'And now you have a taco.' She smiled up at me. 'Very Mexican.'

Later, when I took the plate back to their caravan, I found Vicky there on her own doing the washing up.

'That was delicious, thank you,' I said to her. 'But there's really no need, you know.'

I was becoming almost embarrassed by their generosity. Vicky carried on scrubbing at the sink with her back to me.

'Mara says you don't eat.'

'I don't usually eat this much lunch, that's for sure.'

'And what do you eat? Lettuce, tomato, cheeses – I don't know.' She scrubbed away at a saucepan. 'In the day, at night, what's the difference? You can't live on that.'

'I don't mind. It's what I like to eat. Anyway, I never seem to have time to cook.'

'Don't have time to cook? I don't have time to do anything *but* cook.' A ghost of a smile passed over her face. 'When your husband's away, you can come here to eat, see?' She half turned her sad face towards me. 'I mean it, any time.'

Vicky knew, only too well, what it was like to have an absent husband. As the circus impresario, part of Rolando's job involved finding new *terrenos* and for this he was obliged to travel continuously. Even so, this was clearly not the only reason he stayed away. Rolando's philanderings were common knowledge and children from a wide variety of other marriages and liaisons were always turning up on the circus doorstep. No wonder poor Vicky looked sad.

When I had first met her, the time when Rolando had invited us to dinner with him at La Villa, I had thought her uncommunicative in the extreme; but as with so many of my first impressions, this was only part of the story. Now, with her charming, blaspheming, larger-than-life husband out of the way, in her own quiet time Vicky started to speak to me. Not with words or sentences, but with food.

Small and shy, like a tiny nesting bird, Vicky never came to my caravan herself. Instead, almost every day she would send Mara round with some new delicacy. Often these were nothing more than the domestic staples common to every Mexican family, maize tortillas, slightly charred from the griddle on which they had been heated, or plates of glistening purple frijoles, but not always. Sometimes she sent a glass of juice, or a piece of some special fruit which she thought I should try, carefully washed and peeled. I learnt to read her mood by the food she sent me. A glass of yoghurt filled with grapes or orange segments meant that she was in a meditative or reflective mood that day. She made the yoghurt herself, rinsing the cultures carefully with water every morning and adding new milk to her big glass jar. In a more creative frame of mind she would infuse handfuls of scarlet *flor de jamaica* petals into a pale pink juice. Chicken soups and salads of watercress were for strength when she felt tired or ill; strawberries were to lift the spirits; chocolate to soothe the nerves.

As the weeks went on and I became more adept at interpreting it, her language grew both subtler and more baroque. Words and phrases became whole sentences, treaties, diatribes. Pollo en mole, I learnt, was a special food for celebrations, requiring an elaborate and precise use of many different spices and chillies; I knew that she would only cook this when she felt strong and clearheaded, or to express some secret pleasure in her life. On the rare occasions when Rolando made an appearance she baked with lemons, apples and honey, ambivalent sweet and sour confections, their deeper patterns disguised with tracings of whipped cream. And when he left again, I knew that in the many flavours of the fiery Mexican chillies which she would sometimes send me to try – red, yellow, green and black; fresh, dried or preserved in special oils – lay both her anger and her secret strength.

Mara, the bearer of these silent epicurean musings, did not share her mother's oblique approach to life. If I was ever wrong in my first impressions of Vicky, I was doubly wrong when it came to Mara. Of all the circus cousins, Mara, beautiful Mara, with her face like a distant snow queen and a head as strong as her tiny contortionist's body, was her grandmother's child. Funny, generous, practical to a fault, Mara believed in spells with the same fervour that her mother believed in recipes. She had Doña Elena's boundless energy and the courage to meet life tirelessly, at full tilt.

With Pamela and Belén's English lessons over, invariably it was time for Mara to come tapping on my door bringing Vicky's frijoles, or yoghurt, or whatever it happened to be that day. As the days went on her visits grew longer. Sometimes we would go shopping in the market together; sometimes she would bring her sewing (all the girls made their own costumes) and sit with me while I wrote up my notes. At nineteen, Mara was quite a few years older than the other cousins, of whom Pamela (fourteen) was the youngest, and Vanessa (sixteen) was the oldest after Mara herself.

It was from Mara that I learnt most of the practical elements of circus life. Where to get water from, how to hook up our electrics to the circus generator, where the nearest washerwoman lived and where the closest shops were to be found (all of which had to be discovered anew every time the circus moved). She also showed me how to heat the bucket of water which we used for our daily bath with a special element which she kept in her caravan, rather than the laborious system I had devised of boiling up pans of water on our tiny stove, an operation which could take up to an hour or more each day, especially if I wanted to wash my hair.

Those mornings at the circus belonged to the women. Because the last performance did not end until ten o'clock, Circo Bell's were naturally late-night people – Karina and Gallo, although they had nothing particular to do, would always moon around until two or three in the morning – but the women were always up early. Before I came to the circus I had always imagined that it would be the smells which I would remember – the smell of sawdust and greasepaint, as the phrase goes, although the latter had no smell at all that I could discover. In fact, what I most remember from those mornings are sounds. The sounds of the circus had many perspectives. Distant sounds, carried faintly in through my window, so familiar I hardly noticed them any more: the tinny wheezings of Mundo's tape blaring out through the megaphone by the box-office '. . . *Elefantes* . . . *Taiii-wan* . . . *Tintin, el Payaso Más Chiquito en el muuuu-ndo*'; the strains of some ranchero music or salsa coming from Gato the soundman's room in the cabin of the stage truck; the monstrous roar of Mexico City traffic. Nearer to hand I could hear the sound of the women gossiping and voices calling: Mara looking for her sister, Olinda; Pamela wanted by her mother, Carmen; Yvonne singing to Taynarí in his pram. I could hear Jovita and Vicky scrubbing clothes in one of their big plastic tubs. Belén reciting her seven times table. And beyond them the sound of hammers on the tent pegs, or the creak of the trapezes as Gordo and Ricky practised some new turn.

In the caravan on the opposite side to us from Rolando and Vicky lived Güera and Chillón. Chillón was the foreman in charge of the *chamacos*, the casual labourers who were hired to do the heavy work such as putting the Big Top up and down. Crammed into one tiny caravan, Güera and Chillón lived with their two small children, Alejandro and the baby Gabriella, and Chillón's sister, Sylvia. Güera, as her name suggests,[1] was a pale-skinned northerner from the state of Chihuahua. She had started her career as a dancer with another circus, Circo Atayde, but after Alejandro was born she had never got back into shape sufficiently to go on performing, and instead had taken on the job of selling tickets at the box-office.

Güera: fat, sluttish and endlessly cheerful. Güera: always laughing and shouting insults, alternately lavishing affection and blows on her small son. Her caravan was always surrounded by a rain of urinous-smelling effluence and, on wash days, which was most days, sprouted curious Heath Robinson growths which dangled with heavy, flapping washing. Her language was so foul it must have curdled her own milk, but it was some of the most inventive I ever heard, an education in its own right. On Güera's tongue the stock-in-trade Mexican insults, *cabrón, hijo de puta, maricón* and so forth, were brilliantly re-worked, threaded on to a linguistic elastic which she then spun into a verbal cat's cradle of insults,

---

[1] *güera* means someone who is either fair or fair-skinned, attributes widely regarded as signs of great beauty all over Mexico.

expletives and mysterious innuendoes, twisting and stretching them, pulling them inside out and back to front, sawing them in half and then reconstructing them again, bigger, better, and a good deal filthier, than ever before.

The word *chingar*, meaning literally to rape, was one of Güera's favourites, roughly the equivalent to our Anglo-Saxon fuck. The famous, and culminatingly insulting, Mexican phrase *chinga tu madre* was never far from her lips but Güera also had a reserve of loving refinements which she used to great effect. Her husband could be a real *hijo de puta* sometimes, a son of a whore, but he could also be *hijo de la chingada*, son of a raped woman. In a more affectionate spirit he could also be her very own *chingón*, while her son, when he was being particularly naughty, was, among other things, a *chingaquedito*. If either of them really over-did it, pulling a *chingadera*, a fast one, we could hear her yelling at them to go to hell, *vete a la chingada*, and if they didn't she would give them a *chingadazo*, a whack over the head with one of her mighty fists.

'Ay, me chingaron,' she would lament if she was ripped off or got the better of in some way; and gossiping with Sylvia or with the other women over some particularly scandalous turn of events we would sometimes hear her gasp, in her cracked, technicolor voice, *No chingues!* You're joking!

Although in a blacker mood the same expression when used to Alejandro could also mean, 'If you do that again I'm going to really wallop you, so watch it'.

As a Mexican woman, to be considered a *grosera*, a woman who was vulgar enough to use this kind of language, usually considered to be the preserve of men, was to walk a particular and sometimes dangerous tightrope, as I later, shockingly, found out. But for the moment, because I liked Güera, who was funny and good-hearted, and also because no doubt as a non-Mexican so many of her allusions must have gone straight over my head, I never thought much about her language, except as a bizarre linguistic joke. Late at night sometimes, after the last performance, a group of us would go up to a small taco bar on the Avenida Lomas Verdes for supper and one of the boys – Omar or Ramón, usually – would take great delight in going through Güera's fruitier turns of phrase, explaining them to us in painstaking detail. But there were some people at the circus who, despite the notorious abrasiveness of everyday circus life, did not think that this kind of thing was at all a laughing matter.

Olga, little Olga the *estrella*, whom I had first met that afternoon with Doña Elena back in San Juan de Aragón, had been a puzzle to me for some time. Even from the beginning, from my first few days with the circus, she had always seemed different to the other girls. Like so many of the circus people – Omar and Gallo, for example – it was well known that Olga had come to the circus for love. Her lover was Ilish, an intense and beautiful-looking young man, slim-hipped and high cheek-boned, who worked under Chillón as one of the *chamacos*. When we first arrived at the circus Tom and I often used to see them together in the cheap *comedors* and taco bars near to the circus *terreno* where we went to eat in the evenings. Later on, during those long, cold and sunny mornings at Lomas Verdes, I grew used to seeing Olga around the circus camp. Despite the fact that we all lived so close together, there was always a feeling of apartness about her. She never seemed to engage with the other women, never went shopping or to the market with Brissel, Pamela or Olinda, or came with us on our occasional outings to a cinema or a fair. Instead, every morning I would see her in the same spot, dressed in immaculate white, sitting on a stone in the sun, her dark head bent gravely over a book.

Olga was small and quiet, very slight in build, with a mouthful of crooked teeth and huge, swimming brown eyes. There was a feeling of great frailty about her; something demure, almost prissy, in the way she walked, in her lowered eyelids and in her butterfly voice, which was utterly at odds with her sensational runaway to the circus into the rough arms of the extravagantly beautiful Ilish.

Even in the wardrobe, Olga was modest to the point of prudery. Instead of stripping off without a thought as the other girls did, Olga would go into elaborate contortions, carefully facing the wall and wriggling into her costume and *mayas* beneath her wrap, rather than expose any part of her nakedness to public view. Olga never talked bawdy with the other girls. In fact bad language, even of a relatively mild nature, made her scarlet with confusion, a fact which was soon latched on to by naughty Olinda, for whom this was the most perfect bait.

'Katty, Katty,' she would say, fixing me with her huge eyes, 'now it's time for *our* English lesson.' She would glance slyly in Olga's direction. 'Come on, tell us how you say ... *pussy* ... *chichis!*' She would compose her face into an expression of exaggerated innocence. 'I've been meaning to ask you for ages ...' another sly glance, '... what does fucky-fucky mean? You see, I kept hearing it in this film the other day ...'

By now I thought I had all the circus caravans more or less sorted out. I knew which ones belonged to which families, and how many people slept in each, but I was still curious to know where Ilish and Olga lived. One day as I watched Olga sitting on her rock as usual, immaculate in her white dress, I asked Mara. She looked at me with surprise.

'*No seas loca*, don't be crazy, they don't have a caravan.'

'Where do they live, then?'

The circus, I knew, was full of odd corners and cubbyholes, in the transport trailers and the trucks, which some of the single boys – Omar and Gato the soundman, for example – had converted into living space. But Mara only shrugged.

'Se acomodan donde puedan,' was all she said. 'They accommodate themselves where they can.'

'What do you mean?'

'Look, that's where they're living now, I think.' She waved her hand vaguely over to the concrete wall beyond Güera and Chillón's caravan, at the far side of the car park. 'Over there.'

I looked to where she was pointing, but all I could see was a pile of debris, pieces of old packing case and coils of rusting barbed wire which the *chamacos* had cleared away from the main site when we had first arrived in Lomas Verdes.

Later on that day, when I was walking round that way with some scraps for the elephants, I took a closer look at the place Mara had indicated. I saw that not all the pieces of packing case and planks of wood had been dumped in a heap after all, but that some of them had been carefully piled up against the wall. No sooner had I noticed this than one of the planks moved and Olga came stepping out from behind it.

'Olga!'

'Hola, Katty.' She smiled and pulled the plank into place behind her, as if she were shutting a door.

'Olga . . .' I tried to hide my embarrassment. 'So this is where you live. I had no idea.'

'Yes, this is where we live.' Olga smoothed her dress with her tiny hands. 'Shall I show you?'

Against the wall they had constructed a kind of wigwam out of old planks and pieces of packing case salvaged from the pile of debris. The 'door' was secured with a piece of bent wire. Through the cracks between the planks I could see that the tiny space inside, just big enough for two people to lie down in, was lined with a fragment of old red carpet. Two mugs, a bottle of shampoo and a few ragged paperbacks were arranged along the back wall.

'It's not much.' She glanced at me quickly, and then away again. 'But lodging is so expensive. I told Carlos' – Olga was the only person in the circus who ever called Ilish by his real name – 'I told Carlos I would rather not waste the money. We're saving, you know – for a caravan.' Flies from the rubbish dump only a few feet away, with its rotting babies' nappies and fast-food wrappers, settled on her white dress. She waved them away patiently.

'Martinelli and Teresa live right beside us.' She pointed to another tatterdemalion shack next to the wigwam. 'José-Jaime and Veronica were here too.' She mentioned another of the *chamacos* and his girlfriend. 'But their baby was ill, so they've rented a room in Lomas Verdes for a few days.' Olga smiled her charming, crooked-toothed smile. 'As you can imagine, it's a little harder with a baby.'

Olga loved to read. It was not just her mind but her spirit which hungered for books. She drank them down, feasted on them as if, like a powerful charm – more powerful than the circus lights, more powerful even than love – only they could take her out of herself, away from the poverty and squalor among which she had chosen to live. I had a few books in Spanish which I lent her, Juan Rulfo's Mexican classic *Pedro Paramo*, some poetry by Octavio Paz and García Márquez's luminous collection of short stories, *La increíble y triste historia de la Cándida Eréndira y de su Abuela*

Desalmada.[1] Sometimes when she came over to my caravan to return a book we would talk about what she had just read, and in this way, little by little, I came to hear her own story too. If she ever saw any resemblance between herself and Márquez's Innocent Eréndira, she never said so, but in its own way her story is just as incredible, and every bit as sad.

'I did not always live like this,' she told me once. 'Things were very different when I was a child. I was brought up by my grand-parents, in a good neighbourhood. The families who lived around us were fine people, professionals most of them, doctors and *licenciados*.[2] My aunts were all well educated, some of them even went to the university. One of my aunts had over a thousand volumes on her shelves. Where I grew up there were always books, books everywhere.

'It was my grandfather who taught me to read. He taught me many things, many more than my own father ever did. When I was with him, I knew I was safe. And I loved him more than any one in the world, except perhaps my brother Umberto.'

'Doesn't he worry where you are?' We had wandered round together to the front of the circus, to the box-office and the en-closure where Luis kept his elephants. I liked to feed them and came round here most afternoons with any scraps I had left over from lunch. 'Your grandfather, I mean.'

'He died just before I came to the circus.' In her neat white dress, with its puffed sleeves and slender tucked waist, Olga picked her way daintily over the sloping ground. 'I was living with my mother again then. Ilish – Carlos – wanted me to run away before, but my grandfather had cancer and I knew he was dying. I couldn't leave him. But after he died,' she shrugged, 'well, everything was different then. I had nothing left to stay for.'

The elephants were used to my visits by now. When Hannibal saw me coming her trunk came snuffling towards me, breathing vaporously and plucking at my pockets to see what I had brought.

---

[1] *The Incredible and Sad Story of Innocent Eréndira and Her Heartless Grandmother*, Gabriel García Márquez (Editorial Diana, Mexico, 1986).
[2] *licenciado* means someone with a university degree, often used formally as a title instead of Mr or Miss.

I took some stale rolls out of a brown paper bag and gave one to each of them, Penny, Judy and Hannibal, in turn.

'So then what did you do?'

'I had thought about running away many times, and had often talked it over with Carlos. I was under age, only sixteen, and still at school, but in the end it was not so very difficult to do. You see, my mother used to take in washing – that's how I came to know Carlos in the first place. He was working for another circus then, the Circo Union, which was playing at a site near our house. Every time he came to collect his washing I would slip a few of my own clothes under his and he would take them out without anyone knowing. In this way I smuggled out my documents and a few books, too, but nothing more. Then one day I found Carlos waiting for me outside the school playground. He said, '*Vamos*, we're going.' So I left with him that afternoon, and never went back.'

'Do you think they are still looking for you?'

Olga and Ilish had arrived at Circo Bell's only a month before we had and there had been rumours of news-flashes about her on the television.

'One of my aunts looked for us, but not my mother, no.' A look, as if she had tasted something sour, passed over Olga's face. 'Not my mother. She never bothered to look for us.'

The elephants had finished the rolls. Hannibal's trunk hovered impatiently, seeking out the fruit scraps she could still smell at the bottom of the paper bag. I put out my hand and felt her trunk. Even though I rode her in the parades every night, each time I touched her it was still with a sense of shock. Her skin had a rough, prehistoric feel to it, more mineral than animal, as if it was an ancient thing, fossilized slowly over a thousand years or more. Her pelt was covered in whiskers, elegant elephant whiskers like lengths of the finest spun steel.

'Do you want to feed her?' I held out the bag of fruit scraps to Olga, but she drew back, shaking her head. Although I had never had any trouble with her, Hannibal, maverick lady, was renowned for her uncertain temper and everyone at the circus, even those swaggering *domadors* Gordo and Ricky, treated her with respect. I emptied out the rest of the scraps from the bag and went to sit down next to Olga, who was perched on a bale of hay safely out of their range.

'Tell me about them, your parents, I mean. What are they like?'

'My mother is small and dark, and *muy agitada*.' Olga thought for a moment. 'I think she must have been very pretty once. My father was a singer in a mariachi band. We never saw very much of him at home. His band was successful and so he was almost always away from home. He was very musical; he played the violin and the guitar, and sometimes the trumpet too. But most of all he would sing. When he sang his voice was melancholy, like a night bird.'

She smoothed her white skirts down over her knees.

'The day I was born was the day my mother found out about my father's second family. He kept them in San Luis Potosí, a town far north of Mexico City. It was an accident that she found out at all. My father's wife – his real wife, because my parents were never married – had died giving birth to a daughter just one day before I was born and a friend of the family called up to get him home for the funeral. Carmen, my half-sister, was the fifteenth child they had had together.

'I think that a great bitterness entered into my mother's soul on that day. I know she could never bring herself to love me. Whenever she looked at me, she must have seen my father's great deception. Her own pain, too. She used to taunt me sometimes that she was going to send me away, back to that other family in San Luis Potosí. It used to make me cry so much. I couldn't bear the thought of them, the thought of my father's other life. My mother used to tell me stories about him, about how he went with other women, and even beat her sometimes. He only came home about once a month, just long enough to get her pregnant, and then he would be off again. Even though my mother knew about the other family, they still had two more children after me, my brothers Umberto and Guillermo.

'People say that I am very like Carmen, my half-sister. I think about her sometimes and wonder what she's like. But I've never wanted to meet her. I've never wanted to set eyes on any of them, not even my grandparents. I wouldn't know what to say. People used to say that my father had many other children besides us.'

Olga shrugged. '*Quién sabe?* Who knows? I never wanted to find out, couldn't bear to. I remember that at my school there was this girl, Teresa, who looked just like me. People used to mistake us for each other, as if we were twins or something. Everyone remarked on it. Our resemblance was uncanny. But I never went near her, never asked her who her father was. I was too afraid to; too afraid what the answer would be.'

Luis, the keeper, followed by Jacaira, one of his daughters, emerged from their little bubble caravan next to the elephant enclosure. He jerked his chin in our direction in greeting and started to break up some of the bales of hay for the animals' evening feed. We sat in silence for a while, looking out over the huddled camp. Late afternoon was one of the times which I always loved best at the circus, a lazy time when there was still half an hour or so to go before it was time to go to the wardrobe to get ready for the first performance. Neither of us were in a hurry to get back and after a while Olga went on with her story.

'Although I lived with my grandparents for most of my child-hood, when I was five my mother married again, really married this time, not just living in what we call here a *unión libre*, and we were sent back to live with her for a time. But I was not happy. It was a very bad area where she lived, the Colonia Guerrero in Mexico City, full of prostitutes and drug addicts. There was a good deal of crime, the streets were not safe places to walk.'

As Olga talked, I watched Luis move among his animals. Soothed by his presence they swayed together, trailing their trunks dreamily in front of them.

'I didn't really like her new husband, even though he always used to be very affectionate with us. I remember that he was always touching me, stroking my arm, my shoulders. Trying to make me sit on his knee. I hated that. Whenever he tried to talk to me, he always stood too close . . .' She broke off, staring past me unseeingly across the circus camp.

'I don't know.' She shook her head slowly. 'I was just a child, a baby almost, but the way he touched me, I think I always knew it wasn't right. Then one day he really tried to touch me . . .' She blinked rapidly three or four times. 'He tried to touch me, you know, in a different way. I tried to call to my mother for help' –

Olga's voice was so soft that I had to lean towards her – 'I called. But she wouldn't help me. No. She wouldn't help me.' She fell silent again; a small frown appeared on her brow. 'The next thing I remember is that my cousins were there, and my aunts. I don't know how they got there. All I remember is that they took me away with them and then later they took my mother's husband away too. She was very angry with me. I know she blamed me, because later they sent him to jail. She even used to go and visit him there. All she wanted was her husband: she didn't care what he had done.'

Down in the valley below us a few faint lights were already beginning to blink. Even though it was not yet dusk someone had switched the main circus generator on, and the sloping red and white striped roof of the Big Top and the wrought-iron trellising of the box-office were now garlanded with lights.

'My own father died in the earthquake in 1985,' Olga went on. 'It was a great tragedy because he should not have been in Mexico City at all that day. He had been *en gira*, on tour with his band, but for some reason he came home a day early. My brother Umberto said he caught sight of him briefly on the street corner, and that was the last time any of us saw him alive. After the earthquake we learnt that his house (he did not live with my mother) had been completely destroyed.

'I remember running down the road with Umberto, running and running. There were people lying in the street, on the pavements, everywhere. I didn't know if they were dead or alive. When we got to my father's house I knew at once that he was there. The house had gone, but beneath the rubble we could hear his voice. He was in there, buried alive. First, we tried digging – with our bare hands, there was nothing else. But then the police came and forbade anyone to go in, it was too dangerous, they said.

'For several days we could hear his voice, growing weaker and weaker, but no one could do anything to help him. It was five days before they managed to get him out, and of course by then he was dead.'

From her enclosure with the other elephants, my Hannibal looked down on us with her two all-seeing little eyes. Her cheeks bulged with hay. Beside me, Olga's face was cast in shadow.

'The day after there was a second earthquake. I was alone in the house with my two youngest brothers. The children started screaming and I could hear the neighbours screaming too; screaming and running outside. I was so terrified I didn't know what to do. We all ran out into the street. I don't remember where. We just ran – anywhere – trying to get away. There were buildings falling all around us. Great cracks opened up in the road. Later I learnt that as well as my father, two of my best friends had also been killed that day.

'I was ill after the earthquake,' she went on in her tiny butterfly voice. 'I don't know what was wrong with me, but I had a fever and I couldn't get out of bed. It was then that I stopped speaking. The doctors tried everything, and my aunts too, but nothing worked. At first words would collect inside my head, but each time I opened my mouth they seemed to freeze on my tongue, miscarrying before they even hit the air. After a while I found out how peaceful it was not to talk. For the first time in my life I was alone with my own thoughts. So long as I did not let anyone else inside, my head was like a secret garden, a calm and gentle place where no one could touch me. It was restful there, so restful. So I decided to stay.

'Of course, my mother was the same as ever. She said that if I didn't get better, she would send me *por allá*' – she indicated with her head – 'up there, to the other family. But I didn't care. So long as I could be alone inside my head I didn't care about anything like that any more. For a whole year I didn't speak at all.'

The evening was calm without a breath of wind. One by one the lights came on in the caravans. Outside Mundo's caravan three-year-old Lely, who occasionally went out in the clown act with her father and brother, skipped past the water butts in her tiny outfit and clown's bubble shoes. Güera, cash box in hand, made her way over to the *taquilla*, to the little office in which she sat every evening selling tickets for the show. Soon it would be time for Jovita to let the girls into the wardrobe. But still Olga had not finished.

'The only thing I liked was my school. There was a teacher there who was very good to me and who I loved very much. I was good at lessons – I even won prizes – but my mother never wanted me to go to school. She preferred it when I stayed at home to help her. I was more use to her at home, because I could cook and clean the house and babysit the little ones while she went out.

'I had an elder half-sister, my mother's first child by some *novio* she had before she met my father, but she never helped me much. She had a job with a small printing press. At first it must have been very hard work, because I can remember how she used to cut her nails very short, and when she came home in the evenings her hands were always dirty and stained with ink. But soon I noticed that she was not doing that kind of work any more. She grew her nails again, and her hands were always clean and white. This happened at about the same time that she started to come home late. She used to stay on to help her boss make out the payments to the employees, at least that's what she told us. After a while she did not even bother to make excuses. Soon it was obvious that she didn't do any real work for him at all. Instead of working she used to go to the cinema with him, and the theatre, accompanying him on all kinds of outings.

'The boss was an old man, over sixty at least, and my sister was not yet twenty, but my mother never said anything. He used to give my sister money and, as long as he did that, she was happy.'

'And what about Ilish, what did your mother make of him?'

'Of course, with Carlos it was different. Carlos was young and did not have any money. We became *novios* in secret at first. When my mother found out she was very angry, but Carlos always defended me against her. They used to have terrible fights.' She lowered her eyes, half-smiling.

'We have already been through so much together. Did you know that when he was with the other circus, Circo Union, Carlos went blind? He burnt his eyes in a fire and the doctors said that he would never see again. But one of the women who cleaned at the hospital knew a lot about herbs and in the end it was she who cured him. While he was recovering, she used to bring him to my house every day to see me, so that he could tell me what I was wearing, what colour my eyes were . . . We grew very close then.'

'Do you ever think about going back home?'

'No. I love the circus. I love all the processions and parades. The lights, you know.' Olga turned towards the bulky silhouette of the Big Top. 'It's exciting, don't you think? We're working on our own act now, in the evenings, Carlos and me, did I tell you?'

In the darkness I could see her eyes gleam.

'What about your brothers? They must miss you, don't they?'

'I send messages to my brother Umberto sometimes, through a schoolfriend.' Little hands clasped together in a smooth, white lap. 'Just so he knows I am safe. But I'll never tell him where I am. I know he'd want to come to the circus too, and that wouldn't be right. He must finish school, do something with his life. It is very difficult here if you are on your own. The people are very' — she searched for the right word — '*rudo*, you know, rough, sometimes. I would not want him to pick up their ways. I'm all right, because I have Carlos to look after me.' As she spoke of him her face became luminous again. 'It is different for me.'

'And he really does? Look after you, I mean?'

I thought of Ilish's nickname. The *güero loco* they called him sometimes, the wild güero.

'Oh yes, I know what people say about him.' Olga smiled. 'But I can change all that, I know I can. He says he will change. He's promised. At La Villa we went to the Basilica together and he took a vow not to drink. And at New Year he has promised that he will take another vow, about drugs this time.' Love glowed from her like a nimbus. 'He helps me, and I help him, Katty. We're together. Safe.' I felt her hand on my arm. 'Isn't that what it's all about?'

SEVEN

Morir y matar son ideas que pocas veces nos
abandona
*(To die and to kill are ideas which rarely desert
us)*

OCTAVIO PAZ, *El Laberinto de la Soledad*

The circus was full of the enchanted: runaways and lovers, like
Olga and Ilish; wanderers, orphans, and the dispossessed. Within
the circus, as within any tribe, there was a complicated hierarchy
of family, performers and *chamacos*, but as far as the outside
world was concerned, we presented a united front. Even if the
ladies of Lomas Verdes regarded us as a caste of untouchables,
for those whom it embraced – little Olga, even Tom and me – the
circus was a place of refuge, our protection from the streets. The
circus looked after its own.

In Mexico City, even in middle-class suburbs, vice and violence
were on every corner. You did not have to look far. It seeped in
like poison gas from the slum *barrios* which collected in the sunless
valleys at the foot of the Lomas Verdes hills. At night the Skate
Mall parking lot, which in the day marked an unofficial no man's
land between the two worlds, became a thoroughfare for undesir-
ables making their way (and their living) between the two. Caravans were broken into, money and possessions disappeared.
Mundo warned all of us to lock our doors when we went out and
to keep an eye on each others' trailers.

The second week that we were camped in Lomas Verdes, the
owner of the taco bar where we often ate in the evenings was
robbed at gun point at his till. A few days after the robbery I was
walking up the road with Mara on my way to the supermarket
when I saw a group of six or seven policemen standing at the
entrance way to the same shop. A small crowd of people, including

Vanessa and Güera just returning from the market, were hovering nearby.

'What's going on?'

We went over to join them.

'Some man was shot.' Güera shrugged her fat shoulders.

'Not Raúl . . .'

'No, I just saw him talking to one of the police over there.'

'Thank God . . .'

Raúl was the owner of the taco bar, a dapper middle-aged man whom we had come to know quite well over the last week or so. He spoke excellent idiomatic English, most of which he had learnt in London, where his chief venues, in ascending order of importance, he was fond of telling us, had been the LSE, the Playboy Club and an all-night drinking venue known as The Candy Box.

Several police cars, their lights flashing, were drawn up on to the pavement outside.

'No one seems to know who the dead man is,' Güera said. She spoke with a strange neutrality, as if she was discussing the weather or the price of beans in the market.

'Look, that's him, there . . .' Vanessa, equally unperturbed, jerked her head. 'Under the sheet.'

Beyond the gathering of onlookers I saw the figure of a man sprawled on the road. Someone had covered him up with a white cloth. It was stained at one end with splatterings of blood. The policemen stood around the body with an air of indifference, leaning up against their cars in their shades and shiny black boots. They made no attempt to disperse the crowd. One of them spoke briefly into a walkie-talkie.

'*Vamos*, Katty. Let's go.'

Mara, who had a healthy mistrust of anything in which the police were involved, pulled at my arm. In the distance an ambulance siren whined.

'Yes, I'm just coming.'

I was looking for Raúl. Inside the shop, which was cordoned off by the police and their cars, I caught sight of him briefly and raised my hand to him in greeting. He did not wave back. From beneath the white shroud a trickling of blood, like black treacle, dribbled across the tarmac and into the gutter.

It was two days before we saw Raúl again and he was able to tell us what had happened.

'You're never going to believe this.' He shook his head. 'This is such a Mexican story – a *uniquely* Mexican story – I still find it hard to believe it myself.'

He sat down behind the bar. Under the harsh electric strip lights, his skin looked pale, tinged with green.

'We heard it was a suicide,' Tom said.

'Suicide? What suicide?' Raúl looked at Tom and then at me. 'You know what we mean by *machismo* here in Mexico, right? All that strong man stuff with pistols and women, just like you see in the movies?' Sardonically, he beat his chest with his fists. 'Well, I'm going to tell you a story about a real macho man, Mexican style.

'Just after I had opened the shop that morning, this policeman comes into the store. I knew him quite well, actually. This section of the Avenida Lomas Verdes is on his beat and I often used to invite him in for some tacos or a fruit juice – it pays to keep the police on your side round here, know what I mean? Anyway, this guy comes in as usual, in uniform and everything, but I can see straight away that he's drunk. And I mean drunk . . .' Raúl smiled grimly. 'Jesus, that guy was on a bender, I should think he'd been drinking for days. Anyway, he bought this bottle of whisky from me' – one half of Raúl's shop was also a liquor store – 'and he started to drink it, right here, out of the bottle.

'At first I was talking to him, you know, trying to humour him a bit. He was clearly upset about something – who knows, maybe his wife had gone off with someone and left him, or he'd been in some kind of fight. I never really found out what was on his mind, but it must have been something like that because after a while he started to come over all aggressive with me. He started saying all these stupid things like: "So you think I'm not a real man, do you?" and "No one is going to tell me I'm not a real man."'

Raúl looked out of the door of his shop with distaste, to the pavement where the bloodied shroud had lain.

'Of course, I'd never said anything of the kind, but he kept on about it. "I'm as *macho* as the next guy; no one messes with me," all this kind of crap. Anyway, by this stage I've got some other customers in here, so I'm not paying all that much attention to him. The next thing I know he's outside in the street, shouting, "*Oye*, Raúl, Raúl." I look up and there's this guy waving his gun at me. Jesus!' Raúl passed a hand over his eyes. 'He says, "*Oye*, Raúl, you want to see what a real man is made of? Well, I'll show you what only a real *macho* man would dare to do."

'And then he shoots himself in the head.'

When I was with the women – traditional, inward-looking in their ways – the outside world receded; indeed, seemed almost not to exist. The circus was our protective carapace. It was only the boys, also traditional in their outlook but raised, like Raúl's policeman, on a diet of Mexican machismo, who ever really confronted the outside world.

Although initially it had been easier for me to get to know the women, I had now been with the circus long enough to know most of the men there too. Circo Bell's was a very young circus and most of the male performers, with the exception of Antonino the *equilibrista*, Martinelli the juggler, and of course Mundo himself, were still in their teens. There were Gallo and Omar, Karina and Mara's *novios*, and then the clowns Ramón and Charlie, who also performed a monocycle and a knife-throwing act; then there was Gordo, Mara and Olinda's brother, and Jorge Morales, the trapeze artists whom we had met on our first night with Circo Bell's, the time we went to the Hermanos Vasquez circus. The only one who I as yet had barely spoken to was Ricky, Mundo's eldest son and the third flyer in the trapeze act.

As Gordo had been at some pains to point out to us, there was no doubt that the trapeze artists were the stars of the show. Their act always came immediately after the interval, the most prominent slot in the billing; and in case there should be any lingering doubts, their music, relayed by Gato from his sound box in the truck 'wings', was the theme music from *Superman*. After their grand entrance, Mundo, the catcher, would climb up to his swing over one side of the net, while the three boys, the flyers, scaled the rope-ladder to their tiny platform on the other. One after the other they swung out on their trapeze, through the spotlights and up into the dark, bodies stretched, feet almost touching the roof of the Big Top. Once, twice, three times they swung, before launching themselves into the void, spinning, somersaulting and jack-knifing with the grace and precision of divers: plunging down again to be clasped, with shimmering split-second timing, by Mundo's outstretched hands. Once 'caught' they continued out with him on the long pendulum trajectory towards the deepest recesses of the tent, swinging backwards and forwards, once, twice, before pirouetting round to catch their own creaking trapeze again and landing neatly on the tiny, perspex platform.

The frisson of danger when they fell (which because they were always trying new and more complicated jumps, they frequently did) was not a trick of showmanship, as I had sometimes suspected. Despite the net, an awkward fall from such a height was enough to break even the most experienced neck, and it was not uncommon in the circus world for trapeze flyers to be crippled, sometimes even killed. As it was, their backs and legs were often lacerated, burnt raw in criss-cross patterned welts by the impact of their fall against the ropes; the palms of their hands a mass of continually re-opened sores.

Although their entrance on to the stage, swirling suddenly into the spotlights in their white and silver cloaks, was always a dramatic moment, it was not until they were in the air that the true power of the trapeze became apparent. Although I watched their act every night, sometimes twice a night, I never really got used to the transformation. In the ring, with the usual sleight of hand of lights and make-up and costumes, it was surprising sometimes, but not entirely improbable, to see these three normally scruffy teenagers transformed into such an exotic triumvirate, but in the air ... In the air their metamorphosis was something more complete, a chemical wedding of light and speed and fear. Poised so high up above their audience, as if by some mutual act of desire between the flyers and the crowd beneath them, they became taller, stronger, more god-like than they ever were when rooted to the mortal ground. They were disturbingly beautiful to watch.

The climax of the trapeze act was the much-vaunted *triple salto mortal*, the death-defying triple somersault, which they had only recently introduced into their act. In those early days they were still taking a lot of falls: their successes intoxicated both spectators and flyers alike.

'Have you noticed,' Brissel said to me one day as we sat together watching, 'how each of them falls quite differently to the others. Gordo is the *le vale madre*, he just doesn't care at all.' She dimpled at the thought of her favourite cousin. 'He just shrugs it off and tries again. Jorge is the sentimental one, I keep on thinking he's going to burst into tears any minute. And Ricky is the *enojón*, the one who gets angry. You don't want to go too near him afterwards, I'm telling you, he looks as if he might hit someone.'

Ricky often looked as if he might hit someone. As the two eldest male cousins in the Bell's family, Ricky and Gordo were not only the heirs to the business, but were also looked upon as the natural leaders of the new generation. All the other boys, Ramón, Charlie, Gallo, Omar and Jorge[1] followed them; and even the girls, especially the younger ones, took orders from them. Despite the bristling young Hotspur act when I had first met him, Gordo was too fundamentally easy-going and had too much of his sisters' irreverent sense of humour to stand overmuch upon his honour. But with Ricky things were different.

Ricky was polite to me, but always very restrained, sometimes even to the point of brusqueness, and I occasionally found myself wondering, perhaps unfairly, if for some reason he mistrusted our presence in the circus. Like his sister Pamela, who at fourteen was already a beauty, Ricky took after his mother, Carmen, and was fairer skinned than Gordo and his siblings, who were all extremely dark. Although he was very small (whenever I was near him, I was always surprised to find that we were about the same height), Ricky exuded a feeling of strength which, for an eighteen-year-old, was shocking in its intensity. At first I imagined that this was due to simple physical fitness – this was particularly so in his upper body, immaculately developed from his training on the trapeze – but soon I realized that there was something more to it than this. After all, Gordo and Jorge, all the circus boys in fact, were athletes and therefore in just as good shape. With Ricky, I realized, the

---

[1] Ilish, of course, was only a *chamaco* and therefore well below the salt in the circus hierarchy, as were Chillón the foreman and Luis the keeper.

feeling was something which came from inside him, something which he purposely projected. An *espantamujeres* was how I once heard him, only half in jest, describe himself, a 'woman-scarer'. But this was not really his intention; or, if it was, it was not his only intention. Like many macho men, Ricky may not have liked women very much, perhaps even, in his heart of hearts, he may have feared them, but he certainly wanted them. There was something deeply, unnervingly sexual in the aura of brutality which he projected. Not only his body, but his eyes burnt with suppressed energy. Even if they did not actively fear him, there was an unspoken feeling among everyone in the circus that, if it could be at all helped, you did not mess with Ricky.

One day, when Tom was away photographing in Puebla, a town just to the east of Mexico City, some friends of Carmen and Mundo's invited a group of us to dinner at their house. Naturally, we had to wait until the last performance had ended and so it was late by the time we left the circus. About eleven o'clock Mundo and Carmen set off in their car with their two youngest children, Augustin (Tintin the clown) and Lely, while the rest of us followed in Ricky's truck. I was sitting in the front next to Ricky, with Mara and Omar beside me, while Gallo and Karina and a couple of the others piled into the open back.

We were just coming out of the slip road which led from the Skate Mall and the circus camp into the Avenida Lomas Verdes, when another camionetta turned in past us. The truck was crammed with university students on their way to a dance which was being held that night in part of the Skate Mall complex. As Ricky pulled into the Avenida we heard voices shouting, and then someone in the back started banging on the roof of the driver's cabin. We came to a halt just in front of Raúl's taco bar and Ricky jumped out. There was more shouting; I could hear his voice, raised above the others, trying to quieten things down.

Opposite us in the taco bar I saw Antonino and Ramón, who had been quietly eating their supper, come to the door.

'Qué pasó?' Wiping his fingers on his trousers, Ramón called over to us. 'What happened?'

Before we could reply I heard a scuffling sound, and then the sound of footsteps running. Ramón ripped off the poncho he was wearing and, thrusting it through the truck window at me, ran off down the road after them.

'Qué pasa aquí? What's going on here?' Raúl appeared in the doorway too, along with some of the other customers.

'Quién sabe? Parece una bronca.' Antonino, serene as usual, shook his head wonderingly. 'Looks like a fight.'

'It was those university kids,' Karina shouted over from the back of the van. 'Drunk as skunks. They started making remarks, insulting us. So Gallo took a swing at one of them . . . Ay, mi Gallito.' She clutched her hands sentimentally to her chest. 'I do hope he'll be careful.'

'Estos muchachos,' Raúl sighed. 'These kids, always fighting.'

He looked at me and shrugged. Since there was nothing more to see, the rest of his customers soon went back inside to their suppers. For a while there was silence. Then we heard voices shouting again, a little less certain this time.

'Which way did they go?'

'I didn't see, did you? I was still in the truck.'

Mara and Omar and I stared uselessly down the road.

'I saw them, they're down there.' Karina pointed into the darkness towards the circus camp. 'Ay, mi Gallito . . .' she squeaked, scrambling out of the truck. 'I'm going to see what's happening.'

'I'll come with you.'

Before the other two could stop us we ran down the road towards the piece of waste land which lay between the entrance to the Skate Mall and Raúl's taco bar. Although the generator had been turned off, the bulky silhouette of the Big Top was just visible behind it. It was very dark. Karina clutched my hand.

'Ay, Katty, Katty, do you think he'll be all right?' She was whispering, but I could hear the excitement trembling in her voice.

'Quién sabe? Who knows?' I found myself echoing Antonino's words.

'Look! There they are.' She pointed below us, to where an old cement mixer had been dumped, just to one side of a small ditch. Three figures, unidentifiable in the darkness, were making off into the bushes behind it.

'Gallo?' Karina made as if to go after him.

'No, don't go any further . . .' I pulled her back.

Just then the three – Gallo, Ramón and Ricky – emerged on to the road a little further down. They were panting and dishevelled. There was no sign of the students. 'What happened, what happened?' Everyone crowded round them. Ramón and Gallo were trying not to look too pleased with themselves, but Ricky was cock-a-hoop.

'Did you see that? Did you see, *prima*?' He turned to Mara. His eyes were twice their normal size, the pupils abnormally extended so that the whole cornea seemed to have turned black. 'Those poor fucking mother-fuckers . . . !' He threw his head back. His laugh, like his voice, was oddly high-pitched. 'You'll have to put that in your book, Katty, won't you?' Ricky grabbed my wrist. 'That'll really be something for your book, won't it?'

He was standing very close to me. I could see the sweat pricking out on his forehead. He was breathing hard. On his upper lip curled the silky, uneven tracing of an adolescent moustache. Droplets of sweat, like tiny transparent seed pearls, gathered between the hairs.

'Ay, qué me encantan estas broncas, qué me encantan.' His eyes blazed. 'I just love these fights, I just *love* them!'

He slammed his hand on to the bonnet of the truck, intoxicated with his own success.

On the drive over to dinner Ricky went over what had happened again and again.

'The thing is, you must never just jump into a fight like that. Never. You have to sum up the situation first. You heard me trying to calm things down at first, didn't you? You heard me, *prima*?'

'Sí, Ricky.' Mara smiled at him indulgently. 'We all heard you.'

Ricky slapped the driving wheel with the palm of his hand. '*Chinga!*' He laughed gloatingly. 'It was never going to be much of a fight really, those fucking *fresas*[1] from the university don't know a thing. We chased them off the road and into the building site there where it was dark. From that moment, I knew we had them. No sweat.' He hammered the driving wheel again. 'But then, all of a sudden one of these bastards suddenly pulls out a knife.

[1] *fresa* literally means 'strawberry', but in Mexican slang is used pejoratively to describe a spoilt or soft person.

Híjole! I'm telling you, Omar, never turn your back on anyone in a fight, you never know what they might pull on you.[1] You must always be watching out, always watching each other's backs. You got that?' Full of importance Ricky turned to Omar. 'Remember what I'm telling you, OK? You might need it next time.'

Omar nodded seriously.

'Anyway, the next thing I know this guy's pulled a fucking knife on us, right? Shit!' Ricky gripped the steering wheel so that his knuckles showed up white. 'I had this penknife in my pocket but that was all, nothing compared to what this guy had. He had a serious blade there, *hombre*, I'm telling you. I was thinking, shit, we've really had it this time, boys. But then suddenly I had this idea. I got hold of my penknife and stuck it out underneath the cloth of my jacket, see? Like this.'

Ricky was so excited he was hardly looking at the road. He thrust two fingers underneath the military-style camouflage jacket which he always wore, pointing them at us like a gun. His lips narrowed.

'I just stood there, just looking at him. Very calm. I said, If you don't get out of here right now, *I'm going to blow your fucking head off . . .*'

He smiled and in the darkness his teeth showed up startlingly, very white and even. '*Chinga!* You should have seen them run.' Ricky threw his head back and rattled the steering wheel. 'You should have seen them *run!*'

Perhaps because Circo Bell's was still very much controlled by a single family, a hermetic body without many external influences, not only the girls, but the boys too were clean-living to the point of puritanism. Their vices were sex and fighting.

I knew that many of the circus boys liked to fight and often did, honour-bound both by the rituals of adolescence and the tribal loyalties of the circus to defend each other at all times, but until now I had never really thought much more about it. Unlike the girls in the circus, who despite the false promise of parades and processions and fishnet stockings, were guarded with Sicilian

---

[1] Ricky had learnt this the hard way. At La Villa he had been involved in a fight with a local gang in which someone had hit him across the back of the neck with a bottle. He needed six stitches and was unable to work for several weeks.

zeal by their fathers, brothers and male cousins, rarely leaving the circus's protection, the boys were expected, and even encouraged, to make forays outside it. And when they did, invariably it was to challenge the outside world as traditional Mexican machismo demanded: either by making love to it, or by fighting it. Conquest, in whatever form, was all.

When we arrived at the dinner, Ricky was still enraptured: flying high, not on his trapeze this time, but as if he had just swallowed half a bottle of amphetamines. For him, I realized with fascination, the fight had been better than any drink or any drug. Better, even, than sex.

Flanked by his lieutenants, Gallo and Ramón, Ricky burst in through the door, his army combat jacket flying open. As the rest of us clattered in behind, we could hear his voice, squeaky with emotion, recounting the story to his father. He seemed completely unaware of the other people in the room – our hosts, a graphic designer and his wife who were old friends of Mundo and Carmen's, and their guests, a handful of respectable-looking middle-class Mexicans. As Ricky told his story, the room subsided into a chilly hush.

'I was holding my knife under my jacket like this, see,' he explained, breathless with the glory of it. 'Then I just stood there looking at the fucker, staring at him right in the eyes. Then I said: If you don't get out of here right now, I'm going to blow your fucking head off, fuck-face . . .'

Mundo, in his unaccustomed suit, flexed his huge hands disapprovingly but said nothing. Carmen looked impassive. Sergio and Maria smiled nervously and started handing round the dips. Their children, on the other hand, two weedy teenage *fresas*, a girl and a boy with braces, were speechless with the thrill of it all. They followed the three strutting boys with adoring eyes.

It was strange to be inside a real house again, a house with glass windows, pictures on the walls, and loos that actually flushed, but the novelty was quick to wear off. Before long I felt bored and restless, oppressed by the weight of bricks and mortar. Sergio and Maria's other guests huddled together on the sofas. From time to time they cast us nervous looks, as if, like creatures sprung suddenly to life from the pages of some medieval bestiary, they could not be entirely sure what any one of us might do next.

Although Ricky had fought as one of a gang, I knew that in his heart he celebrated his victory as a personal one. Unlike the Mexican Indians, for whom a sense of community is all-important, mestizo Mexicans are a nation of individualists, at once traditional and yet unrestrained, often anarchic in their ways. They do not readily adopt a group mentality. Their society, still blooded by their violent past, is based on the unspoken, but widely held view that any unit larger than the extended family is essentially untrustworthy: whatever lies outside the family, therefore, has become a rich and lawless picking ground, to be plundered, pillaged, beaten or seduced at will.

This attitude does not only apply to individuals – after all, young boys like Ricky who turn themselves on by flexing a little muscle are by no means unique to Mexico – but extends right through society, a rot which has crept into every body with any authority within the country. In Mexico not only politicians, but the entire judiciary, the armed forces, the civil service and the police force are corrupt on a scale with which it is difficult to think of any reasonable comparison. As foreigners living only temporarily in Mexico this did not usually affect us, although with the circus we were often aware of minor abuses, particularly from the police: on the spot 'fines' for speeding or driving without a licence and so forth. Before I left England I remember reading a report in the *Independent* newspaper which said that a recent Mexican study had found that the majority of the country's most serious criminals, including bank robbers, rapists, kidnappers and drug traffickers, were *police*. At the time the claim seemed so absurd that I was not inclined to take it very seriously.

One afternoon a few days later I was in my caravan getting ready for the parade as usual – I had learnt how to do my own make-up by now and, although I usually changed in Jovita's wardrobe with the other girls, if I was ever in a hurry it was often quicker to do it here – when Tom arrived back from Puebla.

'You'll never guess what happened to me,' he said, kissing me.

'Not the car?' My single greatest dread while Tom was away, since he always drove huge distances, was that he would have an accident. Driving on Mexican roads was always a lethal occupation.

'No, not an accident.' He pushed to one side a pile of clothes and the bits and pieces of make-up, lipsticks and bottles of foundation, which I was slowly acquiring, and put his cameras down on the table. 'I was robbed.'

'Robbed! Who by?' I put on an old shirt and a cardigan over my costume to keep warm. 'Did you report it to the police?'

'The police?' Tom laughed sourly. 'How could I report it to the police. I was robbed *by* the police.'

'*What?*' No amount of dark comments from people in the circus about the viciousness of the police force – and there had been plenty – had really sunk in up until now.

'Hola, hola, qué pasó?' A gravelly voice just outside the door. 'Tommy, Tommy!' Rolando, who was making one of his rare appearances at the circus, embraced Tom enthusiastically. 'Where have you been, you *vago*[1] you?' He winked at him roguishly.

'He's been robbed.' I sat down on the bed. 'By the police.'

'By the police, eh?' Rolando seemed to think this was a good joke. 'Where?'

'In my car. On the highway just outside Mexico City.'

Tom explained what had happened.

'I was driving along when this traffic policeman started signalling to me to pull up on the side of the road. I pulled over and he got in beside me into the passenger seat. Then he asked for my keys, which I gave him, and for my documents, which of course I showed him. I noticed that he didn't really look at them properly, but straight away started to say something about how I didn't have permission to have the camper top on the open back part of our truck. It was all a nonsense of course, I realized that immediately, but after a bit he gave me back the keys and asked me to drive off the main road and down this little side street.'

Rolando listened with a look of amusement. His hands were

---

[1] *vago* means literally a vagabond or a tramp, but used here it has a picaresque sense, to describe one who has many adventures, sexual and otherwise. *Se fueron de vagos*, they went off like vagabonds, Mara would often say with some fatalism, when the boys stayed out late.

like Mundo's, the hands of a trapeze artist, as huge as hams; from time to time he rubbed them together so that they gave off a faint trace of aftershave.

'I drove down this road, like he said,' Tom went on, 'and stopped on the corner where there were another three policemen. I had the distinct impression that they were waiting there for us, as if the whole thing was a set-up. One of the other policemen, who they all called *capitán*, now got into the car too. This "captain" didn't bother to mention the camper top at all. He just said, "Are you going to pay or not?" I said, "What do you mean, am I going to pay? Pay for what?" But he didn't reply to my question, just kept on saying "Pay up, pay up, it'll be better for you if you just pay us now".

'Of course by now, I knew what they were after, but I kept up the dumb act as long as I could. Eventually I said, more out of curiosity than anything, "How much do you want me to pay?" "Four hundred dollars," he said.'

'Four hundred dollars!' Rolando could contain himself no longer. He gave one of his gravelly hoodlum's laughs. 'Huh, huh! That's because they saw your number plates; they must have thought you were American.' He was enjoying himself. 'They think all Americans are rich.'

Outside the pre-parade music started up. From the window I could see the now familiar sight of the other performers gradually making their way round to the back of the Big Top. Brissel and Gordo dashing, late as usual. Yvonne, emerald feathers in her hair, pushing Taynarí in his little pram. Antonino went by carrying his props, various swords, candelabra and collapsible ladders balancing on a metal stand. He saw our truck parked outside, a sure sign that Tom was back from one of his trips, and waved in at us through the window.

'So what did you do?' It was nearly time for me to go. I peered at myself in the mirror, putting the last touches to my make-up. 'You couldn't have paid them all that, surely?'

'Don't be ridiculous. There was no way I was going to pay them $400. I said, "Look, let's go to the police station and sort all this out there." That's when they started to get really nasty. They started swearing at me, very aggressive. All the *chinga* bit started, *chinga tu madre, chinga tu madre.*' Tom, warming to his story, gesticulated crudely.

'So now it's *chinga tu madre*, eh?' Rolando rubbed his hands, delighted. 'You've been living next to Güera too long, I can see.'

Tom, who had been boiling some water for coffee, passed Rolando a cup.

'By now there was not even the smallest pretence that this was anything to do with a legitimate fine. They were robbing me, and that was that. Both of the policemen were wearing guns. I tried not to look at them, wondering if they would dare to threaten me that way, but instead they made me drive even further down through the side streets. I had no idea where we were, or how to get back on to the main road. Then we stopped again. They said, "OK then, how much money have you got?" So I took my wallet out; I had about 200,000[1] pesos in it, which they took from me immediately, but I could see that it wasn't enough for them. They frisked me, made me empty out every pocket, shirt, trousers, jacket, the lot. They cleaned me out of every last peso, didn't even leave me enough to make a phone call. Then they directed me back to the main road. When we were a block away they got out and that was the last I saw of them.'

'Ay, Tommy.' Rolando clapped him gaily on the back. 'Te chingaron.' He shook his head. 'You were fucked, good and proper. No doubt about it.'

'Surely there must be something we can do?' I said. Rolando's attitude was beginning to irritate me. 'We should call our embassy, report it to them at least.'

'Your embassy!' Rolando honked with laughter. 'And what would they do, pray? If you tell them, all they can do is to report it back to the police. And then what happens? The guys who did you get hold of your address, or your licence plates, and they'll come after you, believe me.[2] Don't make trouble for yourself.'

'Well, I don't believe you.' I was really angry now. I could not believe that we had no recourse against this kind of abuse.

---

[1] About £40.

[2] He was right. We did eventually ring the embassy, whose only comment was to repeat, almost verbatim, what Rolando had already told us. Their official advice was to do nothing.

'Oh, don't you? This is *Mexico*, Katty. It's the same with everything, even with politics. No one votes for PRI[1],' Rolando shrugged, 'but they always win. It's the way the system works here, that's all. And in its own way it does work,' he smiled, 'despite what you *gringos* say. You just have to learn how to take advantage of it, that's all.'

There is an interesting notion, popular amongst Mexican intellectuals, that all time is present simultaneously in Mexico, that all history happens, and can happen, today: a Lacandon Indian sips the slow hours in his hut, or goes hunting with bows and flint-tipped arrows in the forest of his ancestors, while at the same instant twenty-first century office blocks, towering obelisks of steel and glass, are inaugurated in its cities. The modern Mexican state, emerging in fits and starts after the upheavals of the 1910–17 Revolution, and by inference modern Mexicans, are still in the process of defining themselves. The Mexican is at once ancient and modern, Indian and Spanish, the conqueror and the conquered. As the poet Octavio Paz has written, Mexico is a country which has still not yet managed to decipher its own features. The fact of Mexicans' *mestizaje*, or mestizo-hood, is central to this dilemma. 'If the *criollo*,[2] born of Spanish blood, was the victim of ambiguity, the mestizo, born of mixed blood, was doubly so: he was neither *criollo* nor Indian – the mestizo was the living victim of illegitimacy. From this feeling of illegitimacy grew his insecurity, his perpetual instability, his tendency to swing between extremes: from courage to panic, from exaltation to apathy, from loyalty to treachery. Cain and Abel in a single soul . . .'[3]

After the Revolution intellectuals and artists, such as the painters Diego Rivera, Freida Khalo and their circle, deliberately exalted the idea of the Mexicans' heroic Indian past at the expense of their Spanish inheritance, in the process helping to forge a new and emotionally satisfying national identity. The Spanish, particularly Cortéz, became the villians of the piece, while

[1] PRI – the Partido Nacional Institucional, the Institutional Revolutionary Party, has been in power in Mexico continuously since the Revolution.
[2] *criollo*: a Spaniard born in the Americas.
[3] From Sor Juana: Her Life and Her World by Octavio Paz (Faber and Faber, 1988).

prominent Indian figures such as Cuauhtémoc, the last Aztec Emperor, were resuscitated as powerful and emotive symbols of Mexican nationalism. Cuauhtémoc soon came to be venerated with almost as much zeal as that still more ambiguous, mixed-blood icon, the Virgin of Guadalupe.

An idealized pre-Colombian Indian past, particularly the Aztec past, was not the only period in Mexican history to be singled out for its political correctness. With oriental, face-saving selectiveness, the Wars of Independence against Spain and the 1910–17 Revolution were also dwelt upon as periods which were in keeping with this vigorous new sense of nationalism. Other eras which conspicuously did not fulfil this role – the entire Colonial period, the French occupation of 1862 which installed Archduke Maximillian of Habsburg temporarily on the Mexican 'throne', and the dictatorship of Porfirio Díaz[1] – were glossed over, sometimes apparently forgotten altogether.

'A society is defined as much by how it comes to terms with its past as by its attitude to its future,' Octavio Paz wrote. 'Although we Mexicans are preoccupied or, more accurately, obsessed with our past, we lack a clear idea of who we have been.' Enshrining some periods, forgetting others, the Mexicans live 'between myth and negation', a people without a memory.

I had come to Mexico, and to the circus, to find magic: not the magic of fairy tale, of malevolent fairies and Seven League boots, but magic as a whole new way of looking at life, a language beyond language. Defined in this way it very closely mirrors what we understand by myth. Free from the childish associations of the word 'magic',[2] a myth becomes not just a story with supernatural

[1] Porfirio Díaz was elected president in 1876, and subsequently won re-election many times although over the years he was to become, effectively, a dictator. His rule, known as the Porfiriato, lasted some three decades and was a time of great economic progress and stability. Minus points were strict political and press censorship, excessive reliance on foreign investment, and the fact that in this period some 3,000 families owned half the country. Little of the newly created wealth filtered down to the mestizo and Indian classes, many of whom lived in a state of virtual slavery. It was Díaz's policies, and the urgent need for land reform, which sparked off the 1910 Mexico Revolution.

[2] Whereas the word 'magic', in the literary term 'magic realism', has come to be regarded as a dubious, even frivolous description, the idea of myth and realism used together is acknowledged by many writers and critics to be one of the most important contributions made by Latin American writers to contemporary fiction.

embellishments, but a metaphor for the origins of an entire people, their social structures, taboos and psychological make-up. A myth is a profound revelation of a culture's collective unconscious.

In Mexico, both history and time are fluid concepts. The Mexican predeliction for myth-making remakes history in its own image, but it is an image which is not yet fully realized. It is interesting that the periods which are most enshrined in popular memory are also amongst the epochs of greatest violence and social upheaval. The peculiarly perverse brand of Mexican machismo is sometimes explained as forming part of an elaborate screen thrown up by many Mexicans to mask their feelings of illegitimacy, their sense of insecurity with their own *mestizaje*, but this has always seemed to me to be a very incomplete explanation. There was something much more disturbing behind it than that. As I was beginning to find out for myself, there is a hidden current in Mexico, a kind of dark underbelly, which finds its most profound expression in violence, in bloodshed, and the contemplation of death.

The border town of Matamoros, Tamaulipas, smells of sex and witchery. Spivvy and streetwise, festooned like a pimp with cheap, gilt trinkets, Matamoros spills along the banks of the Rio Bravo opposite its neat Texan neighbour Brownsville, before petering south, without a backward glance, into a squalid, semi-tropical scrubland.

Heading south from the States, nothing quite prepares you for the moment of re-entry into Mexico. Even if, as we had, you had already been through that same town on your way over the border in the first place, it makes no difference. In Corpus Christi, where we had spent a week buying our caravan and a small Ford truck, I told the sales manager that we were about to join a Mexican circus. 'A circus? Hell, that shouldn't be a problem,' he smiled his slow southern smile. 'Why, that whole goddamn country's a circus.'

Mexico might be geographically close: mentally it was like contemplating a black hole. We were in Corpus a week, but even a few days would have been enough for their fear to infect us. After a while it seemed as if the whole town knew where we were heading. 'Aren't you guys *afraid*?' they asked at the Trade Winds Motel, at Leisureland, at Denny's Up-All-Night. 'I mean, *Mexico*...' The unfinished phrase would hover delicately between us, like a trembling bubble, fraught with I don't know what shibboleths. The danger. The disease. Perhaps, quite simply, the dirt. It had never occurred to me to be afraid. After all, we had already been living in Mexico for several months before we came up to Texas, but by the time we headed south again ... I could not help wondering.

The Mexican border with the States is two thousand miles long. Its very length, and the extremes it has come to represent – First World to Third World, Protestant to Catholic, Anglo-Saxon to Latin – are the source of frequent, more pejorative comparisons: to cross the border has become a metaphysical act in which a traveller passes from credit into debt, from order into chaos, even, as some would have it, from light into dark.

Now that we were finally over the border again, I felt infected by America's fear. It clung to me, seeped from my pores. I could smell it on my skin like sour milk. I could not shake it off. Matamoros was like a giant mirror, compelled to reflect back everything the US, in its ignorance and dread, cared to project on to her. This was no longer simply the seedy little town that it had been just a week ago. Matamoros with its tawdry, overgrown plaza and its parking lots, its ancient cars belching exhaust fumes, its fruit and vegetable shops spilling over into the street, the stalls selling everything from tourist tat to fruit juices and *licuados*, was a new and sinister place.

I nursed my bag close to my body. When a man stopped to ask me the time, I jumped back from him like a nervous cat, expecting treachery. I saw a cripple shining shoes; saw how the men looked at me, covering my body with lustful eyes. And there was another thing. Mexico smelt. In the States, I realized, nothing had really smelt, not even the food. In Matamoros I could smell at once if a restaurant was dirty, but I could also smell the food cooking. I could smell drains, but I could smell flowers too. There was dust. And flies. In Corpus Christi I don't remember seeing a single fly. I don't remember seeing jasmine or hibiscus, either. I felt fear here, but I felt desire, too. There was something lustful and carniverous about Matamoros which made Corpus and Brownsville seem like pale, workaday places beside them.

I passed a shop which had a sign in the window: 'Tarot cards read here, 10,000 pesos.' I went in, and was sent to a tiny cubby hole at the back of the shop. The cubby hole was hung about with a mish-mash of occult paraphernalia, magic pyramids, amulets, and pictures of the Virgin of Guadalupe. On the floor votive candles flickered in glass jars. I was nervous, I had never had the cards read before. A man sat there who called himself El Gitano, the gypsy. El Gitano wore a white shirt slashed open to the waist. His chest was covered with a mass of amulets – an ivory tooth, a clenched fist, a gold dragon – all on heavy silver chains. In his tinted spectacles, I thought, he looked more like a drugs dealer than a magician. 'The cards never lie,' he said. 'Everything comes out in the cards.' But his reading was not convincing. He looked most of it up in a book.

After I finished with El Gitano, I lingered on in the front part of the shop. This was given over to a *hierberia*, a herbalist, of the kind you find in markets and travelling fairs all over Mexico. The sham of the Tarot cards might have been put on for the tourists making their day trips from across the border, but the *hierberia* most definitely was not. While El Gitano lurked alone in his cupboard, at the front of the shop trade was brisk.

Almost all the customers were Mexicans. As well as herbs and spices to prepare every known infusion and natural cure, the shop had a strong line in magical and religious oddities: charms and amulets – including replicas of some of the ones sported by El Gitano himself – rosaries, pictures of the saints, strange aphrodisiac powders and roots. Their speciality, however, was candles. There were candles of every size and colour. You could buy a candle to the Miraculous Humming Bird, which would give a man the choice of any women he wanted; to the Chameleon, to the Black Cat or to the Five Powers, for power over your enemies; to the Black Sleep, to make someone love you, or to the *Santa Muerte*, Holy Death, to rid yourself of them again.

The most popular candle of all was also one of the most unusual: to Pancho Villa. Pancho Villa, one of the most famous bandits of all time and hero of the Mexican Revolution. Pancho

Villa, the 'Centaur of the North', who like Robin Hood robbed from the rich to give to the poor, but who was also responsible for some of the cruellest and bloodiest atrocities ever committed in that bloody era. Pancho Villa, who trounced the Americans and became one of their most wanted men with a $5000 bounty on his head; who, even with Pershing's punative mission of several thousand US soldiers on his tail, was never caught.

Villa's candle, inscribed with plain black lettering, lay between the banks of voluptuously perfumed saints and virgins, between all the magical beasts and potentates ever dreamt of by the exuberant Mexican psyche.

Pancho Villa, read the simpole invocation, *Watch Over Me*.

EIGHT

Yo soy soldado de Pancho Villa
de sus Dorados soy el más fiel,
nada me importa perder la vida,
si es cosa de hombres morir por él.

(I am one of Pancho Villa's soldiers,
of his Dorados I am the most faithful,
I don't mind dying
because it is a man's thing to die for him.)

POPULAR MEXICAN SONG

Six months later, in the town of Chihuahua in northern Mexico, I went looking for Pancho Villa myself.

Through one of the Chihuahua societies I contacted a local historian who agreed to meet me in the *comedor* of our hotel. Edelmiro Ponce de León was tall for a Mexican, and very thin. He wore cheap socks and dirty thick-soled shoes. His eyes were sad and heavy-lidded, very round and brown. The corneas were fixed high up in his eyeball so that too much white showed at the bottom, giving him the sad air of a hypnotist. We sat for a few minutes exchanging pleasantries while two sulky girls, their fringes lacquered like cockatoos, served us with stale cakes.

I felt rather ashamed of the venue. The hotel was in a poor street, cluttered with blinking neon signs and lottery shops, but we had chosen it because it was central and for the beauty of its old courtyard, which was decorated with antique blue and yellow tiles. We had stayed in cheap hotels like this all over Mexico – 'the dingy room, the symbolic dead beetle and the smell of urine,' as Graham Greene describes it in *The Lawless Roads*. Usually there was nothing to distinguish between them, except here in Chihuahua where at night mysterious women with deep voices and high-heeled shoes lurked along the corridors. The concierge, all seeing and beady as a *tricoteuse*, had been well trained and clearly turned a blind eye to these nocturnal comings and goings.

The day I met Edelmiro there were only a few other people in the *comedor*. On the other side of the courtyard was a cantina which, although it was only eleven o'clock in the morning, already jangled with the sound of *musica ranchera* and wild, tequila-riddled carousing.

'And so, which Pancho Villa is of the most pressing interest to you?' With long fingers Edelmiro lifted one of the cakes and bit into it. A delicate shower of stale cake fell on to the dirty tablecloth in front of him. 'Pancho Villa, the Man. Or Pancho Villa, the Myth?'

He brought out this phrase with a kind of pride, as though he had been waiting a long time for just this opportunity to use it, rehearsing it often inside his head.

'Is there such a difference?'

'Oh, yes, very much so.' He took another bite of the cake. The crumbs fell as before, becoming tangled in his soft moustache. 'You see, Pancho Villa – the Man, so to speak – was not always popular in Mexico. In fact it was only quite recently, when the Americans decided to adopt him as a kind of folk hero, that certain people here in Mexico started to take him seriously at all.' Outside, from the cantina, I heard the distant tinkle of glasses shattering. 'You see, Villa made a raid on Columbus, just across the US border in New Mexico in March 1916. Killed some people, roughed up the town a bit. An act of revenge against the *gringos* who refused to supply him with arms. He felt betrayed by them for siding with Carranza against him. Even with a five-thousand-dollar price on his head, they never caught him. Even Pershing and his men, regular US army troops who spent nine months trying to track him down in the mountains, never caught up with him. Villa was the only man ever successfully to have invaded the United States, they say. It's quite a claim.'

Edelmiro stared at the empty plate with his hungry, hypnotist's eyes. There was something at once so refined and yet so famished about him. I called over one of the girls and ordered another plate of cakes. The sound of more breaking glass came from the cantina and the rowdy refrain of a popular song, 'La Cucaracha'. Whether from indifference or politeness, Edelmiro did not seem to notice the noise. Instead we went on talking about Pancho Villa.

'Villa was a bandit for many years before he joined the revolutionary cause. He did not join the Revolution because of altruism, but because as a bandit it suited him to become respectable again. Here in Chihuahua they used to call him the Attila of the North. He was a cruel and opportunistic man. He committed many atrocities, not only against Mexicans but against foreigners too, the Spanish and the Chinese. He hated the Chinese especially. At Torreón three hundred of them were massacred after some of his men died of food poisoning from one of their restaurants. He called them 'enemies of the revolution', but that was really nothing to do with it. He just hated the Chinese. It was a racial thing; like Hitler and the Jews.'

From the metal briefcase which he had brought with him Edelmiro bought out his collection of old photographs and press cuttings of Villa. There was Villa swashbuckling in a Mexican hat; Villa with some of his men, swaddled in bullet belts; post-Revolution Villa, dapper with a waxed moustache, posing stiffly in an unaccustomed dark suit; a copy of the newspaper *Extra* printed on the day, 20 July 1923, Villa was assassinated; Villa's body, punctured with bullet holes, slumped over the side of his Dodge.

As I looked at the photographs, Edelmiro talked on about Pancho Villa and his many guises. His hands, long, elegant hands, if not quite clean, lay in repose on the table in front of him. The cakes came. Occasionally, when pondering another sentence, he would put his hand out furtively, as if hoping not to be noticed, and take another cake. More crumbs, gentle ones, dropped on to the yellowed clippings. His surname, Ponce de León, I remembered, was both noble and Spanish, the name of conquistadors. Something of its faded gentility still clung to him, despite the socks and the cheap metal briefcase, some dim Renaissance aura of parchment, goose quills and candle grease. Across the old courtyard a man and a girl came staggering out from the bar, the girl giggling, the man bleary-eyed, blinking owlishly in the sudden sunlight. Among these rough people, among the cantinas and the lottery ticket-sellers, Edelmiro was oddly displaced. His hungry look, it occurred to me, was perhaps more intellectual than physical: a Don Quixote still tilting vainly at the imponderables of the Mexican Revolution.

The group photographs interested me particularly. The faces of the men were hooded, their clothes thick with dust beneath swaggings of leather bullet belts. I was surprised that they should have been persuaded to pose so formally, in so orderly a fashion, in the middle of a battlefield. In some they were arranged in rows, like a football team, with Villa in the centre, the tough coach with the heart of gold.

'Ah, yes, you see, here is Pancho Villa. And here, his *Dorados*.' Edelmiro pointed to the photograph.

'His *Dorados*. Pancho Villa and his Golden Ones. Like Robin Hood and his Merry Men, you mean?'

'Exactly so.'

He gave the ghost of a bow.

'Who were they?'

'The *Dorados*? Who knows?' he shrugged. 'Desperados. Murderers and wanted men like him, most likely. Villa had great charisma. He drew men to him, persuaded them to fight not just for the Revolution, but for *him*, for Pancho Villa. Villa's troops were always intensely loyal to him, but the *Dorados* were more than that. They were special, the élite; Villa's own personal bodyguard of a hundred handpicked men. During the fighting they made up the heart of the *villista* cavalry, but even when they weren't fighting they were always with Villa, protecting him wherever he went.'

I looked at the picture again.

'I bet some of them had a story or two to tell.' I turned the photograph over in my hands. 'I suppose they must all be dead by now.'

'Almost all of them,' Edelmiro nodded.

'You think some of them may still be alive? They'd be too old, surely. If Villa was alive he would be, what? Well over a hundred.'

'He was born in 1878,' Edelmiro calculated, 'so he'd be a hundred and fourteen. I doubt if there are any *Dorados* left of that age. But the Revolution years turned the whole country upside down. Some of his men would have been little more than boys when they joined him. I have a friend, an ex-army man who I know used to keep in touch with some of them. There was some organization which used to raise money for revolutionary veterans and their families. He was involved with it for a while, knew all the old boys. I'll take you along to meet him if you'd like. Maybe he will have some information for you.'

Edelmiro's friend, Lieutenant Hugo Navarro, was studying at the Institute of Anthropology, not far from our hotel. We walked there through the dusty streets of Chihuahua snarling with midday traffic. We were in luck. We found Navarro immediately, waiting in between classes in the courtyard of the Institute, an open place trellised prettily with vines. He was an unexpectedly young man with a small, gnomish physique, heavy-bearded and barrel-chested. Edelmiro explained to him why I had come to Chihuahua. The lieutenant thought for a moment.

'There are a number of old veterans I can think of who certainly served under Villa in the División del Norte, but as for the *Dorados*.' He shook his head. '*Difícil, muy difícil*. There were only a hundred of them, you know. Most of them didn't survive the Revolution anyway.'

'There was one, though,' Edelmiro put in. 'I remember you telling me about him once. The one that was living in Jiménez, what happened to him?'

'José Meléndez?' Navarro nodded. 'I suppose it's just possible that he's still around. But if he were still alive, he would be a very old man, you know. I am not sure ... there are plenty of other men who knew Villa.' He looked at me doubtfully. 'These men, these *Dorados*, they were not like regular soldiers, you know. Are you sure? I mean these men were *rough ... muy rudo ...*' He tailed off. I saw him glance at me and then toward Edelmiro with unease. I thought I knew what he was getting at.

'That's OK.' I smiled. 'I'd like to try, if you had some kind of address for him or something. Just to see if he is still there.'

I had hoped to meet someone who knew Villa, maybe even someone who had fought with him, but the thought that I might have the chance of meeting one of his *Dorados* had never crossed my mind. I tried not to sound too eager. 'If he doesn't want to talk to me, then that's fair enough. But I'd like to try.'

When he saw how serious I was, Navarro did not try to dissuade me.

'I don't have an exact address for him. Go to Jiménez and ask for the Colonia Campesina.' He gave me a street name and an approximate number. 'I can't remember the exact number, but it's around there somewhere. Ask the neighbours. If he's there, you'll find him all right. And if you do find him, tell him I sent you. Teniente Hugo Navarro. Remember that. You'll be all right.' He shook me gravely by the hand. 'You'll be all right if he knows you were sent by me.'

In search of the last *Dorado*, Tom and I drove to Jiménez, south from the town of Chihuahua towards the border with Durango. The vast open spaces of northern Mexico, particularly the desert lands east of the Sierra Madre, defy the imagination. Before the Revolution a few powerful Creole families, *latifundistas* as they were known, the Terrazas, the Creels, the Cuiltys, owned most of the land: vast, semi-autonomous holdings worked by Indians and mestizos, many of them debt peons. The combined *haciendas* of the Terrazas family alone are estimated to have covered a total of six and a half million acres.

All day we drove through these ruined kingdoms. Like the landscape, the road was dusty and hot. Occasionally we passed through corridors of blonde grass. Once, in the distance, we spied a glitter of green which at first we thought was water, but which turned out to be an expanse of acacia bushes as big as a lake, but for the most part the land was scrub-like, thirsty, as uncompromising as the people it spawns.

Towards three o'clock we stopped to have lunch in a roadside *comedor*. The building was a solitary, ramshackle cabin made out of wood, with nothing more than a rusty Coca-Cola sign over the door to announce itself. Inside a woman served us with fried eggs, frijoles and tortillas. There was nothing else to offer us. While we ate the woman sat watching us silently from behind the beaded curtain which led into her kitchen. She was completely alone. She sat patiently, not moving, her hands clasped in her lap. I tried to read her expression: curiosity, envy, indifference? I could not tell. Somewhere, in a corner behind us, an ancient refrigerator hummed and juddered, but apart from this and the scraping of our knives and forks against our plates and the occasional buzzing of flies, there was no other sound in the whole place. There was no television, not even a radio to break the long silence of afternoon and heat. Even if we had not been there, I could imagine her sitting behind her curtain still, watching that empty room and the vast, empty landscape beyond it. There was nothing else to do.

I thought of the circus, of Güera, Jovita, Luis the elephant keeper, northerners all of them, like this woman: Güera from just outside Chihuahua, Jovita from a village near Torreón, Luis from the state of Nuevo Leon. Looking out towards the distant sierra I thought I could read them in this landscape. Tough, self-sufficient, beholden to no one. It might have been any one of them sitting behind that bead curtain, staring out at the sky.

Before we left I went round the back to use the privy, a crude hole in the ground fenced off by a canvas screen. In a paddock beyond it was a horse, still saddled, chewing at the scrub. Perhaps there was someone in the house with her after all: a husband or a father come home for his bellyful of beans and to sleep out the worst of the midday heat.

The north of Mexico is horseman's country. Even now in Chihuahua and Durango where there are so few roads and so much land, a man is nothing without a horse. In a place like this it is easy to see why the myth of Pancho Villa should so easily have supplanted anything else the man might have been.

Pancho Villa, the Centaur of the North: a legendary being, half man, half horse. According to the myth, his horsemanship and cunning were such that even if he was sighted by his enemies in one place one day, he would confound everyone, even his own men, by reappearing a hundred miles away or more the next, having ridden secretly all through the night. He never slept, trusted no one, not even his closest companions and followers. Pancho Villa was the ultimate man of action in a land where patience and endurance were often the only recourse against injustice and poverty; the very incarnation of the Mexican macho.

Villa's exaggerated masculinity – individualistic, tough, courageous to a fault (which, naturally, made him irresistible to women too) – had passed into Mexican folklore well before he joined Madero's Revolution and became General Francisco Villa, commander of the División del Norte. Even in his youth, hiding out in the hills as plain Doroteo Arango,[1] an everyday bandit and a cattle-rustler, Villa was larger than life. A kind of collective fantasy of romantic bravura grew up around everything he was and did. Every train robbery, every hold-up, every outrage committed on his territory was attributed to him as a matter of course; but so, too, were acts of charity just as extraordinary. John Reed, the American war journalist, gives an account[2] of how Villa, fired by the misery of the peons on the Hacienda Los Alamos, gathered together a band of men and raided the house, which he thoroughly looted before distributing the spoils among the poor. No two stories I ever seemed to hear about Pancho Villa were the same. Even the account of how he first became an outlaw has many versions. The most popular of these is that he came home one day to find the local landowner, on whose land Villa's family worked as sharecroppers, on the point of violating his sister, Martinita. Villa, then aged just sixteen, slipped into his cousin's house, took hold of a pistol and before anyone could stop him, fired three slugs straight at the *hacendado*. By this account Villa is a common cut-throat no longer, but an innocent man, even an honourable one, instinctively challenging the injustices of a corrupt society.

Was it ever possible to say, in those violent, self-interested times, where the real Villa ended and the popular imagination began? Tales of Villa's prowess, in love and in war, his good deeds to the poor, the loyalty he inspired, are part of Mexico's deepest language – her poetry and her music. Stories, ballads and literally hundreds of *corridos*, popular songs still sung by mariachi bands all over Mexico but which during the Revolution were the principal sources of news for a largely illiterate people, were composed about him. More so than any of the other great revolutionary leaders and generals from the north of Mexico, most of whom were either middle-class thinkers, like Madero, or aristocrats and soldiers, like Carranza and Obregón, Pancho Villa personified the

[1] Pancho Villa was born Doroteo (Dorothy) Arango, changing his name to Francisco Villa, thought to be the name of another notorious bandit, only after he became an outlaw in 1894.
[2] *Insurgent Mexico*, John Reed (Penguin, 1983).

Revolution for the common man. Because he was one of them, he showed ordinary Mexicans, the poor and the oppressed, that they too could rise up and take control of their own destiny. Historians may still argue the whys and the wherefores, but ordinary Mexicans have always known exactly what he was.

Pancho Villa, watch over me.

The Colonia Campesina in Jiménez is a poor district on the outskirts of the town. We drove slowly along its scrubby streets which were patrolled by mangy dogs and a group of children kicking a punctured football. The houses were low, one-storeyed affairs. On their windowsills geraniums dangled from old paint pots, the ubiquitous gardens of the poor. We asked around, as the lieutenant had advised us, and found Meléndez's house with alarming ease. Across the door was a rusting fly screen. I pulled it open a little and knocked. We listened. No reply. I knocked again and then, seeing that the door was unlatched, pushed it ajar. I put my face as close as I dared to the crack and called, 'Señor Meléndez . . . ?'

'Any reply?' Tom was standing behind me.

'Señor Meléndez?' I tried again a little louder this time. 'No, nothing. But I'm sure . . .' I listened again. 'I am almost sure I can hear someone moving about in there.'

I looked cautiously in through the crack, but could see nothing. All the shutters were closed and I was blinded by the blazing sun outside in the street which bounced mercilessly off the white walls of the houses. A sinister, musty smell, which I could not identify, came from the dark interior.

'Here, you try. Your voice carries further than mine.'

I stepped back, feeling suddenly extremely nervous. The fact that we had found the *Dorado*'s house with such ease had thrown me off balance. I had not had a chance to prepare myself properly. If he was there, what would I say to him? And what – oh, God – would he say to me?

'Está mal, el señor.'

A man's voice behind us. We both jumped. Tom sprang away from the door, pulling it guiltily shut behind him. Opposite Meléndez's house was a scruffy general store. Two men were standing outside it, watching us.

'We're looking for Señor Meléndez. José Meléndez? Is he ... does he still live here?'

'Sí, pero está mal. He's ill, that's why he's not answering.'

'I can't believe it,' Tom muttered to me, 'then he really is still alive.'

'Uhuh!' I coughed into my sleeve. 'Just.'

'What do you want with him anyway?'

The owner of the store was a young man, large and fleshy in build. He wore a dirty singlet tucked into a pair of Levi jeans. We crossed over the road towards him and explained briefly why we had come. When we had finished the two men glanced at each other. The second man, the older of the two, started to laugh. It was not a pleasant sound.

'Es muy mal hablado, el señor. What do you want with him? He's a foul-mouthed old man.' He shook his head at us. 'You don't want to talk to him, believe me. Everything is *chinga*-this and *chinga*-that, if you'll excuse the expression.'

'We've come a long way,' Tom said. 'All the way from Chihuahua. Is he too ill to see us, do you think?'

'From Chihuahua, indeed.' He looked hugely amused.

'We were told, in Chihuahua, that he was one of Pancho Villa's *Dorados*. The last one, in fact, who is still alive,' I said.

'That's right,' the young man in the singlet, whose name was Fernando, nodded. 'He was one of Villa's men. He was very close to him. They used to call him *el verdugo de Villa*.'

'Verdugo?' Tom said to me. 'What does that mean?'

'Uhuh!' I coughed again. 'It means hangman,' I said in English. 'Apparently he was Villa's hangman.'

A nervous knot had appeared in the pit of my stomach.

'Whenever Villa wanted someone killed' – with something like pride, Fernando swept his arm towards the old man's house – 'he sent this man, José Meléndez, to do it for him.'

'Oh, yes. He's very violent, even now,' the second man chipped in. 'I saw him in a fight just the other day. Fernando, you remember, *hombre*? In the cantina. They say his strength is still amazing. It took two or three men to pull him off. Imagine, at his age.'

'So how old is he, exactly?'

'Ninety-one.'

'What was that?' The men both spoke in heavily accented Spanish, too fast for Tom to catch every word.

'He's ninety-one and very violent,' I translated, smiling. 'He was in a fight last week. In the cantina. It took three men to pull him off.'

I turned to Fernando again. 'Does he, er . . . does anyone live with him?'

'No, he lives alone now.'

'No one else could stand him, the old bastard.'

'Look, I tell you what,' Fernando was warming to the subject, 'I know him quite well, seeing as how my shop is just across the road. There used to be a bench just here.' He pointed under the window of the little store. 'All the old men from the *barrio* used to come and sit here, to pass the time of day – until they stole the bench, that is.' He shrugged in a good-natured way. 'Anyway what I'm saying is, why don't I go across and speak to him for you? He knows me as well as anyone. Maybe it would be best. My friend is right, he's an old man, know what I mean? A little . . . capricious, shall we say?'

'Is he well enough to see us?' I asked. 'I mean, will he understand why we've come?'

'Oh, he'll understand. There's nothing wrong with his mind, he's clear as a bell. And if he isn't feeling like visitors, don't worry, he'll let us know.'

We followed Fernando through the tattered fly screen and into the house. Inside, as before, it was very dark. We were immediately engulfed by that same sinister, musty smell – the smell, I now realized, of an old man dying.

There were only three rooms in the house. The principal of these, which we entered immediately from the street, was a long thin room, obviously the kitchen, although apart from a sink and a few pots and pans on a table up at the far end, it was almost entirely naked of furniture. Two other rooms led from this. One, nearest the door, was a bedroom; a formal room with a dressing table, looking glass, a lugubrious wooden cupboard in one corner. There was nothing in the room to suggest that it was ever used. The heavy, womb-coloured damask on the bed was unwrinkled, the space around it shrouded in spectral, midday darkness.

Fernando went on ahead of us into the third room, which led off from the top end of the kitchen. Greyish daylight, grey like the appalling sick-bed smell, filtered through the doorway. Beyond it I could hear the sound of voices, the creak of bed springs. From where I stood waiting I could see just a little way into the room. There was a movement, a groan. In a trick of light the old man's shadow – black, angular, abnormally large – loomed suddenly on to the wall beside me. I flinched as if I had been hit and jumped backwards, my heart in my mouth. The shadow vanished again.

'He will see you.' Fernando stuck his head round the door. 'You can come in now.'

The old man lay, long and thin under his blankets, in the greyish half light. A fierce, old man's face – shaggy, vulpine – stuck out from beneath the covers: long, sunken cheeks beneath bushy eyebrows; a vigorous thatch of grey hair which stuck up defiantly from the top of his head; and the most enormous ears I have ever seen. Their lobes, thick and fleshy, hung pendulously down the side of his face. Wiry, greyish whiskers sprouted from their gristly, cauliflower shells like some ancient growth. *My, what big ears you have, Grandma*. Tom and I approached the bed slowly, perching ourselves on two stools which Fernando drew up for us alongside it. Beneath his greasy blankets the old man stirred.

Although at first he had appeared frail, closer to I could see that he was a big man still, and that his limbs were strong. I remembered what Fernando had said, that despite his ninety-one years, when he was well and standing, José Meléndez could fill any room with his physical presence, towering over much younger, fitter men. His hands, huge, hirsute, flexing and unflexing, plucked at the rough material by his sides. Some time ago the Mexican government had outlawed the carrying of firearms, but according to local lore this man still carried one every day of his life, not in a holster like in the old days, but tucked into his waistband, or hidden secretly in the folds of his clothes. *My, Grandma, what big hands you have*. I could imagine those hands handling a gun familiarly, lovingly, much as I would my pen or the pages of a book.

Beneath the bed a chamber pot was filled nearly half full with dark yellow urine. Outside in the back yard I could see an old-fashioned wooden privy, and a number of cockerels with glossy feathers picking in the dirt. Even though the door was wide open to the outside, the stench of stale urine from the chamber pot clung to the room, filling our nostrils with its nauseating sweetness.

José Meléndez, Pancho Villa's last *Dorado*, was dying alone. His wife had preceded him to the grave three years ago but, perhaps because he was so familiar with death, he did not seem at all to mind her passing.

'Solo, uno vive más a gusto,' he told us. 'I am more comfortable living on my own.' He pointed outside to the yard where his cockerels strutted. Occasionally, with an ear-splitting noise, one of them would crow. 'You see. They sing to me,' he said with satisfaction. Until recently he had kept a cow, too, a *lechera* or milking cow, but it was 'mucha mortificación' to bring her in and out of the house every day, so he had finally put her out to pasture on a friend's land.

We were in luck. The old man was in a good mood that day. In fact, Fernando whispered to us, impressed, he had never seen him so predisposed to talk. Normally, he had warned us before we went in, he never talked about the Revolution. Even when all the old men in the *barrio* gathered together on the bench outside Fernando's shop to talk about the old days, he had hardly ever joined in, but had kept his own counsel throughout the years; little by little, his own myth, as salty and reeking as Villa's own, growing up to fill the silences.

José Meléndez had joined the Revolution to avenge the death of his brother. He did not give us the details. When I asked him who had killed his brother he merely said, 'It was the Revolution, wasn't it? It was like that in those days,' and would be drawn no more.

'And Villa?' I asked, 'what made you decide to join up with Villa?'

'Where I came from it was always Villa,' he replied. 'Pancho Villa, Pancho Villa. Siempre.'

Although he did not seem to be offended by my questions, he spoke in a kind of shorthand, which if it had not been for the patient Fernando, familiar with his old man's mire of ellipses and silences, would have been almost impossible for us to understand.

When he spoke he made violent gestures with his hands, punctuating them with a strange guttural sound, a *pah!* or a *tchah!*, wrenched from the visceral depths of his old man's belly.

'Pancho Villa,' I tried again, 'what was he really like?' I realized that I had to seize the moment. 'Was he a bandit like some people say?'

'Villa? *Pah!*' Meléndez snorted, bringing his fist down suddenly against the side of his bed. 'Siempre fue bandido, antes y después. He was always a bandit, before and after.' He spat on to the floor. 'He was good when he had to be; and bad when he had to be. That's all.'

'And you were General Villa's right-hand man, weren't you, Señor?' Fernando spoke to him encouragingly.

'*Tcha!*' The old man snorted, but he did not seem displeased. He turned his sunken gaze towards us. 'We were like this.' With one of his sudden, fierce gestures, he held up two fingers. 'Like brothers!'

'And the day he was assassinated? Do you remember that day? It must have been a terrible blow.'

'Sure I remember it.' He glared at me from beneath shaggy eyebrows and shrugged impatiently. 'We all have to die someday.'

'Señor Meléndez was with Pancho Villa at Canutillo, weren't you, Señor?' Fernando said. 'After the Revolution General Villa was given this *hacienda* by the government, not far from here, near Hidalgo de Parral. He was also given the right to hand-pick fifty of his most loyal *Dorados* who were to live with him there and act as his bodyguards, isn't that right, Señor? You were one of General Villa's men, right to the last. One of his *escolta*.'

'So it's *General* Villa now, is it?' The old man sneered. 'Oh yes, I was at Canutillo all right. Fucking Canutillo, no one knows what hard work that was,' he grumbled tetchily to himself. 'Villa was a regular slave driver at Canutillo. We had to get up at four in the morning and he would keep us working sometimes until seven or eight o'clock at night. Here, boy, pass me one of those cigarettes, will you?'

Fernando reached into the drawer of a scrofulous old bedside table where Meléndez kept his cigarettes and respectfully lit one for him. The old man inhaled, coughed fruitily.

Mara Bell's, contortionist and queen of the
circus, performing her aerial ballet act. This
was the act she tried to teach me, although
I always found the simpler task of riding
Hannibal much less daunting

Above: Gordo Bell's, who with his cousin Ricky was the star of the trapeze, in mid-flight

Augustin Bell's, Gordo and Mara's first cousin, also known as Tintin the clown. At six years old he was one of the circus's most popular attractions, billed as 'Tintin, the smallest clown in the world'

Tom in performance
as clown Fatty Fatty

Below: The Finale.
Front row, left to right:
Jorge Morales, Ricky
Bell's, Mundo as Mr
Bell's the clown, and
Gordo Bell's. Behind
them, just visible, are
Pamela and Karina

The *chamacos*, as the circus hands were known, putting up the Big Top in Toluca. The *chamacos* were at the bottom of the circus hierarchy and, apart from a few stalwarts, would often change at each new site we went to

Tintin's sister Lely, aged three, made up for the clown act, plays on the guy ropes before the start of the show. When we joined the circus she had just started her career and at this tender stage was still only an occasional performer

Mr Bell's (Mundo) in his caravan, helping his daughter Lely to dress. Mundo was the circus's 'artistic director' as well as one of its principal performers

Above: Olinda Bell's with her grandmother, Doña Elena, eating ice cream between performances. Behind them are Ramón and Brissel practising on her monocycle

Below: Backstage, waiting for the parade to begin. One of the circus trucks doubles up as a behind-stage area, from which the performers make their entrances into the ring. The elephants use another entrance, just to the right of the truck. *Left to right:* Mundo, Charlie, Mara and Omar

Above: Mundo, made up as Mr Bell's the clown, with Katie. The circus camp, arranged in a semi-circle around the back of the Big Top, is in the background

Below: Washing day. Every drop of water we used, whether for drinking, bathing or washing had to be brought into the camp by hand. Jovita *(far left, in curlers)* presides over an ancient washing machine, although most of the laundry was done by hand. Mara, with her back to us, is in the foreground, and our caravan, the Pop-up, is just visible to the right

Luis, the elephant-keeper, accompanies Hannibal, 'my' elephant, on one of the circus trucks on which the animals are transported between *terrenos*

Making up in Jovita's wardrobe. The wardrobe
consists of the front section of a converted bus.
Jovita, the wardrobe mistress, also lives in here
with her prize possessions, a black and white
television, and a framed picture of the Virgin
of Guadalupe

Karina, my first friend in the circus, with Gallo

Above: Luis the elephant-keeper with his wife María-Magdalena and their daughters Lupita and Jacaira. Along with Jovita, Luis is the circus's longest-serving non-family member. He always keeps a loaded gun in his caravan and is known respectfully as Don Luis

Below: Tom with his dancing girls, the *bastoneras* – known to us as the Kentuckys because of their fondness for eating Kentucky Fried Chicken. *Left to right:* Pamela and Olinda Bell's, Tom, Brissel and Karina Bell's

Little Olga and Ilish. Olga was one of the circus's many runaways. Ilish, her lover, had worked with circuses in Mexico since he was just seven. He was orphaned when his father and eight brothers were all killed in a car accident

Omar, Mara and Katie sitting on top of Mara's *caja*. Mara would fold herself inside this tiny box as one of her contortionist acts

'I should have been with him that day, the day they assassinated him. He drove into Parral in his car with some of the boys. The assassins were waiting for him there, in a house overlooking the street. They had been waiting for him a long time, more than a hundred days, they say, for him to pass by. When they saw him coming someone on the street, a peanut vendor, shouted 'Viva Villa!' And then they just gunned them down. Villa, the lot of them. I should have been there too. The only reason I didn't go was because it was my wedding day that day.'

'His wedding day! One of Villa's men, you see, right to the last.' Fernando repeated with pride. 'And tell them, tell them, Señor, what you had to do to become a *Dorado*. Just like you told me once, remember?'

'*Pah!*' The old man turned away again. His cheap cigarette crackled into the fetid air.

'You see, not just anyone could become a *Dorado*,' Fernando explained. 'You had to have done something special, something to prove that you were different from the rest.'

'What did you have to do, Señor?' I took up Fernando's cue. 'Señor Meléndez?'

The old man did not seem to have been listening to us, but after a while he said dreamily, 'After my brother died, I decided that I would kill all of them. All of them. Whether they gave themselves up or not.' He reached up and stubbed out his cigarette against the bed-head. Then, leaning back against his pillows, he added in a whisper to himself, 'Viboras! Vipers, vipers everywhere.'

José Meléndez, the last *Dorado*. Looking around that little room, with its hopeless stench of urine and old age, I found myself wondering what difference all those years of revolution and death had really made to his life. Apart from the creaking bed, the chipped bedside chest, the space around him was pitifully bare. On one wall was a small crucifix, on another a calendar with a picture of a clown. Over the bed he had hung a very small framed photograph of a woman in old-fashioned evening dress, one of his sisters he said, with her daughter, his only surviving relative. It was the only personal detail I saw in the entire house. Behind the bed was stacked a pile of ancient suitcases, and hanging from a nail on the wall behind it an old nylon shopping bag in which he kept his papers.

Did he choose to live like this, I wondered? Was it poverty and old age which forced it on him; or perhaps just simply familiarity? What had the Revolution really taught him? What had it changed? Once, like tens of thousands like him, he had fought for Pancho Villa. Perhaps that was enough. For even Villa himself, as his critics are quick to point out, was no idealist, no passionate reformer like that other great man of the people, Emiliano Zapata. A young boy like José Meléndez can have had very little clear idea of who or why he was really fighting. He was for Villa, because Villa, as John Reed once put it, 'had the knack of absolutely expressing the strong feelings of the great mass of the people'. Men fought for Villa because he focused their strongest and darkest impulses: he was their violence, their machismo, their revenge. He made an inarticulate people eloquent, with the only means that they knew. And yet when he was gone, I wondered, what was really left? Votive candles and a new, swashbuckling, secular saint.

Pancho Villa, watch over me.

In fits and starts our conversation proceeded. As the Lieutenant had suggested, we asked him about the battle of Zacatecas and the battle of Torreón, two of Villa's most famous victories over Huerta's federal army in which Meléndez, then aged just thirteen, had also fought. But his heart was never really in it.

'What do you want to know about that for?' he would ask sometimes. 'Son cosas muy viejas; esas cosas que pasaron, ya volaron. Those times are gone, they're flown.' And then he'd change the conversation to some domestic subject, to his chickens, or the merits of his new mattress.

'You must watch out,' he would often add in a dark undertone, 'there are vipers, vipers everywhere.'

Despite all our efforts, it was difficult to keep him on the subject of the Revolution for any length of time. At first I thought that his mind was simply wandering, but when we had been talking to him for longer, a different pattern began to emerge. We were talking about Pershing's punitive expedition to capture Villa, after the raid he and some of his men had carried out on the American town of Columbus, New Mexico.

'Villa fue siempre muy listo,' he began. 'Villa was always very clever, he knew all sorts of tricks. He would make us put the shoes of our horses on backwards, so that the *gringos* thought we were travelling in the opposite direction. Sometimes he even made us put the soles of our shoes on the wrong way round . . .' He stopped in mid-sentence, as if recollecting himself.

'I'm only telling them because they're foreigners,' he said to Fernando, 'and they will be taking all these things back to their own country. They won't be telling them here, not in Mexico.' He turned to us again. 'You must be very careful,' he said with great emphasis, 'I have known people like you be killed because you knew too much.'

For a while his remarks like this continued to puzzle me. His conversation was full of them: references to many dangers, both to himself and to us, and to the 'vipers' which were lying in wait for us everywhere. I realized then that for all his insistence that these were old subjects, things which had 'flown' as he put it, a part of him was still living the Revolution. For him there was no time gap, perhaps there never had been. When he talked about the Revolution it was not from the perspective of an old man, but from that of someone quite different, someone still living with the weight of those days.

Fear of betrayal had been one of Villa's obsessions. José Meléndez, his last *Dorado*, had learnt his lesson well. Trust no one. Speak to no one. Not to your woman, nor your neighbour, nor even your closest friend. The room in which he lay dying, with only his cockerels for company, stank of his fear of betrayal. It rose from the stale yellow urine under the bed, seeped from the lonely, peeling walls, from the unkempt little yard with its crowing birds. Long after we had left the old man it clung to us too, to our skin and hair and breath, and it was many days before we could wash it away.

NINE

Mexico is a state of mind.
GRAHAM GREENE, *The Lawless Roads*

The time which it took to move between *terrenos* was known in the circus as *días perdidos*, 'lost days'. The ancient, tatterdemalion procession of the circus on the move, and the taking down and putting up of the Big Top, could sometimes take two or even three days, depending on how far we had to travel. Unlike the 'lost days' in the Maya calendar, which were considered unlucky times, the circus's 'lost days' were often the only times of liberty from the long evening round of wardrobe, make-up and performance.

No one was sad at the prospect of leaving Lomas Verdes. Mexico City, perhaps the most polluted and overpopulated city in the world, is not a healthy place at the best of times, but living on the edge of a rubbish dump, among the debris and effluence of the Skate Mall car park, was a positive health hazard. Oly and Belén both had such bad coughs that Vicky had confined them to their caravan for several days. Nearly everyone else had some kind of ailment, usually respiratory in origin: a sore throat or a cold or a wheezing chest. Even the tiniest cuts, I noticed, took a long time to heal, and unusual care was required to make sure they did not turn septic. Karina, who even in the healthiest places enjoyed all manner of ills, both real and imaginary, was in and out of our caravan four times a day, for elastoplast, throat pastilles and quantities of aspirin which she usually, exasperatingly, sicked up again almost immediately.

Because we were so high (Mexico City is nearly eight thousand feet), at night, as Mara had so cheerfully predicted, it was often bitterly cold. Since we had bought it in Texas, our caravan was equipped with the very latest air-conditioning system, but the only heating we had was in the form of the two small gas rings on which we did our cooking and heated our water. To keep warm Tom and I were often forced to sleep in two layers of clothes. On several occasions we woke up in the middle of the night to find the canvas roof over our bed frozen solid on the inside.

We had been in Lomas Verdes nearly a month and everyone was ready for a change, although as usual no one, not even the brothers, seemed to know where the next *terreno* would be. As a result the days before a move were always electric, the camp humming like a medieval court with rumour and counter-rumour, whispers and surmise. Even though in theory he was the one who was responsible for the decision to move, Rolando, as richly perfumed and paunched as any Medici Prince, seemed to have no more idea than anyone else where the circus was heading, largely, I suspected, because he enjoyed the plotting and counter-plotting more than anyone. Rolando was positively Machiavellian in his wheeler-dealing over new *terrenos*. Even though I knew he abominated PRI, in Lomas Verdes he had managed to come to some mysterious but mutually beneficial arrangement with the local party headquarters whereby, in return for letting the circus off its taxes, PRI were allowed to give out large quantities of complimentary tickets – with the result that in Lomas Verdes we had been playing to the largest audiences the circus had seen for many months. His next target, he told us, came from an even more unexpected quarter, the Red Cross.

The Red Cross branch in question was based in Guadalajara. For a few heady days Rolando allowed a shining vision of this city to appear, fresh and green as an oasis mirage before our parched eyes. Tom and I were ecstatic; Mara knew better.

'Don't believe a word of it,' she said, putting her arm around her father's neck. 'He always changes his mind, don't you, Papá?'

Brissel, practising her new monocycle act, came speeding jerkily around the corner. She jockeyed unsteadily on the spot, holding her arms out to her sides to balance herself.

'Where are we going, Uncle?' she asked him hopefully. 'Oly said it might be down south, to the Yucatán?'

'The Yucatán, eh?' The whites of Rolando's eyes glittered. 'Fancy the beach, you three?'

'I thought you said we were going to Guadalajara,' I reminded him. I have never known anyone so brilliantly adept at evading a question.

'Uncle, Uncle!' Pamela spotted her uncle from the door of her caravan. Although she was half-way through making-up – one eyelid blue, the other still white with powder – she ran lightly over in her *bata* and clogs and tucked her arm into his. 'You said you'd have us in Acapulco by my birthday, remember, Uncle? You promised!'

'Did I indeed?' Rolando twinkled at her. 'Well, that settles it then, doesn't it? Acapulco it is, *mi princesa*.'

'So we're not going to Toluca, then?' Mara said slyly, her arm through Rolando's other arm. 'Papá! Yesterday you told us Toluca!'

Mara stamped her foot, but I could see that she was laughing. The charade – for such it was – was clearly following an old and familiar pattern. 'Papá, you know how much Omar was looking forward to it.'

Omar's family lived in Toluca.

'You think I wasn't looking forward to it as well, *mi hija*?' Rolando tried, and failed, to look repentant. Instead, all he managed was his usual sleepy, sexy smile. Omar's mother, I remembered, was an old girlfriend of Rolando's and one of her elder daughters, Alma, Omar's half-sister, was rumoured to be one of his many natural children.

In the end of course, in spite of all the speculation, we did not go to Guadalajara at all, or Toluca, or Acapulco. Instead, Rolando had found another location still further north-west into the outermost suburbs of Mexico City. I thought of all the energy I had expended in the past trying to discover, with any degree of accuracy, where the circus was headed. I knew better now. The whole process was like a game: now that I knew the rules, I knew better than to expect any definite answer. One night after the last performance (sometimes even during it, if the audience was small), without any real warning at all, the *chamacos* would begin to pull down the Big Top; the location of the new *terreno*, by some mysterious process of osmosis between the caravans, would suddenly be on everyone's lips; and by the next morning we would be gone.

I stopped worrying whether we would be in Acapulco by Christmas, by Pamela's birthday, or whether we would even get to Acapulco at all. The circus would be the same wherever we were. The circus was its own world, sufficient unto itself. I remembered Jorge, the third brother's story of his grandfather, Refugio Encarnación, who gave up everything for love and to follow his destiny. 'If you really want to join the circus,' Jorge had told me that day, 'the whys and the wherefores are not important. It is what is in your heart that will decide it.'

And it was true. Besides, this way of life suited me. In the circus you lived for today: tomorrow, if it came, would look after itself. Despite the taboos and restrictions of being a woman, there was a sense of liberty, of sheer physical freedom here, the like of which I have rarely experienced, either before or since.

It turned out that there were to be two whole 'lost days' between Lomas Verdes and the new *terreno*. Rolando suggested to Mara that we should make a trip to Toluca after all, which was not far from Mexico City, so that Omar could see his family and so that Tom and I could visit the Nevado de Toluca, a snow-capped mountain and local beauty spot on the outskirts of the town.

There were seven of us in the expedition in all: Tom and myself, Mara and Omar, Gallo (without Karina, who had been gated by her sister that day), Antonino and Ramón. Even though we were late setting off, at Mara's insistence we stopped to eat at a place called La Marquesa just outside Toluca, a series of unprepossessing huts by the roadside which were nonetheless renowned for their quesadillas – a kind of deep-fried tortilla filled with melted cheese – and mushroom soup.

'My father drives all the way out here sometimes just for lunch,' she told us. 'And then all the way back again. He thinks nothing of the distance.'

In Mara's eyes, whatever Rolando did was perfect. There was an intensely practical streak in Mara. Whatever we needed – a new pair of shoes, a certain shade of lipstick, sequins for a new costume, even a spare part for the car – Mara always knew exactly the best (which often meant the cheapest) place in the whole of Mexico where these things could be acquired. At La Marquesa, it was quesadillas and mushroom soup.

We chose one of the roadside huts where a couple of plump Indian women in check pinnies presided over two steaming vats, one of fragrant broth, the other of boiling oil.

'Just look at those!' As we went in Tom pointed over the women's heads where great strings of sausages were draped decoratively like carnival streamers.

'No-o, Tom,' Mara was insistent. 'We didn't come here to eat *sausages*. You must try the soup.'

'But look, they've got green ones. Green sausages!' Tom, who adores sausages, was fascinated. 'You must let me try one of those.' Suspended in one corner, the sausages hung like bunches of swollen fluorescent fingers from the darkened space between the rafters.

'Oh, *those* sausages.' Mara saw where he was pointing. 'Of course you must try *those*. Those are specialities of Toluca.' She looked pleased. 'They flavour them with special herbs, that's why they're green. But should he eat them here?' She turned anxiously to Omar. 'There's that place in the *portales*, in the main square in Toluca, remember? Wouldn't it be better if we waited to buy some when we get there? I will take you to the *portales* later, Katty.' She tucked her arm through mine. 'There's a shop I know there which, I promise you, does the best cakes in the whole of Toluca!'

Wrapped up in her mother's old camel-hair coat, which was several sizes too big for her, its old-fashioned peaked collar framing her face, and with her eyes kohled into two sweeping Egyptian points – what she called her 'street' make-up – Mara looked like a tiny but exquisite fairy who had somehow made her way into the overworld where she was now assuming a not very convincing disguise.

Hanging out with our circus friends outside the circus environment often took on this slightly surreal quality. When we had first arrived at La Villa I remember being disappointed by how ordinary the circus people looked out of their make-up and costumes. Whatever I had been expecting – a cast of fairground freaks, abnormally muscled, shrunken or hirsute (the strongmen, dwarves and bearded ladies of my imagination) – it was certainly not this flock of charming teenagers. It was only with time, when I got to know them better, that I came to realize just how extraordinary each of them really was.

Antonino came from a family of peasants and mystics whose village, what he could remember of it, lay in retreat from the world, high up in the mountains of the rural province of Galicia in Spain. From our first weeks with the circus I had always felt an affinity with Antonino. Like so many who had chosen the circus life, Antonino was one of life's true wanderers. He had learnt his trade of *equilibrista* as a boy from the maverick Spanish priest, Jesús Cesar, in whose travelling troupe, the Revolution Circus, he had first come to Latin America, spreading the priest's message of love and peace amongst men.

Antonino had spent two years travelling with *los muchachos*, as the priest's troupe were known, but eventually decided that it was time to see what else was going on in the world. With only twenty-four dollars in his pocket he had made his way to the Dominican Republic, working in a biscuit factory, a bakery, for the electricity board, as a mime artist, a painter, any odd job which came his way, and at the same time drifting slowly southwards towards Mexico. Although he was able to turn his hand to most things, Antonino had always missed the life with *los muchachos*, and so when one day, in the Yucatán, he saw that a circus had come to town he immediately bought a ticket for the performance. In the parade that night who should he recognize but one of his old friends from the Revolution Circus. The friend had a word with the management and the next day Antonino began his second circus career. Circo Atayde, Circo Vasquez, Circo Magico Frances, Circo Modelo: without papers, visas, or even a passport (stolen by a colleague from the electricity board), Antonino slipped into that twilight world again, wandering the length and breadth of the Mexican circus world, before finally ending up with Circo Bell's.

Antonino, pale-skinned, slender and slight of build, had the singular aura of a man who has seen God. There was nothing immediately distinguishing about him – his face was long and thin, his teeth crooked, his eyes, despite their extraordinary brilliance, were no more than an everyday hazel – but there was an air of tranquillity about him, the feeling of a still centre, which drew everyone to him.

Antonino had many friends in the circus since, like us, he was of an age which bridged the gap between the two generations of the Bell's family, but it was principally those who had ended up at Circo Bell's without a family of their own – Ramón, Gallo, little Olga, all the runaways and waifs – who seemed particularly to gravitate towards him.

Antonino shared a caravan with Ramón, a tiny van decorated with peeling clowns' faces which was always known as La Chuchina. Inside was a bed, just big enough for the two of them to share: the whole of the rest of their tiny space was packed, in much the same way as the wardrobe, with spangled costumes and stage props: monocycles and juggling balls and clown paraphernalia for Ramón, an elaborate collection of ladders, candelabra, swords and bowler hats for Antonino. Despite the almost intolerable proximity this threw them into, the two were inseparable, 'like brothers' Ramón told me.

In Toluca the *portales* which Mara had talked about, the colonnades which run round the main plaza in the centre of the town, were full of stalls selling Day of the Dead[1] mementos, sugar skulls, toy skeletons and tiny chocolate coffins piped with coloured icing, but we did not have time to stop there for long. As we stopped at a traffic lights on the outskirts of the town three small boys, street urchins no more than six or seven years old with ragged clothes and grimy skin, appeared from the undergrowth and started to juggle with a collection of broken tennis balls. Beneath the dirt their faces were smeared, in a parody of clown's make-up, with red and yellow chalks. They did not juggle very well. Their skinny little arms, protruding sharp as needles from their tattered T-shirts, were hopelessly uncoordinated and it was as much as they could do to keep two balls in the air at once. Even so, we cheered and applauded them. As soon as the lights changed Ramón

[1] The Mexican Day of the Dead coincides with our Hallowe'en, but is a predominantly Indian celebration in which the souls of the dead are believed to return to visit their loved ones on earth.

leaned out of the window and gave them a big handful of coins. Nothing delighted the people from Circo Bell's more than other circus acts, however *ad hoc*, and the front row of the stalls was often filled with whole troupes of little beggar boys such as these, their faces still traced with paint from their stint working the traffic lights. It did not matter how badly the circus was doing, Jorge and Rolando, those big-hearted mavericks, always let them in for free.

'That's what you looked like, Ramón, when you first came to the circus,' Mara said as we drove off. 'Te acuerdas, Antonino? Do you remember? Tan sucio! So dirty! Covered in grime from head to foot he was.'

Baby-faced Ramón sat in the back of the truck, his arms clasped around his long legs.

'I remember very well.' He turned to her. 'I was in love with Vanessa and you used to taunt her and say, How can you go with that *squinkle*, with that ugly little *chamaco* who's so dirty all the time. How could I forget it?' he mocked her.

'Ramón, would I have said that!' Mara opened her Egyptian eyes wide.

'Oh yes, you would. You know you would. Besides Vanessa told me.'

'You were so little then, nothing but skin and bone,' Antonino said in his soft voice. '*Bien* "baby", isn't that right, Mara?'

'That's right. We all remember. Tell Katty and Tom how it was, Ramón, when you joined us.'

'I was working on the games then, at a fairground,' Ramón said. 'Circo Bell's was tented next door, that's how I met them. I was only thirteen then, but I had already been on my own a long time.'

'Ran away from home,' Antonino added, 'just like Olga did; and Ilish, too.'

Ramón looked back towards the little urchins.

'It's true though, that's just what I was like at that age. There was nothing for me at home, not even enough to eat after my father left. I did everything, all that kind of stuff' – he pointed towards the juggling boys – 'washed cars, shone shoes, worked in a *churro* bakery. I even worked the buses with one of my brothers.

We would get on to a bus together and one of us would sing a song while the other collected money in a hat. Until I ended up at the fairground, that is. That's when I really ran away. Until then I always used to go home to my mother every few days or so, to take her some of the money I had earned. But I was earning good money at the fairground – six hundred pesos a day – so when they moved on, I decided to go with them. I told no one, just hid in the back of one of the trucks.

'We went to Zacatecas. It was so cold down there, not like in Monterrey where it was still summer. I had taken nothing with me; I had nothing to take. At night I used to sleep under the machines, without even a blanket to cover me. It was a dirty job too, working the machines. Isn't that right, Gallo?'

Gallo nodded. Like the street urchin Ramón, he too had come to the circus from a fairground.

'I started off each day clean, but by the end of the day . . .' he shrugged, '*híjole*, with all the grease from those machines, it was just impossible. After a few weeks of that kind of work you get dirt beneath your nails, dirt ingrained so deep that it's almost impossible to get out. Worse than living on the streets.' He held out his hands, which were pale-skinned and delicate, studying them minutely as if to reassure himself, a practised, fastidious gesture. 'Not like with the circus. Clowning is clean work. That's why, when I met Gallo, I told him that he should come away with us, join the circus like I had. I'll never forget what it was like working those machines: *bien feo* . . . ugly work. I said, *vente para aca*, Gallo, come with us, come with us. Until finally he came.'

We started to drive up towards the *nevado*, up through forests of dark green pine. After Mexico City the air was as clean and cool as snow. We drove on and on, up past the tree line, until the whole valley of Toluca lay stretched out beneath us, desiccated and brown, like a vast map made out of old parchment. The huge distance made us contemplative, and little by little, as we watched the valley unfolding beneath us, we fell silent.

Tom drove the truck along a rough track which led nearly all the way to the summit of the mountain. There, two crater lakes lay, as cold and still as mirrors. Their waters – unruffled, pale and mineral greens – flared briefly in the sun, but towards the middle of the afternoon, when the sun dropped, their surfaces dulled to a fathomless matt.

'Do you think anyone can tell how deep the lakes are?' Mara asked.

'Who knows?' I shook my head and shivered. 'We must be very high up here; fourteen or fifteen thousand feet at least.' Out of the truck the air was cold and thin. 'Can you feel what an effort it is to walk uphill?'

Our little group dispersed, walking in ones and twos around the shores of the lake. We were together, and yet apart. There was no need to talk. After the sluggish city, the pure air, the silence, the space, were intoxicating. The walls of the crater valley were full of the cold, stone colours of very high, desert places. We started to climb up to a ridge, speckled with a thin powdering of snow, which overlooked the lake, but by now we were so high that in the end only Ramón and Antonino made it to the top. We watched them, waving and calling to us, their two tiny silhouettes illuminated, as if with manuscript gold, in the setting sun.

'Mexico is at once a world of mystery and clarity,' the Mexican essayist Alfonso Reyes once wrote, 'clarity in her landscape, mystery in the souls of her people.' What he fails to point out, of course, is that the two have always been connected.

The landscape, the desert traversed by the circus mules, may be clear – but what of its *effects*? Ancient gods trod these mountains. Their names might be forgotten, but their echoes – the spirits and demons which they left behind them – still inhabit some vital space. In Mexico, rock and river are still imbued with them. However urbanized many Mexicans have now become, the shadow of this landscape is never far away. Their history and their myths, their poetry and song: all are the fruits of its beauty and its terror.

In Mexico there are times when the natural world takes on the flavour of hallucination.

In a small wood in the state of Michoacan, for a few months each year, thirty-five million Monarch butterflies come to rest. I went there with Tom, very early in the morning. At first the wood was just like any other wood. There were many butterflies around, it was true – all Monarchs, with their distinctive bright orange wings – but in nothing like the numbers we had been led to expect.

We had been walking up through the wood for some time when we came to a grove of about twenty pine trees on the hillside. Unlike the clean, spare branches and trunks of the other trees in the wood, these trees were suffering from some kind of fungal growth. A strange brown cobwebby substance hung from their branches and stuck to the sides of their trunks. In places the growth was so thick that the branches, even the thickest, strongest ones, sagged beneath their weight. Apart from a few orange butterflies languidly flitting in the watery morning light, the wood was utterly silent and still.

We sat down to rest on the stump of an old tree trunk. It had been quite cold that morning but now the sun was rising steadily, piercing through the thick cover of the trees. I began to take off my jacket and as I looked up I noticed something stirring in the trees above me. As the sunlight warmed the branches of the trees, the lichen, or whatever it was, had started to move.

At first this was no more than the faintest pulse, but as the sun increased in strength it became a quiver, a trembling, and finally an extraordinary, fully fledged flapping. The growth was not leaves, or lichen, or Old Man's Beard after all, but millions upon millions upon millions of sleeping butterflies. Awakened by the light, the butterflies gradually disengaged themselves from the branches, where they had massed together a foot or more deep, until the whole wood was full of them. There were so many that the air crackled with the sound, like distant electricity. Occasionally as we watched, with a faint *plop* a pair of butterflies, locked in lovers' combat, would drop on to the ground beside us, writhing together in the soft dust.

But this was only the beginning. We had been standing for several minutes like this when the real miracle happened. Above us there was a sudden rushing noise like wind through the trees. When we looked up we saw that all at once, in one spectacular golden shoal, one of the trees was releasing its burden of butterflies towards us. From a single point on one of the branches, at first a river, then a torrent, then a very waterfall of butterflies was tumbling towards us. In a shimmering, tinkling, king's ransom of shining copper they poured down the gully, until there were so many it became impossible for the eye to focus. The air around them dissolved, as it does when heat rises, until there were so many creatures on the wing that the sky became black with them.

And then they were upon us. Closing my eyes at the centre of the maelstrom I felt the wind of a hundred thousand wings brush my cheeks; felt them touch my cheeks, eyelids, lips, hair. I was blinded, deafened, struck dumb by butterflies. For a few moments the entire physical world was blotted out. I could not move, could not think. I was entirely made of butterflies, for they were all that existed; a soft, golden galaxy of spinning proboscis, antennae and fronds of copper silk.

For a long while I stood with my eyes shut, arms outstretched, laughing and laughing and crying out in ecstasy.

What feats of the imagination could possibly be proscribed to the guardians of this enchanted wood? When André Breton first came to Mexico he said that there was no need for a surrealist movement here: Mexico was quite surreal enough already. To use Carpentier's phrase again, you do not need to go far in Mexico to find the marvellous: the smallness and brilliance of humming birds, the profligacy of butterflies, the light on mountains, the vegetable whimsies of jungle and desert.

The extravagances of nature are the most visible of all Mexico's magical properties. Nutured by them, the landscape of the Mexican mind has become perfectly adapted to the contemplation of the natural world around it. The visionary architecture in the forests of the Yucatán, the daydreams of the Lacandón, the deranged wall paintings of Actopán (an interesting example of a mind as yet imperfectly prepared for Mexico's full impact), even the myth of Pancho Villa, all have in some way been coloured and inspired by it. As I have said, in a country in which even nature so overreaches herself, a new language altogether is required to describe it.

The language of violence and the language of love: in the circus, as everywhere in Mexico, both became clues to the Mexican psyche, as indelibly linked as Reyes's equation of clarity and mystery.

The day after we came back from the Nevado de Toluca was the day I learnt about the rape. It was another 'lost day', one of those strange, dreamy times in between new *terrenos* whose quality, like a Sunday or a birthday or Christmas, was always so utterly different from all other days. The new site turned out to be another car park, mercifully cleaner than the last, just outside a *centro commercial* in the suburb of Atizapán de Zaragoza.

I woke to the sound of hammers in the Big Top. As usual on these days, it was here where all the circus activity was concentrated. I looked in on my way to fetch our water for the day. The *chamacos* (many of them new faces) were putting in the last of the tent pegs; Ricky, Gordo and Jorge Morales were putting up their trapezes and fixing the nets; Gerrardo the welder and Viejito the old handyman were repairing and cleaning some of the canvas that had been ripped in the move.

The same activity was not evident from the caravans. Except for Jovita padding around in her curlers, a somnolent silence enveloped most of the other trailers. I was about to move on with my buckets when I saw Ricky come running out of the Big Top towards Charlie's caravan.

'Oye, flojo.' He kicked open the door with his foot. 'Hey, you lazy bastard, Gordo and me are on our own out here,' he shouted inside. 'Get up and come and give us a hand, will you?'

A sleepy-faced boy came to the door, yawning and rubbing his eyes.

'What's going on? What time is it?'

'Time you got off your arse, *hombre*.' Ricky's mouth turned down dangerously at the corners. He was in an ugly mood.

'OK, OK.' None too pleased, Charlie shambled back into his van. 'I'll just have my wash and something to eat, and I'll be right with you.'

'Didn't you hear me? I said *now*, you lazy bastard!'

Ricky kicked the door, harder this time. His eyes burnt with cold light, only there was no ameliorating euphoria now as there had been on the night of the taco shop fight.

'Where are the others?' he snapped. 'Omar and Ramón?'

His eyes were bruised with dark shadows, his skin unusually

pale and unhealthy-looking. These days he and Gordo went off nearly every night, 'as *vagos*' as Mara would put it, until the early hours of the morning.

Charlie shrugged, scratching his upper arms sulkily. 'Ramón said they were going to camp out for the night on the Nevado de Toluca,' he yawned. 'I guess they're not back yet.'

We had left the boys, except for Tom and Gallo, with some tents and sleeping bags borrowed from Omar's mother, to make their own way back.

'*Chinga!*' Ricky slammed his hand against the side of the caravan so that the television aerial, the rusting bicycles and various pieces of junk strapped to the back with string, rattled violently. He caught sight of Brissel and Olga, who had been watching this exchange, and pointed his finger at them menacingly.

'No one's to talk to them, you hear me? No one's to talk to them when they get back. I'll soon sort them out.' Yelling at Charlie to get a move on, he strode off back into the Big Top.

Still holding my water buckets, I stared after him. Brissel and Olga, sitting on the steps of Brissel's caravan, stared after him too. They leant their heads together, whispering in low voices.

'*Sangrón!* He's got no right to order the others around like that.' Brissel's usually plump and smiling face puckered. 'They're *artistas*, not *chamacos*. It's not their job. Besides, after . . . *you* know . . .' She glanced at Olga with some secret meaning. 'After *that* . . . I'm surprised he has the nerve to show his face at all, let alone go around bossing everyone else around.'

Brissel, always the most petite and feminine of the Bell's cousins, sucked in her pretty cheeks. Although they would never have dared say so to his face, many of the younger circus people, the girls in particular, resented Ricky's high-handed treatment.

'Here, Katty, come and sit with us.'

Olga and Brissel squeezed up on the caravan step to make room for me.

'Qué pasó?' Sensing some fresh circus gossip I sat down with them. 'What's up?'

Brissel and Olga looked at each other.

'Don't you remember about Anna?'

I shook my head. Who was Anna?

'You know Anna.' Brissel seemed sure I must have known her. 'Teresa's sister. The girl who was raped.'

'Raped?' I stared at them. 'Who by?'

Brissel and Olga looked at each other again, more seriously this time.

'By the *chamacos*,' one of them said.

'But they say it was *he*' – the other nodded towards the Big Top – 'who made them do it.'

'*Ricky*?' I could not believe what I was hearing. Ricky had a vile temper sometimes, and he loved to fight, I knew. But rape? Surely not.

'Anna was the sister of Teresa. You know, Martinelli's *novia*.'

'Yes, I know her, of course.'

Every evening Teresa and her friend Veronica helped Brissel's mother, Rosalinda, the telepathic Professora, to sell her toffee apples at the Big Top entrance. Along with Olga and Ilish, they too had made their home among the rotting detritus of the Skate Mall rubbish dump. Despite Martinelli's status as an *artista*, the two girls were among the poorest and the least regarded in the complicated circus hierarchy.

'Anna was from a very deprived family. Her father used to beat her up and I don't know what else.' Olga spoke softly, remembering, perhaps, the vagaries of her own confused childhood. 'When she decided to leave home, she had nowhere else to go. So she came here, to the circus, to live with her sister.'

'After she got here Anna started to go out with Chino – you know, Veronica's brother, the *chamaco* with the curly hair – but they were always having rows. That's when Ricky got involved. He said she was a troublemaker and he wanted her out of the circus. That's when they . . . that's when it happened. He wanted her chased off.'

'And you really believe this?'

'Some say he paid the *chamacos* to do it.'

'But others say he was there too. That he was the first. They covered her eyes, so that he couldn't be recognized, but Anna knew. She knew it was him by his voice.'

'I can't believe it.' I felt sick.

'Of course his plan backfired.' Brissel was almost whispering, her voice hoarse with indignation. 'When they raped her they broke her arm, too. After that she couldn't work and so she couldn't leave the circus either. Martinelli used to give her some food to eat, so she knew that by staying with him and Theresa at least she wouldn't starve.'

Now I remembered that I had seen Anna before, although I had never spoken to her: a skinny, feral-looking girl with sly, dark eyes. I remembered because she had always worn her arm in a sling.

'Is she still here?'

Brissel shook her head.

'I think she stayed behind when we left Lomas Verdes. Pity,' she shrugged. 'My mother was fond of her. From time to time we used to give her food to eat too, you know. Now we'll never know what happened to her.' For a moment Brissel looked sad. Then her eyes lit up. 'Look, there's Pamela and Oly. My Tía Carmen has promised to take us to the Kentucky Chicken place for lunch.' She pronounced it *Ken-Tooky*. 'Vienes, Katty?'

Kentucky Fried Chicken was Brissel's idea of culinary nirvana. She sprang up, Anna and her troubles forgotten, and ran off, her russet curls bouncing. Olga, more measured in her demeanour, rose daintily to her feet. She looked at me with mournful eyes.

'It's true, you know. One of the *chamacos* who did it told me all about it. He said he felt very bad afterwards. What had she ever done to them?' Softly Olga smoothed her white skirts. 'Poor Anna. I bear her no ill will. They were jealous of me, you know: Teresa, Veronica, Anna. They had been with the circus much longer than I had, but no one ever asked them to take part in the parade. It was not my fault, although sometimes they did make me feel that way. It was the way they looked,' she explained. (Olga was not necessarily better looking than the other girls, but she was distinctly whiter). 'If Anna had been prettier, Ricky would never have tried to chase her off like that. Either that, or if she had had a man to protect her. Teresa has Martinelli; Veronica has José Jaime; I have Ilish. Poor Anna had no one,' she said sorrowfully. 'It's like that, you see. In the circus.'

For weeks the story of the rape obsessed me. Discreetly – as far as anything could be discreet in the circus – I asked around. I asked everyone: Mara, Teresa, Martinelli, even Chino, Anna's ex-*novio*.

Everyone, that is, except the two people I most needed to ask: Anna and Ricky. I could not ask Anna because she was no longer with the circus. But I could not ask Ricky either. Several times I screwed up my courage. Each time I remembered the cold, dark blanks of those eyes, the pearl beading of sweat along the adolescent lip – and the question withered on my tongue.

I reminded myself that one of my own conditions for living with the circus was a strict policy of non-interference. I must be strictly neutral at all times. I must not allow my English, liberal sensibilities to cloud my judgment, or use it unduly to try to influence theirs. If I was going to live like one of them, I reasoned, if they were to be a true focus through which to see Mexico, then I had to learn to think like one of them too.

The lessons of the circus are hard. My arguments were not enough. I could not get the thought of that tortured girl out of my mind, could not suppress my horror and revulsion. But still I could not find it in me to ask Ricky. The truth was, I was afraid.

Mara was philosophical. 'It happened at San Juan de Aragón, just after you arrived.' She shook her head. 'Poor Anna. The trouble was, she was *muy grosera*. You know, she used bad language, swore a lot. *Y se metió con los chamacos*, she tried to be one of the boys.' This, I knew, was considered the ultimate sign of waywardness in a woman. 'She was always with them, at all hours of the day. If they told a crude joke, she laughed as loudly as they did. Can you imagine?' Mara dropped her voice. 'She even used to *drink* with them sometimes.'[1]

Mara's attitude was typical of the circus. They were shocked and felt sorry for the girl, but they were not unduly scandalised. The idea of reporting it to the police would not have occurred to anyone. I thought of Yvonne and her tales of the difficulties of being a woman on her own in the circus. Her response had been to become hermetic. She had sealed herself off from the rest of the world, proudly preferring to suffer on her own than to seek

---

[1] There was no concept of social drinking in the circus. Those who drank were considered drunkards, and that was that.

help from any man. Anna had chosen the opposite course altogether in her fight for survival. She 'went in' with the *chamacos*, as Mara put it, and had paid grievously for her mistake. By opening herself up to the dangerous charge of being a *grosera*, a vulgar person, she lost her right to any respect she might have had as a woman. She became nothing more than scum, fit only to be abused, and then chased from the circus like one of Luis's curs. With Chino she had had some degree of immunity from the whims of the others. Without him her tenuous connection with Martinelli had not been enough to protect her. Without a man, she was, literally, nothing.

What was the truth about the rape? The answer is: I don't know. I heard many versions, all of them different. That Ricky incited it. That he was there all the time. That he wasn't there at all. That they all raped her; that Ricky raped her; that only Chino raped her (this from Chino himself). Even, inevitably, that it was all a figment of Anna's sad and persecuted imagination.

Afterwards, I could only conclude that no one really knew what had happened. Despite myself I thought of it often. The sound of voices at the door – those hating faces, familiar and masked; rushing floorboards; hands holding, wrenching, crushing; the smell of the hunt on stale, excited breath; ripping clothes; ripping flesh. The exact act, perhaps even for Anna, is lost now, obscured by her pain and her fear. Like so much about the circus, about Mexico, it remains an ultimately ambiguous act. An act from the dark side and a glimpse of the underbelly.

TEN

It is a proposition of Mexican geographical logic
that the nearest way between two points is by a
distant third. The only way, in fact. If one wishes
to get from one place to another, one must first
go somewhere else . . .

SYBILLE BEDFORD, *A Visit to Don Otavio*

The language of violence and the language of love. In the butterfly
wood it had been hard to tell the difference. Occasionally as we
watched, a pair of butterflies, locked in lovers' combat, would
drop on to the ground beside us, writhing together in the soft
dust. Butterfly rape? Or butterfly ecstasy?

In the circus, too, there were times when it was difficult to tell.
Often aggressive, occasionally violent, Circo Bell's was charged
with strange, erotic currents. People came to the circus for many
reasons, but almost always for love: Olga's love for her Ilish; Gallo
for his Karina; Ramón for Vanessa. Love could be many things –
capricious, vengeful, erotically possessed – but it was never half-
hearted. In the circus love struck with all the violence and drama
of Greek tragedy. I thought of Karina and Gallo, tossing tempestu-
ously between fights and passionate reconciliation. I thought of
Mara and Omar: she, a diminutive silver fairy spinning wildly on
the end of her rope; he, in the front row of the stalls, gazing up
at her with his soft brown eyes, both struck dumb with love in
the same, single instant.

The zeal with which the girls were guarded by their brothers,
fathers and cousins, was largely aimed at the world beyond our
camp. Inside the circus itself, love, young and yearning, was on
everyone's lips. The lack of privacy, even between husbands and
wives, was no impediment, but rather added spice, taxing lovers'
ingenuity and fanning their ardour to fever pitch. During the day,
when vigilant mothers, fathers, aunts and uncles were at large, the

younger lovers were as chaste as children. Their languid kisses, cool and white as milk, dropped casually on to un-erogenous cheeks and foreheads; arms and hands, with calm and unrequiting fingers, came together as innocently as kindergarten partners. It was only at night, beneath the cover of darkness, that childish innocence gave way to something more red-blooded. At night, I came to understand, the sighs from the Big Top were not merely the phantom creakings of the trapeze or the pull of the guy ropes. At night the circus pulsed with secret rendezvous: the darkened corridors between the rows of sleeping caravans, the silent silhouette of the deserted box-office, a bush, a tree, a hidden flap of canvas.

Everyone had their lover or their *novio*, if not in the circus then in another of Mexico's many circuses, a great number of which were intimately known to Circo Bell's through the elaborate circus network of family ties or old friendships. While we were still in Mexico City, Oly, Mara's younger sister, was often visited by the tightrope walker, Bruno Vasquez.

Tom and I had met Bruno on our first night at Circo Bell's, the night Gordo and Jorge Morales had taken us to visit Bruno's family circus, the Circo Hermanos Vasquez. Bruno was a pale, good-mannered young man, a *güero* with a thin face and light-brown hair cut short at the sides and left to grow long and wispy at the back in the latest American fashion. Like his sophisticated cousins, Bruno dressed in expensive leathers and jangling biker's boots, spoke English with an American accent, had, in fact, all the trappings a Mexican girl could possibly wish for. And yet somehow, despite all this, Bruno never quite managed to be cool. He was, for a start, far too nice.

I was sitting in Vicky's kitchen camper one day eating lunch when I spotted Bruno out of the window.

'Oye, Oly.' I nodded in Bruno's direction. 'You've got a visitor.'

'Quién?'

'Bruno, of course, who do you think?'

'Oh.' Oly went on eating her lunch unenthusiastically. 'Bruno.'

'What's wrong? Have you fallen out with him?'

'No.'

'What then?'

'Oh, I don't know.' Oly rolled her eyes, glancing out of the window with a bored expression. 'Just . . . Bruno.'

Rolando looked up from his newspaper. 'Bo-ring Bruno, that's what.' He winked slyly in my direction.

'Ay, Papá, how can you say that!' Oly tossed her head impatiently, but I saw her peer out of the window again, a little more anxiously this time, to where Bruno had stopped to talk to Ramón and Gallo. Satisfied that she still had a few more minutes, she helped herself to more of Vicky's frijoles.

'Bruno's too nice to you, that's what,' Rolando went on brutally.

'Rolando, how can someone be *too* nice?' I tried to defend Bruno, whom I had always liked.

Rolando shrugged. 'Not for a little English girl, maybe.' He pointed at Oly with his fork. 'But for a little Mexican girl . . . well!' He shook his head and laughed. 'Olinda has always been the rebellious type. She needs someone who will stand up to her, hit her around a bit.' He made an eloquent slicing gesture through the air. 'Like her father and her brother.'

He was quite unembarrassed by this confession; if anything rather the reverse, I thought. While Oly was really too old now to be thrashed by her father, unless she had committed some really heinous crime, her fights with Gordo were frequent, noisy and as much a part of their mutual domestic life as eating or sleeping.

'Isn't that right, *mi hija*?' Rolando shouted after his daughter as she disappeared out of the door. 'Isn't that right, *mi amor*?' he appealed to his wife. Vicky, who had her back to Rolando and was heating up some fresh tortillas on the griddle, appeared not to have heard him. She said nothing and Rolando went on eating calmly.

'That Vasquez boy won't last another week, you mark my words.'

He picked up his paper and started to read the bullfight reports.

It was Sunday, Doña Elena's day for visiting. I always looked forward to Doña Elena, although I suspect that I was one of the few to harbour such uncomplicated feelings towards her. She would sit in Karina's caravan or Vicky's kitchen like an ageing Arab Scheherazade, a little stout now, rolling her enormous kholblackened eyes and weaving a fantastical monologue of gossip, scandal and chilli-spiced anecdote.

On that Sunday Doña Elena, *soignée* as ever in her *grande dame* silks and pearls, heaved herself up the steps into the camper and sat down, puffing slightly, at the table. She had just been to see the matinée performance. As usual, everything was wrong. The girls had all been positioned incorrectly; they were showing their tummy buttons and too much leg.

'You know, *hijo*,' she addressed Rolando severely, 'I don't at all approve of this new way the girls have of hitching their costumes up so high. In my day we never showed so much leg, it would have been considered quite indecent. And as for . . . well, you know . . .' she lowered her voice with uncustomary squeamishness, 'the *buttons* . . . I don't know how you can allow your own daughters to be seen like that.'

'But everyone does it like that now, *abuela*,' Mara protested. 'Things are different now. Besides, it's the fashion.'

'Fashion!' Doña Elena looked round at us disapprovingly. 'And as for that stupid boy . . . what's his name? . . . that Gallo. He has no business not announcing just because he has a cough.' She pronounced the word 'cough' in tones of flagellating contempt.

'*My* sons,' she glanced, gimlet-eyed, at Rolando who was surreptitiously still reading his paper, 'my beloved Yanko anyway, used to announce every day, no matter what.' Yanko was Doña Elena's eldest son who had died, in mysterious circumstances, having fallen from a sixth-storey window. 'And that was in the days before megaphones too. A *cough*, indeed. Milksops and weedlings! Who hired these useless boys, anyway?'

'Here, *abuela*, have one of these.'

To sweeten her grandmother's temper, Mara had been to the *panaderia* in the shopping centre to buy her some cakes.

'Cakes!' Doña Elena sounded as if she had been offered a plate of live worms. 'Good heavens, girl, I can't eat cakes. Couldn't possibly. Do you know why I am so fat, Katty?' She turned to me, showing the whites of her eyes. The tone of her voice took on a dying fall. 'It's because of all the pains and sufferings I have had in my life.' She put her hand to her silken breast. Brilliants flashed on her strong old woman's fingers.

'It affects your metabolism, you know. That's why I need to lose seven kilos in weight.' She nodded. Sighed. Rolled her eyeballs again. 'Still,' she eyed the tempting plate, 'perhaps just one wouldn't hurt.'

'Here, Katty.' Mara offered me the plate too. 'Have a *cuerno*. Do you know what a *cuerno* is?'

'You know, of course you do. A horn, like the ones Rolando puts on Vicky.' Doña Elena bit into her cake, removing the crumbs daintily from her lips with one perfectly manicured talon. There was a silence, short but thoughtful, while we all followed suit.

'Well,' Doña Elena finished her cake, 'this *is* nice. Just like old times.' Fastidiously she brushed a few invisible crumbs away from the front of her dress, licked her enamelled fingertips. Her little exercise in spitefulness had made her more cheerful. All at once she was full of charm and smiles again.

'You know, Katty, we were not always a little struggling circus like this, oh no!' She settled comfortably into her chair. 'There was a time when we were the biggest circus in Mexico, and the most famous too. None of your Fuentes Gasca, or Hermanos Vasquez, or Circo Atayde. *No, no*, none of them counted for a thing.' She made a dismissive gesture with her fingers so that her rings flashed.

The rivalry between these families – most of whom had started off as *cojineros*, the people who hired out cushions at the door, with Circo Bell's – was famous in the Mexican circus world, containing all the twists and back-stabbings of a real-life soap opera.

'In those days we had a huge menagerie.' Doña Elena reminisced happily. 'Not just the three sad elephants we have now, but a rhinoceros, a hippopotamus – you remember Miss Tequila, Rolando? In the end we had to swap her for a new tent – lions, bears, leopards, camels, chimpanzees, gorillas, zebras, horses, ponies, Russian wolves . . .' One by one she ticked them off on her fingers.

'We had many more acts in those days too. There was Rolando, Jorge and Ricardo on trapeze, of course, *Los Invencibles*, The Invincibles, we used to call them. Deyanira, my eldest daughter, was The Beautiful Cosmonaut. Another daughter, Rosalinda (Brissel's mother) was the Queen of the Circus – she's still here of course, although you probably know her as the telepathic Professora these days. We had clowns and dwarves and jugglers.

'Then there was the Invisible Man. Yolanda, the Girl Wonder. Los Aztecas, Olympic acrobats. Los Corzos, the Living Statues. Jim Bell's (no relation) the fearless animal trainer. Calvin and Frank, the Lords of Suspense, with their incredible high-wire act . . .' Her eyes clouded. 'My children, my daughters, all of them were great *artistas*. So graceful, so elegant . . .' She brought her hand to her chest. Then catching sight of Olinda slouching past with Bruno, a grubby jeans-jacket over her *bastonera* costume and a large rip in her fishnets, her expression turned briefly sour again.

'Piernas, piernas,' she groaned. 'Too much *leg*, I'm telling you, Rolando. And . . . *buttons! Dios mío*, I don't know what this place is coming to.'

'Look, have some coffee, Mamá,' Rolando said soothingly. 'Vicky made it specially. We all know how much you like coffee.'

Obediently Vicky poured her mother-in-law a cup. The coffee was black, scalding and so bitter it made one's flesh crawl.

'How delicious!' Doña Elena took the cup and sniffed at it elegantly. 'But you have none, *mi hijo*,' she said, suddenly solicitous. 'I know, you have this cup.'

'No, no, Mamá, it's for you. Vicky can make some more.'

'No, no, *mi hijo*, you have it, you have it.'

They tussled a little and some of the angry liquid spilt on to the table between them. 'Take it, please. Besides, I know I won't sleep if I drink it. You'd be doing me a favour, really you would.'

'Bueno,' Rolando shrugged and took the cup. 'A real Mexican mamá, you see,' he said to me, smiling. 'Nothing is too good for her sons, isn't that right, Mamá ?'

'Dios mío, Rolando,' Doña Elena said, recovering herself. 'It's only a cup of coffee.' Her eyes narrowed. 'Just because you push Vicky around doesn't mean you can push your luck with me, my boy.' Her voice was tart. Sitting up very straight in her chair she turned to me again.

'Have you ever stopped to wonder, Katty, why it is that we, who once had leopards, bears, zebras, lions and Russian wolves in our circus, not to mention Invisible Men, Living Statues, Olympic Acrobats and Girl Wonders, are now reduced to three mingy elephants?'

'I've heard it was the South American tour,' I said.

Back in the seventies Circo Bell's had gone to South America on tour for two years and had come back all but bankrupt. This fact was part of circus lore, but I had not as yet been able to unearth any more about it.

'The South American tour, ha?'

Doña Elena gave Rolando, who was stirring his coffee nonchalantly, a meaningful look.

'Did it go so very badly for you there?' I asked.

'*No, no, al contrario*, quite to the contrary. It went very well for us, extremely well, you could say. What happened was that all my sons are *very bad* administrators.'

Doña Elena gave her son one of her best drop-dead-at-a-hundred-yards glares. Rolando chuckled.

'Vagos, todos. Layabouts, all of them — except me, of course.'

'I can't believe that,' I said.

'*Sí, sí,* it's true, it's true. They spent all our money, that's what. Women . . . cabarets . . .' Doña Elena's rings flashed.

At that moment the music indicating that the next performance was about to start struck up. Through the window I could see Luis coming slowly round the side of the Big Top; the three elephants swayed slowly behind him, sweeping the floor dreamily with their trunks looking for scraps. He was treating Hannibal for an infected sore and I could see a violet patch of iodine just above her ear. As a consolation prize I pocketed the rest of my cake to take to her, and stood up.

'Ah, the six o'clock.' Doña Elena looked at her watch. 'Tcha! That Mundo, late as usual. Still, I must be off.' She struggled to her feet. 'One day I will tell you all about it, and you will write it all down in your book, Katty.' She put her arm round me. 'But aren't you going on? Quick, quick then, or you'll be late.' She shooed me out of the door. '*Piernas* and buttons. Her too . . .' I could hear her still muttering behind me, '*Tcha!* That Katty's as bad as the rest of them.'

With Tom away for whole days, sometimes as much as a week at a time, I was spending more and more time with Rolando's family. I had become particularly close to Mara, who often used to keep me company by sleeping over in our caravan while Tom was gone. The other person whom I was getting to know much better now was her mother, Vicky.

La típica mujer abnegada, 'the typical self-denying wife', is a cliché so common in Mexico as to have earned its own sad epithet. Neglected by her husband, scorned by her mother-in-law, a skivvy to her son, I sometimes used to think that only Vicky's dreams were truly her own.

As a young wife, Vicky had dreamt each of her children into being. Before they were born she had known exactly what each of them would look like. She knew whether they would be a boy or a girl; she knew what qualities they would have, what skin, what hair, even – all-important in the circus – the exact strength and suppleness of their bones. She had dreamt of each of her four children this way, and she had never been wrong.

'Before Belén was born,' Mara remembers, 'my mother told me that it was going to be a tiny little baby, another girl, and that she would be very, very hairy and dark. And when I first saw Belén, that is exactly what she looked like – as small as small could be, covered all over in fine dark hair, like a little monkey girl.'

Vicky did not believe in witchcraft, in spells, or even in *limpias*, as Mara so passionately did, but she had known from an early age that her dreams had the power of premonition. Sometimes, if she dreamt of death or disaster, she would wake in the night with a clammy film of fear behind her neck, praying that if she could only forget them in time, dissolve them quickly like the stuff of ordinary dreams, they would not come true. It seldom worked.

Earthquakes were her speciality. Whenever there was to be any kind of eruption, tremor, rumble, even the faintest seismic palpitation in the earth, Vicky always dreamt it first. 'The earthquake of '85 was the worst,' she told me. 'What dreams! I will never forget them. I even dreamt of our house in Guadalajara, right down to the very cracks in the walls.'

Vicky was Rolando's second wife. His first, a beautiful spendthrift who had squandered all her time and his money buying herself the latest new outfits, among them a startling collection of coloured wigs, had not lasted long with Circo Bell's. Their daughter, an exquisite nymph named Jacqueline, ran wild around the circus camp and, in the absence of her mother's ministrations, it was Vicky who often tended to the little girl, changing and bathing her and soothing her in the night. Soon it was not only the child who came creeping to Vicky in the hours of darkness.

Tending to the needs of others was a virtue which had been instilled into Vicky from an early age. She also was *del circo*, from a circus family, and, as her own daughter was to become after her, had been a contortionist by training. When Vicky was very young her natural father died and her mother soon married again. Her step-father, according to the family lore, was as brutish, lazy and concupiscent as it was possible for a wicked step-father to be. By the age of seven Vicky had become a little slave, washing, cleaning, cooking and generally servicing her new family's every hunger and desire. Her mother, thinking only of the comforts of her new husband and their children, was mightily pleased with this arrangement and did her best to see that Vicky stayed at home. She was rarely allowed to go out with her friends or even to leave their caravan at all. Even at the age of seven she was still so tiny that she had to stand on a special little box in order to reach the sink and the stove. I have often wondered if it was at this time that Vicky began to evolve her own secret language, her gastronomic codes of bitterness and fire.

Into this scenario, some thirteen years later, steps Rolando. In the circus world a prince and in any world at all, it must be said, quite charming. Mother and wicked step-father are trounced. Step-brothers and step-sisters are cast down. Cinderella *shall* go to the ball.

If Mara, spinning in silver at the top of her rope, was a creature of the air, Vicky was a creature of the earth. The earth entered her dreams and coloured her days. From the earth came the grains, fruits and spices with which she cooked and found her truest voice. Her understanding of their properties was not confined to the kitchen, but extended to their most antique spiritual and healing powers. She was a skilled and passionate herbalist (often to her children's dismay, who would have preferred to use the chemist's prescriptions, like everyone else).

Of all the people in the circus, Vicky was the only one we ever talked to about Bhutan,[1] knowing that she would instinctively understand it. When we showed her our books, especially Tom's photographs of the simple agricultural life there, the milking and the weaving, the harvesting and winnowing of grain and corn, she would examine them with rapture. Once she told me about a doctor friend of theirs, an old man, who, when he knew that he was going to die, had built a hut at the bottom of the garden in which to live out his last days. 'In it were a wooden bed, a table, a jar of water and a Bible. Nothing else. Such few, such simple things, but everything necessary for life.' She often looked at Tom's book. With her finger she would trace the outline of a Bhutanese woman's back, bent double over her crop of buckwheat. 'That is how I would like to live,' she would sigh gently. 'One day, *quién sabe?*' And her face would soften at the thought.

It was the city which sapped Vicky's strength. The city and Rolando's peregrinations within it. I thought of the erotic freedom which continued to illumine his life; the way in which it had soured and distorted hers. There was something so pure about Vicky and her yearning for simplicity – an austere Gregorian chant to Rolando's sensual baroque flourishes – but even if, from revenge or desire, she had ever wanted to take a lover of her own, it would have been all but impossible within the gossipy confines of the circus. Rescued briefly by Prince Charming, in later life she had reverted to being Cinderella again – only a Cinderella with wrinkles this time, and a thickened middle-age waist.

Vicky had few friends within the circus and received even fewer visitors. Occasionally, while Rolando was away, her relations came to stay to keep her company for a few days. There was a cousin, a slovenly dark-eyed woman (who because of her scandalous stories was always known to Tom and me as the wicked aunt) and, despite everything, Vicky's mother.

Vicky's mother was a parody of her daughter, a tiny, shrewish-

---

[1] Tom's and my travels by horseback across Bhutan are recounted in my first book, *Dreams of the Peaceful Dragon* (Victor Gollancz, 1987).

looking woman with grey shoulder-length hair, so impish in stature that she looked not so much like an old lady as a grotesquely shrivelled little girl. Apart from Vicky herself, no one rejoiced very much to see her. She had none of Doña Elena's presence: neither her charm, nor her resourcefulness, nor her dangerous, spicy wits. I remember her best for the shoulder-brace which she wore for her back, a strange jerkin made of Hieronymus Bosch-inspired whalebone, which at night she would hang up from one of the cupboard handles in the caravan. I would see it still hanging there some mornings like the husk of some monstrous, disembowelled insect.

With Rolando, of course, privileged as a man to come and go as he pleased, things were quite different. My friend the impresario, primped and perfumed, with his hoodlum's voice like silk on gravel, was the roving spirit of the Mexican male incarnate. He had many children, both in and cheerfully out of wedlock, although no one, not even he, seemed to know quite how many.

'Have you met my sister?' was always the cry from Mara and Olinda on Sundays, their arm around the waist of yet another unknown girl, Maria or Isabel or Alma or Lise. Vicky, kneading tortilla dough in her kitchen camper, kept silence. Sometimes she turned her back so as not to see them; but occasionally, when she thought no one was looking, I would catch her following them round the circus camp with expressionless eyes.

Women and cabarets. Women and song. Once, entirely by accident, but in a way which always seems infinitely possible in Mexico, we inadvertently came across both, and with them a strange ghost from Rolando's past.

It was in San Luis Potosí, before we joined the circus, when we were on our way back to Mexico City from Texas where we had been to buy our caravan and our truck. We stayed at the Hotel Progresso, a vast, decrepit building full of rickety furniture and potted palms. The reception was tucked into one corner of an extensive, marble-floored area which had obviously once been an open-air courtyard, but was now sealed off against the inclemency of the elements with some planks and a dubious-looking expanse of tarpaulin.

We soon discovered that, despite the tarpaulin and the planks, every time it rained (which it did, torrentially, every day, this being still the end of the rainy season), the Hotel Progresso became instantly flooded. No one except us seemed to notice the inconvenience. Instead, when we came back from dinner on our first evening we found the receptionist, her hair in dripping rat's tails, dancing a watery lambada across the marble entrance floor, apparently oblivious to the rain, which spread like a shining lake across the vast marble expanse of the reception area, lapping and rippling over the dancers' bare ankles.

This was not the only eccentricity of the Hotel Progresso. Like our hotel in Mexico City, the Monte Carlo, sighing soap operas flickered day and night from a lobby under the stairs. The upper part of the hotel was haunted by the sisters Emilia and Maria, two elderly maids. Emilia and Maria wore brightly coloured wigs covered in saucy little girl ringlets which jigged and trembled as they pranced and preened and chattered their way around the hotel's ever-dustier corridors.

And then there was Veranéa. Veranéa was a singer and it was she who had been dancing the lambada with Rosa, the hotel receptionist, on our first night at the hotel. Veranéa was middle-aged and frog-throated. She wore tight white trousers over bulging, mellow-thighed legs, with a curious white tunic over the top which made her look rather like a hospital orderly. Nevertheless, Veranéa was a singer.

Veranéa, as her name suggests,[1] had a gift for making a fiesta. It was Veranéa who had rescued Rosa from her buckets and mops, who had made her forget the blotted paper-work and the fused switchboard and her ruined hairdo in a wild and sensual lambada. It was Veranéa, too, I suspected, who had transformed the two varicosed old maids, Emilia and Maria, into saucy sirens with Marilyn Monroe curls. And when she heard that we were going to press on to Mexico City the next day, it was Veranéa who persuaded us to stay on an extra few days in San Luis Potosí to see her sing.

Under the stage name Michelle Carlson, Veranéa was per-

---

[1] *veranear* means to spend the summer holidays.

forming at a place not far from the hotel, a bar with the unlikely name of Cherry's Grill.

'Cherry's is full of interesting people. You will like it.' Veranéa gave me a sideways look from beneath her stubby eye-lashes. 'I know everyone there. If you come I can introduce you to all my friends,' she promised us, smiling her frog smile.

'Cherry's Grill' was another rambling, colonial-style building, an exquisite place of delicate columns, vaulted ceilings and arch-ways. Despite its outward beauty, inside most of the building was either derelict or deserted. Piles of rotting planks and a musty cobwebbed darkness greeted us as we stepped inside, and we had to walk up two flights of stairs before we found any other sign of life apart from the man selling tickets at the door. The bar itself turned out to be the covered-in section of what was once a central well, that would originally have looked down over an internal patio on the ground floor. Rows of columns supported soaring moorish arches, and the walls were decorated with antique blue and white tiles. Despite these architectural details, the bar, or cabaret as it turned out to be, had been done up in furious seventies kitsch. There was a dance floor in the centre of the room covered in coloured glass squares; silver and glass mosaic revolving globes dangled from the columns overhead. Red plush banquettes, like something out of a Victorian brothel, lined the walls.

Veranéa introduced us to her party. There was Rosa from the hotel, a girlfriend of hers, and a young man named Gregorio. Gregorio, one of the other singers in the cabaret, was plump and queeny, and wore a curious costume rather like Veranéa's hospital orderly outfit, consisting of a loose black tunic top and slacks. His hair, which was very thick and bobbed, was hennaed to a deep shade of purple. On his fingers he wore many rings, mostly made of silver. On one of his hands he had grown the little fingernail very long and painted it gold. A thin chain ran from a hole in this nail to a ring in the shape of a serpent which curled around the base of his finger.

When he saw me looking at his rings, he leaned towards me confidentially.

'I am from Veracruz, on the coast, you see,' he said, as if this explained something, 'and the Veracruzeños are trrr-opica-ll . . .'

He laughed voluptuously and, thrusting his arms over his head, gave a little shimmy. 'Not like these Potosinos.' Balancing daintily on the banquette, his jewelled hands linked around one of his knees, he looked round the room and gave a barely suppressed yawn. 'These Potosinos are something else. They like to educate themselves.' He nodded sagely. 'You know, I really believe most of them'd prefer to stay at home at night and read a book than go out on the town.'

It was true to say that Cherry's Grill was not very full. Some girls, either single or in pairs, sat around glumly on the banquettes at the other side of the room. Every so often Gregorio would give them little tinkling waves.

'They get so bored, you know, the poor dears,' he explained. 'And wouldn't you if you had to wait around here all night?'

At the table next to us were a group of men, rather small, paunchy types dressed informally in T-shirts and jeans. They had bought a bottle of whisky from the bar which they were mixing together with Coca-Cola. They were already very drunk. After a while they were joined by some of the girls and before long the whole party was riding high. One of the women, who was tall and dressed completely in black, was making toasts all round, throwing her head back and laughing theatrically. She had long hair and long eye-lashes and, although she was not beautiful, there was a kind of exotic energy about her which drew my attention. After a while the party got up to dance. When she stood up I saw that the long-haired woman was at least a head taller than her partner. The man staggered blearily and lost his footing, and I watched as she guided him expertly across the dance floor, his head coming to rest lovingly between her two magnificent, scantily covered breasts.

It was clear that Cherry's Grill was no ordinary cabaret. There were too many unattached girls, wearing too unusual a collection of garments – corset tops, leather boots and mini-skirts – for there to be much doubt as to their real business here. But there was something else about the place which I could not work out. The air was filled with a strange smell which I could not identify, sweeter and heavier than either dope or incense. I looked at the dancing couples. Neither of the other girls was particularly remarkable. One had a shock of curly black hair and a face painted crudely with make-up. The third was slighter and smaller than the other two. She wore a very tight black lycra mini-skirt through which the curves of her buttocks were clearly visible, small and rounded and protuberant as a negro's. Her partner kept running his hand up her leg, not lecherously but tentatively, almost diffidently, as if he were trying something out. Once he put his fingers into the top half of her corset, feeling for her breasts. The girl seemed completely absent, neither enjoying these attentions nor trying to stop them. When her partner pulled away from her at last, repelled by her passivity, she adjusted herself calmly, as if nothing had happened.

There was something odd about her, but what was it? Then I knew. Her face. Her face, I realized, was the most peculiar shape, quite out of proportion to the rest of her body. I looked again. Her nose. Her nose was far too big. And her cheeks were too wide. Her whole face was somehow too thick . . . heavy . . . wrong.

Gregorio looked at me slyly, an amused expression on his plucked mulatto face.

'Do you like her?'

'Like her? In what way?'

'She's had the operation, you know.'

'The operation?'

'*You* know,' Gregorio tinkled at me. 'The *operation*.'

'Of *course* . . .'

It all made sense. The crude, heavy-boned features. The pert, over-muscular buttocks. I looked over towards the dance floor again. The first girl, the tall one, was dancing with abandon now. As I watched she lifted her arms and her substantial breasts spilled, voluptuously rounded and milky, out of her blouse. If she noticed, she was not at all inconvenienced by it. Her partner, pop-eyed and already less than steady on his feet, lost his footing completely and nearly stumbled to his knees in front of her.

'She's had one too.' Gregorio indicated the woman with breasts. 'The operation.'

'A very successful one,' I said, 'by the looks of it.'

Gregorio threw back his head and hooted theatrically.

Veranéa had colic. She sat with her arm around Rosa's friend looking like a frog diva with an attack of melancholy. Although it was not fashionable at Cherry's, where the favoured tipples were either whisky or *cuba libres*, we had been drinking tequila.

'After three tequilas,' Laurie Lee once wrote after visiting Mexico, 'I knew the secrets of the world.' I had drunk two, rather rapidly, and the secrets, if not of the world then at least of Cherry's Grill, were ripening fast.

'These girls,' I said to her, 'do they have rooms here?'

Veranéa smiled her sideways frog smile.

'No, no, they don't turn tricks here. They own the place. The three of them,' she nodded towards the two women on the dance floor, and then to a third serving drinks behind the bar. 'The cabaret belongs to them. Those men pay to dance with them, that's all. As for the others,' she shrugged. 'Well, I guess we all have to make a living somehow.'

It was three o'clock before '*La voz romántica de Michelle Carlson*' finally took to the stage. Her voice, surprisingly, was small and bird-like, distorted by a badly wired, twanging sound system. She was followed by three middle-aged dancing ladies in bulging swimming costumes, the wistfully billed 'bailarinas esculturales'. Gregorio, his languor increased by the tequilas, said he simply could not be bothered to work that night. From his careful perch on the banquette he yawned neatly like a cat, revealing a small pink tongue.

After her performance, Veranéa's spirits were restored. She ordered more tequilas and settled down for a chat. She had been singing professionally from the age of twelve, she told me, having been born into a theatrical family. Her father had been a clown, a musical clown, who had worked with many circuses when he was younger.

'How extraordinary. We're going to Mexico City to travel with a circus,' I confided to her. In the States this confession had produced many reactions, from incredulity to a kind of fascinated horror. Here, amongst Veranéa and her friends, it sounded almost mundane, a mere workaday thing. 'Circo Bell's, perhaps you have heard of them?'

'Oh, yes, Circo Bell's,' Veranéa smiled to herself. 'Jorge Bell's.' She laughed, as if at some private joke. 'And Rolando Bell's. As a matter of fact, one of my sisters had a child by Rolando.' She mentioned this as if it were a casual thing, such as borrowing a library book. 'Or was it Jorge?' She frowned briefly, unable to decide. 'No, on second thoughts I'm almost sure it was Rolando.'

'Probably.'

I finished the last few drops of my tequila. I knew how Laurie Lee had felt. By now there were no secrets, really none, which could surprise me.

I never did discover if any of the Almas or Lises or Marias or Isabels had an Aunt Veranéa whose *voz romántica* could be heard each night in a transvestite brothel in San Luis Potosí, although after only a few weeks with the circus I knew enough to realize that it was, on balance, more likely than not. Once I mentioned the story to Doña Elena who always claimed, with some justification, that she had no idea how many grandchildren she had.

'Ha! That Rolando, don't tell me.' She made a slight gesture, elegant but dismissive, with her perfectly manicured hands. 'Este siempre pegaba su chicle en cualquier lado. That boy always stuck his chewing gum in any old place.'

But even she had to admit it was a good story.

With an outward semblance of demureness the younger members of the circus lived out their erotic lives richly among the canopies and secret places of the circus. The camp of squalid caravans, with their dejected air, their rusting aureola of bicycles and water butts and dangling television aerials, was transfigured by their power.

By day the kids dressed discreetly, if anything rather more conservatively (with the exception of rebellious Karina) than the average Mexican teenager. But the nights were a different matter. By night, with perfect propriety, naked flesh was everywhere. Tender thighs pressed though latticed *mayas*, protruding lasciviously, in bite-sized chunks, from rips and tears. Naked shoulders and plump white arms sloped, Salomé-like, beneath jewelled headdresses and nodding feathers. The frowsty costumes of Jovita's wardrobe, scrofulous and sweaty, shedding sequins like rusting silver dust, were transformed, born again each time they were slipped over a slender waist or pulled up to cup a bud-like breast. Amongst the girls the customs that Doña Elena so deplored, the hitching up of costumes high over hip bones, the new-fangled baring of 'buttons', were acts of innocent seduction, carried out not for their effect in the public ring at all, but for their more private allure. When Karina bent over, displaying the roundness of her splendid bottom, when Mara's floor-length white and silver cloak slipped from her shoulders, or when Pamela stretched out her beautiful legs in their tasselled boots, it was not for their effect in the public ring at all, but part of an intense and private lovers' song.

The Grand Parade through the streets of Atizapán de Zaragoza was as shambolic as it had been at Lomas Verdes. This time only two of the long trucks took part, one carrying Luis with his three elephants and the other holding a large trampoline on which Gordo and Jorge, in their spangled trapeze costumes, gave a display of jumps as we rode along.

Mara, as circus queen, as usual rode at the front of the procession on the roof of Mundo's ancient Chevrolet. As befitted my new role in the circus I sat on the cabin roof of the elephants' truck with Karina. This time I knew better than to wave at the crowd as I had done last time. Instead I took my cue from the others and spent the time chatting to Karina or just watching the world go by.

As suburbs went, Atizapán de Zaragoza had seemed at first to be about as dismal and grimy a place as I had yet seen in Mexico City, an anonymous hell of thundering traffic, evil-smelling exhaust fumes, open drains and telegraph wires. But the cabin of the elephant truck, with its extra height, proved to be an unexpectedly good vantage point. We drove up the high street, scarred with a familiar chaos of *vulcanizadores*, mechanics' workshops, shops and taco stalls in make-shift shacks. Behind them, from the truck roof, I could now see the remains of what had once been country life, lingering on like a fragile dream just behind the urban sprawl. A hammock slung between two trees; a dairy (amazingly) behind a shop selling three-piece suites, their gaudy damasks covered in protective plastic sheeting. We passed the remains of village plazas, with their crimson and pink bougainvillaea, acacias and palms; their park benches and curlicued wrought-iron kiosks, the last remnants of a gentler age.

Behind the façade of tumbling concrete walls, splattered with green and red PRI graffiti, I could see plots of scrub land where cows and donkeys grazed, where chickens and turkeys scratched in the dust. In places there were even plots of maize and behind them, when you looked up into the hills, whole swathes of land with as yet no buildings on at all – the countryside.

Ahead of us Gordo and Jorge were somersaulting and tumbling on their trampoline. Karina saw me watching them and nudged me in the ribs.

'I have a message for you, Katty.'

The pink feathers of her headdress nodded and fluffed in the breeze.

'Oh yes?'

'From Gordo.'

'Oh yes.'

I wondered what was coming.

'He says he likes you very much.'

'Really?'

'Yes, really.' Karina looked at me expectantly.

'Karina!' I laughed. 'I'm married. As he well knows.'

'He says to tell you that he does not mind. He is not jealous.'

'Well, that's very kind of him.'

I suppressed a desire to really laugh this time. If Gordo saw Karina and me whispering together he gave no sign of it. I could see him, dark haired and slim, tucking and bouncing, his body arched against the sky. The whole thing was absurd: the boy was nearly half my age. The possibility of him, in some other lifetime, glimmered briefly, erotically, at the edges of my mind. I thought for a moment.

'Tell him I like him too,' I chose my words with care, 'as I like you all. As a friend.'

Karina looked at me blankly, her head to one side.

'Don't look at me like that. I'm married, remember.'

'In Mexico that's never made any difference,' she said innocently.

'So I've noticed.'

As the poet said, there is no pleasure without sin, a motto the Mexicans seemed to go to absurd lengths to fulfil.

'You don't understand.' Feeling prissy and English, I tried again. 'I *love* Tom.'

'You are in love *with your husband*?' Karina sounded shocked.

'Of course I am. What is this, Karina?'

I looked at her sharply, thinking that she must be mocking me, but I could find no emotion in her face other than genuine surprise.

ma´gic, a. & n. (Of) the pretended art of influenc-
ing course of events by occult control of nature or
of spirits, witchcraft; inexplicable or remarkable
influence producing surprising results.

Oxford English Dictionary

We were in Jovita's wardrobe, getting ready for the six thirty
performance. Brissel and Pamela were struggling into their *mayas*.
Mara, who was always the first to be ready, and Olga, both had
their noses in a book. Beside them Oly squatted on the floor, half
dressed, peering into her make-up box to find the right colour
eyeshadow. The light, which shone dingily from a forty-watt bulb
and was never really bright enough to show up all the colours
properly, was partly obscured by the piles of costumes and props,
among them Tom's clown suit, still waiting to be collected.

'Last night I mixed up the orange and the pink,' she grumbled,
still peering. 'I ended up looking nearly as weird as Karina: as if
I had just gone ten rounds with Pepino Cuevas.'

'Your eyes are so big anyway, Oly, you hardly need any make-
up on them at all,' I said.

It was true. I don't think I have ever met anyone with such huge
eyes as Olinda's.

'Katty! No make-up! You can't be serious.'

My minimalist approach to make-up never failed to shock the
girls, who treasured and tended their make-up boxes with the
jealousy of religious zealots.

'Oly has Jalisco eyes.' Mara, who knew everything, announced
without looking up from her book. 'Girls from Jalisco are famous
for the size and darkness of their eyes.'

Olinda opened hers still wider.

'My eyes are no bigger than any of yours.'

'Of course they are.' Mara was firm. 'You are the only one of
us who was born in Jalisco.'

'Ay, Mara!' Oly, the tomboy, shook her Cabbagepatch-doll curls. 'All right then, we'll measure.' She fished out a tape measure from the debris in the bottom tier of her make-up box. 'Come on, Katty, you first.'

So we measured. We measured our eyes both lengthwise and upwards, and then we measured the length of our eye-lashes, top and bottom rows. We even took Jovita's measurements. As long as we did not interfere with her enjoyment of her *telenovelas*, or with the arrangement of her curlers, Jovita was usually a willing victim on these occasions. Sitting as she sat at the entrance of the wardrobe every evening, hunched and sniffing, squinting at the television from her little stool, her eyes never wavered from the screen despite the girls with their tape measure hovering round her in their costumed finery, like delicately hued dragonflies.

Only Mara, still intent on her book, refused to be drawn into the game.

'What are you reading, Mara?' I asked her.

'Oh, nothing important. Just a book.' Hastily she stuffed it away between the folds of her silver cloak which was hanging up just overhead, and got out a new costume, on to which she was sewing rows of coloured sequins. I was surprised; it was unlike Mara to be so retiring. I knew that she and Omar had had several arguments recently and, although they had soon made it up, over the last few days I had noticed that she was more subdued than normal. Tom was preparing to go away on another one of his trips that evening and so it wasn't until the next day that I had a chance to find out why.

For some time now Mara had been wanting to teach me a proper act. Although I was perfectly happy just going out in the parades, which I continued to do every night, in Mara's eyes riding Hannibal was not enough. After many weeks of consideration, she had finally decided that one of her own acts, the aerial ballet, would be both the most appropriate for me and the easiest for her to teach.

'Really, Mara, I'm quite happy with Hannibal.'

Over the weeks I had become increasingly fond of the elephants; and the times I spent with them, and with Luis their keeper, wait-ing in the wings before the parade began were some of the best I ever had in the circus. They recognized me now and would wind their trunks inquisitively around my waist whenever they saw me, feeling my pockets for the scraps I collected for them each day.

'Tcha! Hannibal's just an elephant!' No one in the circus, with the exception of Luis, ever really understood my English affection for these animals. 'You really should do something more. Besides, the aerial ballet is so easy, Katty. I could do it in my sleep, I promise you.'

'Ye-es.' I was a little more dubious. 'But it's different for you, Mara. You've been doing it all your life.'

'Tcha!' Mara waved her hand dismissively. 'All you have to do is climb up the rope and do a few figures at the top. Honestly, it's like falling off a log. Not difficult at all.'

We started early that morning in the Big Top, before the *chamacos* were about or the boys wanted to put up the net for their trapeze practice. It was always strange to be in the tent in the daytime. If the weather was fine it was often aired during the day and that morning the tarpaulin walls had been hitched up, cleated like the sails of a vast, circular sailing ship. Even so, without the stage lights it was dark and strangely echoing inside. By day the stage curtains, normally a deep midnight-blue velvet with the Circo Bell's logo picked out in shimmering silver, showed up in their true colours, the ancient fabric faded and moth-eaten. It had rained in the night and there was a pervading smell of damp sawdust.

At first Mara's lesson was easy enough. We started with some warming-up exercises and stretches, which even I could manage with ease. Mara looked on approvingly.

'Next we should work on trying to strengthen your arms, Katty. The whole act depends on them.' She felt my upper arms consideringly. 'Hmm.' Her expression became pensive. 'I know, we'll do some pull-ups. If you do some of these every day your arms will soon be as strong as mine.' She smiled encouragingly. We went over to the tiered benches at the back of the Big Top and Mara demonstrated the exercise by pulling herself up and down on the wooden slatting just above her head. Tiny and slim, with her little girl's figure, I watched her bobbing up and down. She made it look so easy. When it was my turn I reached up and grasped on to the tier above my head. With extreme effort I managed to lever myself an inch or two into the air. I tried again, with the same result.

'Try to pull yourself right up, until your nose is level with your hands. Look, like this.' Still smiling encouragement, Mara showed me again.

I tried a third time and with superhuman effort managed to raise myself to within an inch or so of the tier. After ten minutes of this the muscles in both my arms were tired out. I knew I could not keep it up for that much longer. Seeing that I was in difficulties, Mara sucked her cheeks in thoughtfully.

'I know, we'll leave the exercises for a while, you can practise them later on your own. Let's get on to the real lesson. The first part is the easiest: how to climb the rope. You'll enjoy this bit, I know. It's not hard.'

I watched as she let her rope down into the middle of the ring, a length of rough hemp about the thickness of a man's arm.

'Right. Now to climb up doesn't only depend on your arms, you'll be glad to know' – she glanced at me slyly – 'you'll have your legs to help you this time.' She showed me how to coil the rope around one leg, using the friction to push herself up and get another grip, a little higher up, with the other leg, and so on, up and up. In just a few seconds she had levered herself the thirty feet up to the loop at the top of the rope from which she hung to do her ballet figures. She slid gracefully down again to join me.

'Your turn, Katty.' She passed me the rope. 'Don't be afraid.'

I grasped the heavy rope in both hands, coiled one leg around it, and pushed upwards. Getting the initial grip was not difficult. What was more difficult was finding the strength to pull your whole body high enough to start coiling again with the other leg. When I was just two or three feet off the ground I could feel my leg beginning to slip against the rope. Through the thin material of my trousers I could feel it like a burn against the backs of my knees. I slid my hands up a little higher and pulled upwards with all my might. But the muscles in my arms were already tired out, wasted from the effort of the pull-ups. My hands are small and the rope was too thick for me to close my fingers around it comfortably. They too began to slide. The rope bit into my palms, rubbing the skin raw. Hopelessly I slithered to the floor.

After a few moments' rest I tried again. This time I made a little more progress, but it was not long before the same thing happened. My legs began to slip against the rope; and my arms, every muscle now screaming for mercy, were simply not strong enough to counter the downward slide. I tried a few more times, but as I became more exhausted, with less and less success. After my last attempt I lay down, defeated, on the canvas matting which Mara had placed on the ground beneath the rope.

'No more, please.' I rubbed my aching arms. 'I'll have to stop for today. I just can't manage any more.' I looked at my poor hands. The palms were scarlet and painful to the touch, scraped raw by the steely rope.

Mara looked down at me. 'But we've only just begun,' she said with surprise. 'You can't be tired *already*. *Ay Chihuahua*, not even you, Katty!' she laughed.

'You only say that because you're used to it. You do it every night. Twice a night and more at weekends. Can't you remember what it was like when you first started?' At that moment, I would have done anything, anything, except climb up that rope again.

Mara thought for a moment, and then shrugged.

'If you are *del circo* no one tells you how to do these things. You see them every day, from the day you are born. Then one day someone says to you, so-and-so is ill, so tonight you will perform the aerial ballet in her place. So you climb the rope and – *ta-ra!* – you do the figures, just like you've seen everyone else do them. Your mother or your sister or your cousin. If I am ill then Oly or Brissel or Pamela will go on for me, although no one has ever exactly trained them. They just know. That's how it has always been in the circus.'

She sat down on the canvas beside me, her hands around her knees.

'Of course to be a *gran artista*, that is something different. The girls (Brissel and Oly and Karina that is: Pamela is different, she could be good one day) are too scatterbrained, too young to be really good. They know the steps, but that's all. To be a *gran artista* you really have to work, to be dedicated. To suffer, even. My brother Gordo, he will be a *gran artista* one day, with the trapeze.' Mara was intensely, touchingly proud of her brother. 'Oh, yes, I know he fools around, plays the *vago* sometimes, goes off all night with Ricky and the other boys, you've seen him do all that.' Mara shook her head wisely. 'But underneath that he's *una persona muy seria*, a very serious person. He trains, practises new jumps, pushes himself just that little bit further than the last time.'

'And you, Mara? Will you be a *gran artista*?'

'I hope so.' Mara looked down at her hands. She was wearing her red outfit that day, a red top and red trousers with a faint black stripe down the legs. The colour had always suited her dark looks.

'I would like to be, one day. But it's very hard sometimes, Katty, you can have no idea how hard. I had another act, you know, apart from the aerial ballet and the *caja*.[1] We call it a solo trapeze act. It looks simple enough, but it's very difficult to do well. I had been practising it for many months before I felt I was ready to perform it in front of an audience. Then, just before I was going to make my debut, Omar was involved in a bad accident and had to go to hospital. I was very nervous all day, not only because it was my first night, but because I was so worried about Omar. I kept on thinking about him, and as the day went on I felt worse and worse. Because it was my first night, and a difficult act, the audience was full of circus people who had come specially to see me. Not only my family – my grandmother, cousins and aunts, and so forth – but friends from many other circuses, and of course you know just how critical circus people can be. There was nothing for it: however bad I was feeling I knew I had to go on.

'There is one part of the act which is particularly difficult. It involves swinging from the trapeze holding on only by your ankles. Difficult, and dangerous too. And for some reason that night, perhaps because I was so nervous, I simply could not make myself do it. Twice I nearly fell, and ended up grabbing on by my hand at the last minute. I just didn't dare to let go. But I made myself go on. I tried for a third time, and that time, finally, I managed it.

---

[1] Mara always referred to her contortionist act as 'the box'.

'The crowd went mad. Everyone was standing up, clapping and screaming. My father, who had taken Omar's place as my 'catcher' and was standing in the ring beneath me – there was no net – shouted up, "*Bueno*, Mara, you can come down now." But I said, "No, I'm going to finish," and I carried right on until I had finished the whole act.

'At the end the crowd went crazy, cheering and whistling, stamping their feet and standing on the seats. I was about to come down the rope to take my bow when I looked down and I could have sworn I saw Omar in the audience, looking up at me just as he did the first time I ever set eyes on him. Of course, the next instant I could see that it wasn't him at all, but the surprise made me lose my concentration. My grip loosened on the rope and I fell. If my father had not been there to catch me I don't know what would have happened. I was all right, but he was very badly shaken, even more so than I was. When we came off at the end of the act he said to me, "You don't go out again." And I have never been out in that act since.'

I remembered how Mara had first appeared to me: a glassy snow queen whose smile had never really reached her eyes. I had wondered then if I would ever know her; if I would ever be privy to what went on inside her head. And who knows? Perhaps it was largely because of her, the glittering ice-maiden, tiny and exquisite and cold, spiralling at the top of a rope, that I been so drawn to Circo Bell's in the first place. For me, she had always been a mystery in herself. It seemed incredible that this could be the same person speaking.

'Omar has helped me a good deal, you can't imagine how much,' Mara went on. 'I used to be so ashamed of my body, I used to imagine that all the men in the audience would be laughing at me because I was so skinny. Look at me,' she pinched her thigh between two fingers, 'no figure at all; and no *chichis*, as Oly would say. Even now I find it hard, which is why I don't always smile in the ring as much as I should do. But now that I have Omar I don't mind what anyone thinks. He has helped me practise my acts, work on new ones. In fact there was a time when he would even get up early to help me with my exercises.' I thought I detected a new note of bitterness in her voice. She glanced towards the box-office trailer where Omar had his tiny cubby-hole, but there was no sign of any of the boys that morning.

'Yes, I would like to be a *gran artista*, but it wasn't always my ambition, you know. In fact if it was not for Omar, I don't think I would even be in the circus at all now.'

Mara's first memories are of a convent in Guadalajara. She was sent to school there when she was just seven.

'The convent was not a boarding school, just an ordinary girls' day school, but my mother went to see the Mother Superior and asked her to make a special concession in our case. She listened to my mother's story, of how we were from a circus and needed this favour very greatly in order to be able to study. The Mother Superior said that she remembered having taught another little girl many years before in another school. The little girl was also called Deyanira and was also from a circus family. She remembered it clearly because she used to go to the circus quite often, not to see the show, but because the girl's mother used to give cookery and flower-arranging lessons in her caravan there.

'"That little girl's mother is my girl's grandmother," my mother told her. "Doña Elena Fernandez de Encarnación. And the Deyanira you used to teach is her aunt."

'Thanks to this curious coincidence, the Mother Superior agreed to my mother's request. What's more, not only did she agree to take me, but to take Gordo too. We were so close when we were young that no one had the heart to separate us.

'Even though I was homesick at first, I loved the nuns and I loved my life in the convent. After the circus it was so peaceful, so serene. We were given a little room of our own, painted white with a small wooden crucifix high up on the wall, and one of the mothers was put in charge of us. This nun loved us so much you can't imagine, and we loved her. She did everything for us, bathed and dressed us, even helped us to brush our hair, although really we were too old to be looked after in that way.

'The next year my mother came to see the Mother Superior again, and asked her permission to send my sister Olinda to the school, and also my cousins Vanessa and Karina, and another cousin who was also with Circo Bell's in those days, Irilen. The

Mother Superior was very kind, she accepted them all, although none of the others, except Vanessa, lasted very long there.

'None of them learned to love the convent as I had. I loved the silence, the clean white rooms, the quiet way the nuns moved, their habits whispering round them, starched quite stiff like autumn leaves, but it must have been hard for the others sometimes. Because it was not a proper boarding school we lived exactly as the nuns did. Every morning we had to get up very early, and of course we had to pray a good deal. I never minded, I liked that way of life, but the others were all very disobedient and were always trying to kick against the system, always breaking the rules or trying to get out of going to mass, especially Karina who has always been rebellious.

'The nuns were very kind, but they were very strict, too. Poor Karina, she didn't take to life there at all! But even the very strictest ones loved Gordo and Oly and me, no matter what we did. We were always the *consentidos*, the favourites, because we had been there the longest.'

As we sat there in the dark, sawdust-scented interior, a light wind stirred the tarpaulin walls around us.

'The school was a long, three-storeyed building with very many windows in each room and a large patio at the back,' Mara went on. 'My favourite place of all was on the third floor. There was a dovecote there where the nuns kept their birds and if you looked out from there you would get a view down over the whole city spread out before you. Even on the hottest days it was cool there, with a fresh breeze always blowing.

'Out of school hours, life at the convent was very monotonous, but I never minded that, I even learned to like it. Every day was the same. In the evenings, at five o'clock, we used to say rosaries with the nuns; then at seven we would walk down to the chapel to say mass. On the way back we always used to stop and buy bread with one of the *madres*. Then, every evening, we would have the same *merienda*: tacos de frijoles with salsa, bread and milk. Every day, exactly the same.

'We were put to bed at eight. Apart from us, there was one other boarder, a charity pupil, the poor niece of one of the nuns, but I don't remember her name. At first Gordo slept in the same room as the rest of us, but when he got bigger the nuns gave him a camp bed which he used to put up in one of the classrooms. Sometimes he would creep out and come up to our room because he was frightened to sleep all alone in that great echoing place. Other times, when the nuns had left us to sleep we used to get up and creep down to raid the kitchens. There were two big refrigerators there, full of *refrescos* and fruit, so we would take what we wanted and then run back to eat them in bed.

'But for the most part nothing much happened. The convent was cool and white and airy, and I was happy there. That's all.'

I looked out through the cleated tarpaulin to the circus camp ranged around us in a semi-circle, sluttish in its early morning torpor. It was not like Mara's convent, but it was unusually peaceful there that day. It was still early and there were not many people about. I saw Luis's two little girls, Lupita and Jacaira, playing with the milk-white goat which chewed the cud at the back of the caravan; and Lely in her frilly pink dress, trailing after her mother with her lollipops and Barbie dolls. I saw some of the circus dogs: two black and white mongrels who slept in the generator lorry and were always covered in soot, and the grey poodle which had once been in a dancing dog act, with three shaved legs and one fluffy one (Luis had been interrupted in the middle of clipping her, and had never got around to finishing off the job); Paloma, Chillón and Güera's shaggy cream-coloured pooch, sniffed around the caravan steps for scraps; and peering from a hatch in the roof of the generator lorry Luis's spider monkey, in a rage, rattling its chain and chattering spitefully.

Inside the Big Top, Mara stretched, rearranging herself in a different position, her hands clasped around her knees.

'I was at that convent from when I was seven until I was sixteen, when I finished in *secondaria. No lo vas a creer*, Katty, you won't believe me, but I had this idea that I wanted to go on studying.' She laughed, as though this was an impossible ambition, an *ilusión*, as she called it.

'I wanted to enrole myself in *preparatoria*,[1] but even though I kept ringing my father, he never sent me the money.

---

[1] The equivalent of A levels.

'In the end I went home to the circus to try to convince him, but my father was bitterly against the idea. He kept trying to persuade me that somehow or another I would always end up in the circus again; that in all likelihood I would marry a man who was *del circo* like me, and then all that learning would go to waste. Besides, he argued, now you are at the age to be learning your circus acts properly, because if you leave it any longer you won't be able to learn anything. You'll be too old.

'I was very sad when my father wouldn't send me back to school. I missed the convent, and the nuns too, so I made up my mind there and then that somehow I would find a way to go back there. For a whole year I begged my father to reconsider. I tried every ploy, every ruse, every argument I knew – and I can be very persistent, you know.' An elfin smile passed across Mara's face. 'By the end of the year I could see that he was beginning to weaken and I knew that eventually I would win. But then something happened which made everything else seem quite insignificant.

'We were in Toluca at the time and I was doing my aerial ballet act. In the middle of the performance, for no reason that I can remember, I found myself looking down into the audience, gazing straight into a pair of soft dark eyes, the sweetest eyes I had ever seen. Even as I was spinning, I felt something quite small tremble and begin to grow inside me. I think I knew even then that I loved him.' Mara's fingers tightened around her knees.

'For a long time we did not meet, this unknown boy and I, but every night he was there in the same seat in the front row and our eyes would meet across the ring. At the end of my act he would stand up, clapping and cheering louder than anyone. One day, after about a week, I saw him talking to my father, but still I did not know who he was. In the wardrobe all the girls were talking about him, saying how good-looking he was, and laying bets as to which one of us he might like the best. But I kept quiet and said nothing.

'Then one day my sister Alma came to visit us. She is one of my father's daughters by an old *novia* who lives in Toluca, and she brought her half-brother with her. I recognized him at once. It was him, Omar. Until that day I had had no idea who he was, or that he was connected to us in that way.

'A few days later a group of us went on an outing to the zoo – Toluca has a famous zoo – and that's when he declared himself. Even though I loved him I said, I'll think about it. I'm not the sort of girl to have a boy in every port, I told him. The circus could move on any day now and if we got too involved it simply might not be worth it. And so that's when Omar decided to join the circus, to be with me.

'When we left Toluca both Omar and his brother Horacio came with us. We were so happy, Katty, *no lo pudes imaginar*, just like two turtle doves. Omar learnt some illusionist's tricks. He used to cut me in half and stick knives through me, all inside a special box, the same act that Karina's mother used to do when she still lived with the circus. After a while Horacio went back to Toluca, but even then Omar stayed with me. We had got all the way to Acapulco before his mother came to fetch him home. Omar had been in the first term of his *preparatoria* when we met – he was going to be an architect – and she had come to take him back so that he could continue his studies. She was very angry to find him still with the circus. She knew about me, of course, but had always thought it was a passing infatuation and that he would soon be bored. But of course that was not what happened at all. He loved me, it was true, but he had grown to love the circus life as well. But his mother was too strong for us. Enough's enough, she said, it's for your own good. You're coming home. And so he went.

'Everyone was sad to see how much we suffered. I promise you, Katty, I was so unhappy I made myself ill. Instead of Omar another boy, Hector, used to do the illusionist act with me. I used to cry all the way through it, from beginning to end. Poor Hector, everything he did reminded me of Omar, and I just couldn't help myself. I pined and pined for my Omar, just as I knew he would be pining for me. It was as if someone had cut out a part of me, that part of me which had fluttered and begun to grow the first time I set eyes on him, a part of me that I knew I could not live without. I became thin and pale. The weeks passed, but time didn't help. I became quiet and withdrawn, so unlike my usual self that even my father was worried.

'In the end, when my father flew up to Mexico City on business he decided to take me with him. He thought the trip might distract me, bring me out of myself again. Of course, when we arrived at my grandmother's house the first thing I did was to ring Omar in Toluca. He came to see me and told me that he had decided to leave his studies after all. He could not stand us being apart any longer; he was coming back to the circus for good.'

Mara glanced down at her hands. She looked so tiny and frail, sitting there crosslegged like a little red genie, her magic rope unfurling into the air beside her.

'That was two and a half years ago. He was fifteen and I was just sixteen. We have never had a day apart since.'

'That's the most wonderful story.' I expected to see her smile at me as usual, but when she looked up her face was completely stricken. 'Mara, what is it?'

'Ay . . .' She plucked nervously at her trousers. 'Nada, nada.'

None of the circus people, with the possible exception of Rolando, were at all sentimental and I had never seen Mara cry – she was not that sort of girl – but I could see that she was struggling to compose herself.

'It's Omar, isn't it?'

'Sí.' She nodded miserably.

As if on cue I saw the door to the cubbyhole in the *taquilla* swing open and Omar's head appear. *Circo Bell's* announced the red and white lettering over him, *El Espectáculo Más Famoso en Todo las Américas*, The Most Famous Spectacle in All the Americas. Omar came down the steps, jaunty in a new shirt which Mara had bought for him a few days previously. He crossed paths with Yvonne who was pushing Taynarí in his buggy and as he walked past her I saw him turn, in that most tell-tale and all-male gesture, to look at her. Omar turned round again, smiling cheerfully to himself. Unfortunately, Mara had seen him too.

'*Omar!*' She stamped her foot, a look of anguish on her face. 'You see – he's always doing it!' she said furiously. 'In the streets, when we go shopping, in the bus. Everywhere.' She leant forwards, clutching her stomach as if in pain. '*Ay*, I can't help it, but I get so *jea*lous.' She gasped as if she had been punched. 'I can't stand it.'

I watched Omar walk towards us past the Big Top. He had

not seen us and Mara for once made no gesture towards him.

'All men look at other women. They wouldn't be human if they didn't.'

'He never used to,' she said sadly.

'Maybe he was just better at hiding it.'

A melancholy feeling, of being old and worldly-wise, swept over me.

'Does Tom?'

'Of course. But never in an obvious way, because he knows it would hurt my feelings.'

'But don't you mind?'

'No. As long as he looks discreetly and doesn't do anything about it. Come on, Mara, don't you look at other men sometimes?' I teased her.

'No.' Mara dropped her head mournfully. 'I love Omar. He is everything to me.'

'I know he is,' I tried to soothe her.

'Omar is not just my lover, he's my best friend. You see, I have always been the odd one out here in the circus,' she explained. 'Always the oldest of the young cousins and the youngest of the older ones. I don't really have any special friends here, not any more. When we were all little I used to play with Ricky, he was the closest to me in age, but of course things are different now we are older. Then there was Vanessa, but . . . well, you know what she's like.'

Vanessa, Karina's elder sister, was a withdrawn girl, corkscrew-curled with very fine, translucent skin. Vanessa kept herself to herself. Apart from her *novio* Charlie she did not seem to have time for anyone much, most especially Karina, whom she alternately bullied and ignored. Their feuds and fights were as much a feature of circus life as Güera's milk-curdling language, Luis's elephants or Jovita's curlers and *telenovelas*.

'Ay, Katty. I don't know what's wrong with me, but I'm sure he doesn't love me as much as he did.'

Mara rocked herself backwards and forwards in despair.

'What makes you think that? Has he said something?'

'No, no, that's just it. He hasn't said or done anything. It's just a feeling I've got, here' – she put her hand against her heart –

'right here. I keep thinking something terrible is going to happen to us.'

In my eyes very few people could ever have been good enough for Mara. Omar, surprisingly, was. Not only was he good-looking and funny, but he had charming rather flamboyant good manners and, like Mara herself, was extremely hardworking. As far as I knew he had always been loyal to her. I felt I should stick up for him.

'Just think of all the things he does for you, Mara. He may not tell you he loves you every five minutes' – amongst other things Mara had complained of a certain (albeit microscopic) cooling in his romantic ardour towards her – 'but you must think of his actions not his words. I promise you, they are what really count.'

In fact, in Mexican terms, Omar was truly a paragon amongst men. Not only did he carry her heavy shopping for her and gallantly help her on and off with her circus cloak or her winter coat when it was cold, but also Omar regularly helped Mara with her housework when she had too much to do. Machismo, that dark code of honour which so tyrannized the lives of the other circus boys, not to mention the lives of their mothers, sisters and girlfriends, was offended at every count by Omar's behaviour. And the beauty of it was – he simply didn't care.

'Marica, marica, maricón! Pansy, poofter, gay-boy! She's really got you, hasn't she? Got you right under her thumb.' I often heard Omar taunted by the other boys for his troubles. For the most seriously afflicted, to be seen to help a woman in any way at all, even by so much as holding open a door or carrying a parcel, was an affront to their frail notions of manhood. Whenever this happened Omar would say nothing: instead, his eyes would sparkle and his lips would twitch as though to some secret joke, and he would carry on unperturbed, as if nothing had happened. Under the circumstances, it seemed to me, to sweep out Mara's caravan for her when she already had a headache, the supper to prepare, the lunch to wash up and Belén to mind that day, was the truest expression of true love I ever beheld.

Omar was the illegitimate son of a woman who in her youth had possessed the face of a Helen, and the variegated love-life to match. Her five children were the casual gifts of three different fathers, only one of whom had cared to bestow his name on her at the same time as his oats. Omar had inherited his mother's milky courtesan's looks, her shrewdness and her adamantine strength of character. He had the prized pale skin of a *güero*; the neat movements and slim, serpentine hips of a dancer.

From his father he had inherited his courtly manners, a certain worldliness – unusual amongst the circus people, particularly the young – and a propensity for bouts of occasional drunkenness. Omar's father had been a politician of some prominence. He had held numerous important posts, both locally and on a national level, but his chief claim to fame was that he had once founded his own political party, the short-lived PP or Partido Popular (the Popular Party), in the process of which he had made some ill-advised and public declarations against the reigning PRI, and been thrown in jail for his pains. He was known both for his honesty and for his insobriety, the latter of which had cost him, in his later years, a promised governorship of Toluca.

The love affair between Omar's mother and his father, Enrique, came about in the most unusual way. The couple knew each other intimately even though for many months they might have passed each other every week in the street and been none the wiser. They knew what it was to whisper into each other's ears, to blow sweet kisses and breathe adulterous nothings at each other long before they knew the colour of each other's eyes, or had even fingered so much as a curl of each other's hair.

Omar's mother was a telephone operator. Once when Enrique made a call to Mexico City, which he did daily in the course of his political work, she happened to be the telephonist who connected him. The next day, by chance, his call came through to her again. And the next day the same thing happened. Bored, mildly aroused by the erotic possibilities of their anonymity, they got talking. Even though it was a long time before Enrique set eyes on her face, her voice alone must have contained something of its promise – sex or solace, or both – for soon he was seeking her out, seduced by her curvaceous vowels, the warmth and strange breathiness of her laugh, the wantonness of her softly rolling Rs.

When they did finally meet it was not long before Omar was conceived.

Omar's father did his best for their child, which turned out to be not much. Since he was already married and already had more than enough children by his wife, another baby had not been in his scheme of things when he had started their affair. When Omar was born he was generous with money to maintain both his mistress and his new son, but at the same time took the opportunity to put a more prudent distance between himself and them. In his short eighteen years Omar had rarely met his father, who never publicly acknowledged him as his son, even though the family, whom Omar was never allowed to meet, apparently did know of his existence.

Mara was obsessed.

'Katty, what do you think I should do?'

We had gone back to my caravan for a rest after our training session in the Big Top. Mara was often here these days; I know she found it a restful place after the cramped hurly-burly, the continuous shouting and fights which went on in her parents' zebra-striped trailer. She sat on the bed, pulling her curls thoughtfully. 'Perhaps I should dye my hair blonde.' She gazed at herself in my little hand mirror. 'What do you think?'

'I think you'd look ridiculous.'

'Yes, but he likes *güeras*, Katty. You don't understand. Blonde hair and blue eyes, like yours,' she added without bitterness, 'that's what all Mexican men want. They don't want *morenas* like me any more.'

'Look, Mara, Omar loves *you*,' I said, 'not some Barbie doll who has to keep changing the way she looks every two minutes.'

But that day it was impossible to convince her. Something, I did not know exactly what, had happened and she was impervious to my reasoning.

'No, no, you don't understand, I must do something.' She clutched her stomach again. 'I *must*.' Then a thought occurred to her. She looked at me consideringly.

'Katty?'

'Yes?'

'I want to show you something . . .' she hesitated.

'Yes.'

'. . . But you must promise not to be shocked.'

'Oh, yes.' I massaged one of my arms, which was still aching from the rope trick. 'What is it?'

'A book.'

'A book?'

'A book' – she thought for a moment – 'which will help me with Omar.' She paused, as if debating something with herself. 'I will show you, but you must promise not to tell *any*one else, most especially Omar. Do you promise?'

'OK. I promise.'

Mara jumped up.

'It's with Jovita. I'll get it.'

With a look of relief, she disappeared out of the door. When she came back she was holding the same book I had seen her reading the day Oly had measured our eye-lashes in the wardrobe, concealed beneath an old dressing gown. She drew it out and handed it to me with both hands. Across the front cover I read the title. *A Book of Spells*, it said, in large black lettering.

Mara looked at me anxiously.

'Only white spells,' she assured me. 'No black magic, I promise. Only good stuff.'

'Where on earth did you get it?' I turned the book over in my hands. It was quite new, although some of the pages were already well thumbed. The cover was wrapped in cellophane.

'From the supermarket.'

'The *supermarket!*'

'Oh yes,' Mara nodded. 'It's a very popular book. A – how do you call it? – a bestseller. You know how it is in Mexico, we believe in witchcraft very much, so books like this are most popular. Anyone can buy it.'

Inside the spells were arranged like recipes, with a list of ingredients in a column at the top, and then a paragraph or two, depending on how complicated the spell was, on how to proceed in its preparation. They were grouped in sections, money, love, the future, *limpias*, and so on, and had titles like, 'Make Yourself Unforgettable with Red Salt', 'Discover the Initials of Your Future Husband', 'How to Make a Love Potion with Boiled Rose Petals', or 'Ensnare Him with a Lock of His Own Hair'. I thought I could see what she was getting at.

'Are you telling me you want to put a *spell* on Omar?'

My eyes fell on the title of another spell, 'Hechícelo con un Suéter', 'Bewitch Him with a Sweater'.

'"First, take a sufficient quantity of pure new wool,"' I read out, '"and at midnight at the next full moon wash it carefully in a silver bowl, with water in which half a kilo of the finest rose petals, a bunch of violets and six hairs from your own head have previously been boiled . . ."' Oh, Mara, you can't be serious!'

But I could see she was.

'*You* may not believe it, Katty,' Mara said earnestly, 'but that's because you are an *Inglesa*, and maybe these things don't work in your country. But in Mexico they do. I *know* they do.'

'You mean you've tried it before? Really?' I could see Mara colouring slightly, and I knew I had found her out. 'And did it work?'

'Yes!' She was adamant. 'Yes, it did. It was before you came to the circus. I had the same problem. I thought Omar was getting bored and so I thought I'd try out one of these spells. It was supposed to make him blind to everyone else but me. And the thing is, it worked, I swear it did. Things were so much better afterwards, for months he never looked at anyone else, not even *güeras* in the street. Things were so good, in fact, that I made a terrible mistake. One day I told him what I had done.'

'What did he say?'

'He was *furious*, so furious you can't imagine.' Mara flushed. 'He flew into a terrible rage, the first time I have ever seen him like that. He made me fetch the book, then he built a fire and he made me burn it, page by page, until it was nothing but a pile of ashes. *Ay Chihuahua*,' she sighed, 'such a waste.' There was a pause, and then she gave one of her sudden impish smiles. 'This time I had to buy a brand-new one and you know how expensive books are here in Mexico.'

I don't know if Mara ever tried out another of the book's strange incantations. *The Book of Spells* on its own held a kind of fascination for her, as it came to for me, and when no one else was around we often used to look through it together. Witchcraft, superstition, belief in the supernatural, all were as much a part of Mexican life as praying to the Virgin of Guadalupe or eating tortillas and refried beans.

In addition to a new religion, the very first Europeans ever to set foot in Mexico, Cortés and his conquistadors, also brought a magician with them, and with him the New World's first experience of European occultism.[1] Not that the indigenous people needed much teaching on the subject. They had always had their own caste of soothsayers, sorcerers and shamans, complete with their own traditions, spells and sacrifices, much the same as they still do. Magical practices were as old, and complex, as Mexico itself.

As I had learnt from Mara, witchcraft was so popular in Mexico that DIY manuals were now available in supermarkets, but traditionally, and to be absolutely assured of its efficacy, it required the services of a third party. In Mexico you never had to look far to find a witch, and naturally that included the circus.

The circus witch was such an unlikely candidate that it was some time before I was really convinced that she was for real. She was. Sylvia Medina, her mother, and her mother before that, came from a long line of witches from Catemaco, in the state of Veracruz. (Veracruz, I was later to learn, was famous for its witches, and of all the towns in that steamy, sleazy, witchy province, Catemaco was the witches' capital.)

Although she had not been with the Circo Bell's very long, everyone, particularly the children, knew Sylvia well. She was the circus popcorn seller. Every evening I would see her sitting in the same spot at the entrance to the Big Top and, while Antonino balanced his swords and his lighted candelabra, while Charlie and Ramón monocycled, Yvonne walked her tightrope and Martinelli juggled, Sylvia could be found patiently selling her paper twists of fresh popcorn – *palomitas*, or little doves, as they are known in Mexico – to the children who buzzed hungrily around her stall.

---

[1] In his *Conquest of New Spain* (Penguin Classic, 1963), Bernal Díaz del Castillo mentions one Botello, a soldier 'who seemed a very decent man and knew Latin and had been in Rome. He was reputed, however, to be a sorcerer. Some said that he had a familiar spirit, others called him an astrologer.'

I knew Sylvia for another reason, too, for at Lomas Verdes she had been our neighbour. It was she who had lived in the urinous-smelling caravan next door to ours with Chillón, her brother, and lovely fat Güera, so cheerful and foul-mouthed, her sister-in-law. Sylvia was dark and rather stout, and looked older than her twenty-seven years. In the mornings I would often see her hanging up the family's washing in her nightdress. Later on, every day at about lunchtime, she would change into an evening dress. She had a succession of these, although they were mostly variations on the same theme: figure-hugging watered black silk with flounced peplums at the waist and fancy sleeves. She said little, although with Güera around all day, singing and swearing at the top of her voice, gossiping, chatting and chastising the various members of her family and friends, perhaps it was unnecessary. As far as I could tell, the two women got along together like true sisters.

Despite her washerwoman's arms, her snub nose and her soft, meaty belly, Sylvia had an admirer in the circus: Chino, one-time lover of the hapless Anna. They were an unlikely couple. Both in age and in body weight, Chino, with his feral, malnourished body and shock of tight corkscrew curls, was barely half Sylvia's size. But neither this, nor the story of Anna's alleged rape, seemed to disturb Sylvia unduly.

From the beginning, she told me when I came to know her better, Chino had proved an assiduous suitor. He had started to court her when we were still camped at Lomas Verdes although in those days, of course, he was still in theory Anna's *novio*. At first, because of Anna, Sylvia had refused all his advances, but when Anna finally left the circus, well, that was a different matter.

Chino was relentless. He bought her presents every day, *dulces* (sweets), fancy combs for her hair and fairground toys: not the most extravagant gifts, but generous considering his meagre earnings. Soon Chino's sister Veronica had started to plead his suit on his behalf and his friend Ilish would speak admiringly of him whenever Sylvia was present. It was not long before she accepted him and soon they were an established couple. Chino was happy with his conquest.

'He says I know how to show him respect. Not like that other girl, you know, Anna.' Sylvia looked at the ground, kicked at a rusting bottle top with the toe of her shoe. 'He says she was *muy grosera* with him; even used to hit him sometimes. He says he is going to marry me and that he will accept my two daughters as his own.' Sylvia had two little girls from a previous marriage, although they did not live with the circus, but with their grand-parents in Catemaco.

'And do you think he will?'

Somehow I could not imagine Chino as a husband.

'Quién sabe?' she shrugged.

She did not seem either pleased nor displeased at the prospect. Poor Sylvia, in Mexico was any man really better than no man? Quién sabe? Who knows? It was a phrase I heard so often I some-times used to think it was the catch-phrase of the circus.

At first Sylvia was shy about her witchery. The entrance to the Big Top where she had her stall was a kind of nucleus area. From it on one side you could see the ring and the artistes performing; on the other, the box-office, with its red and white circus logo, 'Circo Bell's, El Espectáculo Más Famoso en Todo las Américas', lit up in lights. Everyone who visited the circus had to pass through here, which made it a good place to track down Rolando or Jorge, always the most elusive of the three brothers, or anyone else I particularly needed to talk to. Having changed into my ordinary clothes, but still in my *mayas* and make-up, as was customary amongst the circus performers, I used to sit with Sylvia sometimes in between riding Hannibal in the parades, watching the perform-ance from the bench next to her. When her popcorn trade had finally slacked off, we would get talking.

She told me that she had learnt her trade from her grandmother who was well known for her skills both in white magic and in black. As a little girl she can remember the room where her grand-mother kept her potions and her herbs, the different coloured candles, the amulets and the flasks of holy water. When people came to her, Sylvia remembers, they would write down their pet-ition on a piece of paper. Sometimes there was a photograph attached, and sometimes a figurine, a tiny miniature of a man or a woman fashioned in cloth or clay or wax. As her grandmother worked she would teach Sylvia as she went along: this herb and that for a love potion; this stone and this root together to cause a miscarriage; walk three times round these candles and say this prayer, like so, to keep away evil spirits. She could neither read nor write – one of Sylvia's jobs was to read her the petitions – but her magical knowledge, both for good and for ill, was encyclopaedic.

'I learnt many things from my grandmother, although many of the things she taught me – the black magic side particularly – I never practised. She would never let me. I was too young and it was too dangerous, she said. Instead my talent, even from the time when I was quite a young girl, was for *limpias*.[1]

'A *limpia* is a ritual cleansing,' she explained. 'You can carry out a *limpia* for many reasons. Sometimes a person might fall ill from a *mal aire*, a bad air, or the *mal de ojo*, the evil eye. Other times it might be for an illness which cannot be explained, but which recurs often and cannot be got rid of with ordinary medicine. Perhaps the person is suffering from bad luck. Maybe their neighbours are envious of them for some reason, or someone they know has asked another witch to put a spell on them. A *limpia* can be used to counteract all these things.'

Sylvia's particular skill was with children.

'I used many things in my *limpias*, eggs and alcohol and herbs, the way my grandmother taught me. But with children I particularly liked to use alcohol. I put it on their heads, inside their arms and on the backs of the knees to ensure that the illness will not recur. I also used to use my own hair – it was very long in those days, and beautiful.' She touched her cropped head softly. 'I used to take my hair and wipe the children's heads with it, passing it all over their bodies to take away their illness.'

Sylvia shook her head as if the memory pained her. 'I had great success always, but it was very bad for me. By using my own hair, I was absorbing their illness into my own body. Afterwards I always used to get terrible headaches. My eyes would become red and inflamed, and used to hurt terribly. In the end my grandmother warned me that I should stop. The *mal aires* and the *mal de ojos* were affecting me, she said, and if I carried on like that I would eventually go blind.'

[1] A *limpia* means literally a cleansing.

Because of this Sylvia practised her art only occasionally, although she admitted that she had been asked to do several *limpias* since she had been with the circus. Vanessa had been present at the most recent one and she told me what had happened.

'It was with José Jaime, you know, Veronica's little boy.' Chino's sister, Veronica, had a son of about six months old. 'He was crying and crying, and no one knew what on earth could be the matter with him. Veronica took him to Güera's caravan when I happened to be in there and when Sylvia saw him she said immediately that he had had *un espanto*, a fright, and that if Veronica wanted she could do a *limpia*, which she said would soon cure him.

'Veronica said yes, so we found an egg from Güera's cupboard and a few other things, and then Sylvia took the little boy on her knee. She passed the egg over him, down his arms and legs and over his head, all the time saying these prayers. When she had finished the little boy was completely calm again. Sylvia said that if we broke the egg, she would be able to "read" it and find out what had really happened. So Güera fetched a bowl and she cracked the egg into it. Ugh . . . !' Vanessa shivered. 'It was disgusting. Half the egg was solid, exactly as if it had been cooked, while the other half was still raw. Sylvia looked at it and said that someone had dropped the baby on the floor, whether accidentally or on purpose she could not tell, and this is what had given the child his *espanto*.'

Although Sylvia promised that I could be present the next time, I never did see one of her *limpias*. A few weeks later both she and Chino were gone, back to Veracruz, Güera told me, where they were headed to collect Sylvia's two little girls and start their new life together. No one seemed particularly sad to see them go, but then that was the way of the circus. Here today and gone tomorrow: sentimentality had no place in this kind of life.

I never saw Sylvia again. At the time I was sorry to see her go, but there came a period, some six months later, when I came to wish that I had never set eyes on her. For if it had not been for Sylvia we would never have visited Catemaco on the first Friday of March. If it had not been for Sylvia we would never have heard of the Mono Blanco, let alone have found ourselves there, at midnight, in the middle of an unknown wood.

In fact, if we had known what we were letting ourselves in for, we would never have become involved in the Witches' Convention at all.

TWELVE

'Tis now the very witching time of night,
When churchyards yawn and hell itself breathes out
Contagion to this world: now could I drink hot blood,
And do such bitter business as the day
Would quake to look on.

WILLIAM SHAKESPEARE, *Hamlet*, III. ii. 413

In Mexico I lost my faith in God. In Catemaco, to be precise, the witches' capital. In Sylvia's town.

On the surface of it, as was so often the way in Mexico, Catemaco was all innocence. A holiday place, in fact, full of childish pleasures, with its lake and its pleasure boats with their candy-striped awnings, its rickety water-front restaurants on stilts. In the evenings the water sparkled and the hills fell abruptly into a smoky horizon, like a distant scene from some quattrocento painting. Men standing upright in the prows of their boats fished with nets in the shape of butterflies and the only thing to indicate that all was not as it seemed was the muttering of the grackles as they came to roost in the trees, a soft subliminal sound like the far-away grumbling of discontented gnomes.

On the surface of it, Catemaco cultivates a jokey attitude towards its witchery. In the evenings, at the stalls along the water-front, you can buy witch souvenirs and trinkets, principally in the stylized form of an ugly old hag on a broomstick, on postcards, key rings, posters and photograph albums. A popular T-shirt design bears the logo 'I laughed at the witches and I was turned into a . . .' with a picture of a frog underneath. Restaurants have names like Las Siete Brujas (the Seven Witches) and El Rincon de Brujos (Witches' Corner). Catemaco has nothing to hide. And by putting on this show, by turning its dark face into a shiny plastic souvenir, it succeeds – almost – in cauterizing it.

It was the first Friday in March, a day traditionally propitious for magic of all kinds and the day when each year, Sylvia had told us, Catemaco holds its Witches' Convention. But once we were there it proved unexpectedly hard to discover exactly what or where the Witches' Convention was. Even Sylvia had been vague. 'Puros brujos, puros brujos,' I remembered her telling me. 'Only witches are present on that day, for it is the time when new witches are initiated. Go to the Mono Blanco,' she told us, 'the hill behind the town which they call the White Monkey, that's the place to be.'

But there were many hills around Catemaco and besides, what were we supposed to do once we got there?

We asked around in the town, but that brought us little information. Most of the people wandering around the plaza were Mexican tourists who, when they were not visiting the local beauty spots by pleasure boat, were more interested in visiting the church to receive the beneficent touch of a miraculous virgin, the Virgin of the Carmen, who resided there, than in local witchcraft traditions. At the stalls which crammed the streets around the church there was not a broomstick to be found. Instead religious icons filled their trays, plastic virgins and pottery saints, garish 3-D pictures of Christ on the Cross, and *ex-voto* amulets, little brass figures like ones I used to have on a charm bracelet when I was a child. These were available in a variety of forms, animals, inanimate objects and, most curiously, various pieces of the human anatomy, arms, legs, fingers, and so forth.

'If you have a bad leg,' the owner of the stall explained, 'and you pray to the Virgin and she cures you, then you buy one of these amulet legs and pin it to the Virgin's skirts when you come back. It's a way of thanking her for answering your prayers.'

I thought of the old distinction between a prayer and a spell: a prayer could have no power in itself, unless God chose to listen to it; a spell, on the other hand, so long as it was performed correctly, was guaranteed to succeed.

'Now I know why there are so many people here. If one bit of mumbo-jumbo doesn't work, you can just move straight on to the other,' Tom, a sceptic on both fronts, pointed out dryly. 'Very convenient.'

Like the taxi drivers, the restaurant waiters and the boatmen whom we had asked, the stall sellers did not know much about the Witches' Convention either. One said that nothing was happening at all, or that if it did it would only be in private rituals, like *limpias*, which were usually carried out in people's homes. Another said that usually the location was advertised on posters in the town, but that he had not seen any this year. Back at our hotel we asked the reception boy who suggested, logically enough, that if we wanted to know about the Witches' Convention, then the best thing to do would be to ask a witch.

The house of Catemaco's most famous magician, Gonzalo Aguirre Pechi, was an ordinary-looking middle-class edifice on the outskirts of town. We were shown into the family sitting room, which was also used as a waiting room. Inside, although otherwise affluent, the furnishings were sparse: two stiff-backed chairs, which we were invited to sit on, a broken plastic sofa and a chest. Against one of the walls was a dresser which contained a stereo set, books and ornaments, but apart from these the room was cool and bare.

Various people came and went into the room and, as is usual in Mexico, there was a large number of small children. Sometimes they sat down, on the sofa or the chest, and appeared to be waiting as we were for an appointment, but on the whole it was impossible to tell whether they were family, friends or some of the witch's other clients.

We waited for a long time. Sunlight filtered into the room through lace curtains. One of the men went out and came back again soon after with fizzy *refrescos* for everyone which he lined up in a row, red and orange and caramel coloured, on top of the chest. It was not a sinister place at all. Rather, there was an air of faintly forced normality, of anticipation, much as you might feel in an expensive doctor or dentist's waiting room. Tom fell asleep, bolt upright on his chair.

After a while a young woman came out of the kitchen at the far end of the room. From the way she looked, I knew immediately that she was a witch. She had thick reddish hair piled up on top of her head, high-heeled shoes and hot pants. She came and sat down near me, fingering a pack of cards. We got talking.

'I am the granddaughter of Gonzalo Aguirre Pechi, the famous magician of Catemaco,' she told me. 'He is dead now, he died about ten years ago, but no one, not even here in Catemaco, has ever been able to match his skill.' Dexterously she shuffled the cards through the air, catching them between her long fingers. 'It is true what they tell you. Like all great magicians, he did white and black magic, of course. "El malo contra el bueno, y el bueno contra el malo", that's what he always used to say. The bad against the good, and the good against the bad. White in the day, and black at night.

'He had no formal training, my grandfather. Instead, every Tuesday and Friday night he used to go up to a special place he knew on the Mono Blanco, and there a white flame would appear to him and from this flame he received his knowledge. Many famous people, including one of our own presidents, and people from all over the world used to come here to ask my grandfather to use his skills for them.'

The woman, who was about twenty-five, was called Lupe, short for Guadalupe. She had a handsome, crude face. Her skin was not good. To disguise it she wore heavy make-up, and her eye-lashes were clotted with thick black mascara.

'It is my mother whom you have come to see.' Without looking up, she carried on caressing the pack. The cards bore the Spanish suites: clubs, cups, coins and swords. Their unfamiliarity was strangely jarring.

'My mother is a remarkable woman, as you will soon find out. I will tell you something about her if you wish.' Her long fingers flexed the cards backwards and forwards, breaking them in, until they obeyed her every movement. 'When my grandfather was alive she refused to have anything to do with his magic. And for nine years after he died, still she refused. Then, about a year ago, she started to have dreams.' She paused for effect. 'That is how many witches are born, you see, when they start to have dreams.' Softly, she started her shuffling again. 'In her dreams my grandfather started to appear to her. Each time it was the same dream. My grandfather appeared at her bedside and said that he was coming for her soon. My mother was very frightened, thinking that he was going to kill her, to take her to the place where he was.

'Around about this time she had started to perform *limpias*, quite spontaneously, and one day this girl came to her from Mexico City asking to be cured – she had bad luck and no *novio*, even though she was quite old. Just as my mother was about to perform the *limpia*, this girl went off into a trance and became possessed by the spirit of my grandfather.

'Through her he started to talk to us again and to send us messages. He told my mother that she should not worry, that he was always beside her – when he was alive, and at the height of his powers, one of his favourite sayings was, 'Hay otro detrás de mí', someone else is behind me. Then he told her that he had left a great treasure, including many of the most occult and secret instruments of his trade, buried on the Mono Blanco. He told her that if she went up there at night, to a certain place which he mentioned, his ghost would come and guide her to it.'

Lupe's voice was slow and soporific. When she spoke of these things it was without a trace of emotion or surprise. It was with effort that I roused myself to question her.

'And did she ever go to look for it?'

'One time, but she never found anything.' She shrugged my question away, as if it was of no importance. 'It was too dark and difficult.' She snapped the pack of cards shut. 'All that was about three months ago now. Every so often the girl from Mexico City brings us more messages from my grandfather and as a result my mother has done more and more healing. She has great presence and great strength when she is working, almost as if there was indeed someone else beside her.'

Lupe's mother, the daughter of the great magician Gonzalo Aguirre Pechi, received us in a small, white room which led off from the sitting room. Rosalinda Aguirre was a strong, handsome-looking mestizo woman of about fifty. She had dark hair and eyes and fine, pale skin. Unlike her daughters, another of whom stood at her shoulder watching us as we spoke, Rosalinda had an unexpectedly benign aura about her, and there was both intelligence and humour in the expression of her black eyes and in the line of her mouth.

When we told her why we had come to Catemaco, she looked at us for a few moments with great concentration, saying nothing. Then she shook her head.

'My father was *un hombre muy recto*, a very upright man,' she said, 'and so I am going to be equally *recto* with you.' When she spoke her voice was precise and warm. 'He never let anyone spectate at one of his black masses, because it would be false. So I am sorry,' she shook her head again, 'but I can't take you with me either.'

'Black masses?' I was taken aback.

Neither of us had any notion that the Witches' Convention involved such a thing.

'That's right.'

I had a fleeting impression that behind her grave, unblinking gaze, she was secretly laughing at our naïvety. The daughter who was standing at her shoulder leaned down and whispered something in her ear. Rosalinda listened briefly and then nodded.

'I cannot help you, but I think I know someone who might be prepared to take you.' In a business-like way she picked up the telephone on her desk, dialled a number and spoke rapidly into the earphone. 'At ten thirty then?' Before we could change our minds we heard her making arrangements for us with the unknown person, whoever it was, on the other end of the line.

'Yes, I'll tell them. They'll be there. Ten thirty.' She put the telephone down again and gave us a brief, professional smile. 'There, it's all arranged. One of my daughters will show you where to go.'

Her manner was brisk.

'Thank you, you've been very kind.'

I had the feeling, not entirely comfortable, that events were somehow sliding out of our control. Rosalinda looked at us consideringly.

'You know, I have to tell you that I don't approve of these goings on on the Mono Blanco at all,' she said as she showed us to the door. 'I tell you this: my father, who has been dead many years now, he was a *gran señor*. A great man.'

'Un gran señor.' The daughter, who up until now had been standing silently at her shoulder, echoed her words.

'But since he died, no matter what you may have been told, in Catemaco now there are no true witches left. These people' – she indicated with her hand, tracing a vague semi-circle in the direction of the somnolent street outside her window – 'they are nothing but *cirqueros*, circus performers. I don't know what they get up to half the time, with their vulgar shows. Eating cats and I don't know what.'

I saw her gaze flitter shrewdly towards us, making absolutely sure that we were registering what she was saying.

'Eating cats?'

'Oh yes, oh yes.' She opened her eyes wide and was, I felt, gratified by my horrified response. 'Eating cats and I don't know what other tricks. Myself, I have never approved of all that nonsense.' She was looking at Tom now, watching for his response, but he, more sensibly, was careful to preserve a neutral front. Again I thought I caught a momentary flicker in her expression, but a moment later she was serious again.

'*Cirqueros*, all of them. Which is why, so many years after my father's death, I have decided to revive the great tradition, a tradition which was still honoured during my father's lifetime, but has been brought into disrepute by so many of the quacks and charlatans operating nowadays in this town.' She raised her hands and held them out, fingers splayed, towards us. 'I have started to be able to cure cancer, you know.' She nodded sagely. 'How is this possible, you ask? She is not a doctor. Well, I will tell you.' She looked at us hard. 'It is a gift from God.'

With her red shift and her flowing black hair there was something magnificent about her woman's strength, her air of absolute wisdom and assurance. I thought I knew why they used to call witches 'wise women'. 'Well, you must go to the mountain if you must,' her tone became brisk again, 'and there you will see what you must see. But don't let it be said that I didn't warn you. This man who has agreed to take you with him tonight, I know him well. My father taught him. He is a good man, not like the others – not a proper witch, of course, not like my father, but a good man nonetheless. No harm will come to you if you go with him.'

Her fingers drummed lightly on the table in front of her. Her hands were large and bony, as Lupe's had been when I had watched her shuffling her pack of cards: a man's hands. Her nails were short and very clean, but pointed, and I wondered briefly of what they were really capable.

'Of course' – Rosalinda waited until she was sure that she had our full attention – 'of course, you do *know* what you are letting yourselves in for, don't you?'

'No, not really.' The truth was that even after all this conversation, we were no closer to discovering what really went on in Catemaco. Clearly the time had come to find out. 'No. The truth is, we don't know.'

'Before you go up the Cerro del Mono Blanco,' Rosalinda spoke the words very clearly in her pleasant, low voice, 'you must first write a letter, asking for all the things which your heart can desire. Then, when everything is ready, you must put a sum of money inside the envelope and seal it up.' She looked from one to the other of us. 'But my advice to you is that you must be very careful before you write that letter. This is not a game. You must think about what I have said, and be very sure you know what you are doing. For when anyone goes to the Cerro del Mono Blanco on this day – on the first Friday in March – it is because they wish to make a pact with the devil.' She nodded slowly. 'Yes, a pact with the devil. Now, are you still so sure you really wish to go?'

Outside Rosalinda's consulting room we sat down on the hard-backed chairs again to collect our thoughts. There is a point, which every traveller must reach at some time or another, which marks a personal limit, it can be either moral or physical, beyond which, however tempting, they are not prepared to go. That day I knew that I had reached mine.

'I am not doing anything which could even remotely be considered a pact with the devil,' I said to Tom, 'and that's that.'

There was a dry taste in my mouth. Someone had shut all the windows and the room smelt airless and stale. Then Lupe was at my side. I had not seen her come up.

'My mother told you about the letter, didn't she?' She was smiling. 'Tcha! You don't want to worry about that.' She flicked her hand dismissively in the direction of the consulting room. Beneath the clogged black lashes, her eyes were enormous. 'Don't look so shocked. It's like a letter to Santa Claus, that's all. All you have to do is write something like, 'I want to be a witness to this ceremony', that would be quite enough. You wouldn't be committing yourself to anything. You can just watch.' She walked away and went to sit down on the sofa opposite. When she moved her hips swayed beneath a tiny, serpentine waist. 'That's all you want to do, isn't it?' Her voice was soothing. 'We all know that.'

It turned out that Lupe was herself going up the mountain that night with the same man who had agreed to take us. She was bringing a friend (she was waiting for him now) who like us just wanted to spectate. Unlike her mother, she seemed very relaxed about the proceedings.

'Es muy bonita, la ceremonia. I've been lots of times, it's no big deal.' She took a comb from her bag and started to comb her hair dreamily. 'It's very pretty on the mountain. You really should come, you know, you may never get another chance.' As she talked, in her soft, soporific voice, I began to relax again. With all her warnings over pacts with the devil and eating cats, Rosalinda had frightened me; but as Lupe explained things they soon began not to seem so terrible after all. Besides, I told myself, as far as Tom was concerned the whole thing could never be any more than a ludicrous piece of pantomime anyway.

'Of course, my mother disapproves,' Lupe explained, 'that's why she's tried to put you off. But you mustn't listen to her.' She went on combing her hair, the same faraway look in her eyes. 'I promise, you won't have to do anything you don't want to do.'

As we had been instructed we arrived at the witch's house promptly at ten thirty. Lupe and her friend, a young man from Mexico City called Fernando, were already there, waiting outside in their car; with them was Elena, Lupe's sister, and a group of about four other people, all dressed in dark clothes. The atmosphere was hushed but convivial, as though some secret party were in progress. There was conversation and even some laughter; one of the women was handing out *dulces* and packets of crisps from a bag.

Even though it was close by, in the same street in fact, the witch's house was very different from Rosalinda's. The front door gave out directly on to a piece of cracked and dirty pavement. To get inside we had to push our way past a piece of sacking which had been crudely tacked to the door jamb. Whatever else, witchery had clearly not brought any great material success to this household as yet.

As Rosalinda had predicted, the witch himself was harmless enough. Since his house had only one principal room, he received us in a kind of closet, an area screened off in one corner by a piece of plastic sheeting. The whole of the left-hand wall was lined with glass jars full of unidentifiable liquids, herbs, desiccated flowers, rock minerals, roots and dried insects. On the top shelf was an owl, stuffed. I felt Tom press his shoe against my foot and glanced up to a spot just above the man's head. Suspended from the ceiling on a piece of wobbly black elastic hung a stuffed bat, wings extended, its tiny face freeze-framed in a fanged grimace.

Unlike Rosalinda's consulting room, which had been like an expensive Harley Street surgery, the effect here was like entering the set of a cheap horror film. I suppressed a wild impulse to laugh – and another one to get the hell out as fast as my legs would carry me.

'Don't forget,' Tom whispered, 'any time you feel at all unhappy, we'll just get up and go. That's the deal, remember?'

'I'm fine, I'm fine, really,' I said. 'Let's just see what he's got to say.'

The witch, who all this time had officiously been shuffling through the pile of papers on the desk in front of him, now put the tips of his fingers together and regarded us solemnly.

'First things first.' He cleared his throat with the air of someone about to make an important announcement. 'The ceremony you are about to witness on the Cerro del Mono Blanco,' he intoned, 'has nothing whatsoever to do with the devil.' He paused for effect. 'No matter what you have been told, I repeat: it has nothing whatsoever to do with the devil.'

'Good.' Tom returned his gaze steadily.

'Where we are going, I will conjure up the Spirit, whom I shall address by the name of Adonai,' the witch pronounced. 'I wish you to understand that the rituals I shall use, both before and during the Spirit's presence among us, can only be used for good. Nothing that I shall say or do can have any harmful effect on any of the witnesses present. Do you understand what I am saying?'

'Yes.' Tom nodded. 'Katie?' he turned to me. 'Are you happy about this so far?'

'I just want to know: shall we see this, er, spirit?' I asked.

The witch was small and wiry of stature with sharp, black eyes.

'It is probable that only I shall be graced enough to see Him,' he said, 'although I have known it happen that others have seen Him too. Of course, there is also a chance that He will appear in the form of one of His familiars.' He pointed, with more than a hint of pride, around at the horror-film stage set. 'A bat or an owl, for instance.'

'A bat or an owl. Yes, of course.'

'Yes, well . . .' The witch drew a pile of papers to him and had another shuffle. He cleared his throat again. 'If you'd just like to fill out these forms stating your requests' – he handed us two sheets of paper – 'and *hrumph, hrumph*, that'll be 200,000 pesos.'

'200,000 pesos!' Now it was Tom's turn to look sharp. He turned to me. 'He must be joking,' he said in English, 'that's nearly forty quid!'

We haggled a bit and finally got the price down to half that, but even so the price was extortionate, as the witch was well aware. As soon as he could he sealed up the money in an envelope and secreted it away inside a large sack on the floor beside his chair. Then, before we could change our minds, he set off nimbly to find the others.

In the woods on the Mono Blanco the night was warm and aromatic. The witch led the way, bent down beneath the weight of his bulging sack. The moon was extraordinarily bright. I was reminded of the nights in the Lacandón rain forest, every stone, every blade of grass, every leaf shining like quicksilver. We walked silently in single file, keeping close together. Every so often there was a scuffle in the undergrowth, the cry of some unseen bird through the blackness around us. We walked upwards, almost running at times to keep up with the witch, across small fields and through spinneys. The trees cast shadows on our faces as we walked beneath them.

Then, without warning, we came to a halt. Ahead of us was a small copse of trees. I could not see the witch anywhere. For a long time we stood around waiting for him to reappear, but nothing happened. There were nine of us altogether in the party. At first we stood together in silence, but we were there so long that after a while some of the others started whispering together in low voices. Lupe, who had more *sang froid* than the rest of us, ohed and aiied, and complained that ants were biting her. Her friend, Fernando, a nice-looking young man if a little weak about the mouth, who, oddly, was wearing a panama hat and a red and white spotted handkerchief around his neck, laughed and flirted gallantly with her and helped her to pick them off. 'He's ready, he's ready,' a whisper went round. 'Who's going first?' A young boy of about eighteen, who according to Lupe had come to be initiated as a witch, disappeared into the undergrowth to our right. I felt my stomach muscles contract.

'Is this it, then?' I asked her. I had not realized that we had come to the place.

'Yes,' she nodded, still holding on to Fernando's arm. 'It'll be all right. Just go in when he calls you.'

'Are you all right?' Tom took my hand and held it tightly.

'Just as long as I don't have to go in there on my own,' I nodded towards the dark undergrowth where the witch lay in wait for us. Absurd thoughts, of being bewitched or turned into a frog, came and went inside my head.

When our turn came we found ourselves walking, in total darkness, along a heavily hedged forest pathway. Neither the moon or the stars penetrated here. At the end of the tunnel we found the witch standing in a kind of lair at the base of a large tree. The trunk of the tree, which is known as an *amate*, was very broad with a split on one side beneath which was a small hollow. From behind the trunk came a glow of light from some candles; dark smoke, smelling strongly of herbs and incense, seeped from a fire which smouldered a little way off somewhere in the undergrowth.

As we approached the witch picked up our letter, which I had written out for him in Spanish, and, facing away from us towards some undefined spot in the forest, proceeded to read it out aloud. He held the letter up high between both hands.

'"We the undersigned wish to be witnesses to this ceremony, without any moral, spiritual or mental prejudice to ourselves, so that we may know better the Mexican way of life. We wish to have inspiration in our work. And for there to be no more war."' These last two 'requests' had been suggested by the witch himself;

without them he seemed to think that the spirit, or Adonai[1] as he sometimes called it, would think the whole thing too vague. At the time they seemed innocent enough and, besides, whatever misgivings I might have had about adding them in, it was too late to change them now.

'There.' He folded the letter up again and placed it inside the hollow part of the trunk. He gave us a polite, expectant look, as if he was waiting for us to leave.

'Is that all?'

I had been geared up for something more than this – fire and brimstone and claps of thunder, at the very least.

'Well, er, *hrrm*,' the witch muttered and cleared his throat again. 'You must come back again next year, see. And renew your requests.'

'And cough up another 100,000 pesos,' Tom said smoothly, in English. 'That's what he really means.'

'I think we'll be back in England by then,' I explained.

'Well, you could always telephone,' the witch added hopefully.

When he had dealt with each of our letters and the ceremony was complete, everyone went crowding down the tunnel to inspect the tree. Tom and I dragged along behind them. Although he did not say so, I could tell that Tom was tired and bored, and thought the whole thing ridiculous. After all Rosalinda's scare stories, all the waiting and the anticipation, I had to admit I was disappointed. The whole thing had been a terrible anticlimax.

The others clearly did not think so. When we joined the witch in his grotto, we found him in a high state of excitement.

'He was here, He was here.' In Spanish, the way he referred to the spirit was as 'El', or 'Him'.

'*El* estaba aquí, *El* estaba aquí. Did you hear that, did you hear? *He* was here.'

An avid murmur went round the group. I saw the pile of letters bunched together inside the hollow and thought, with regret, of our 100,000 pesos. With all the others crowding round and chattering together the place had lost its mystery. It was just a hollow tree trunk in a clearing in a wood. It was not even so very dark anymore.

[1] Later I discovered that Adonai means 'lord' in Hebrew.

'This is the very tree where your father used to do many of his *trabajos*,' the witch was explaining to Lupe and Elena. 'See here.' He pointed to the uppermost part of the split in the trunk. 'In his day there was even a picture of Him grafted on to this very spot.'

'Qué bonito! How beautiful it must have been.' I could hear Lupe's dreamy voice.

The witch did not explain why the picture was no longer visible, or what had happened to it. I began to feel impatient with them all. How could we have been so stupid as to have been conned in this way? The man was a quack after all, just as Rosalinda had warned.

Behind the trunk, I could now see where he had built a little archway of leaves, like a tiny shrine, in which more candles burnt. In front of it was the fire from which thin ribbons of incense-scented smoke were still secreting. I had a good look around, but there was nothing much else to see.

'What else, what else?' The group was hungry for more news of 'El'. The witch, still exulting in his success at having been able to 'summon' the spirit, was only too happy to oblige.

'He says that there are not enough of us,' he exclaimed, 'and that next time we must bring more people with us!'

'Yes, He's right, He's right!' The fat lady who had handed round the crisps and who was the mother of the young boy witch – and quite possibly, I realized, a witch herself – grew very excited. 'There should be more of us, it is true.'

'Yes, yes, next time we must be more!' the others agreed, looking at each other with glee.

But Tom and I could not share these feelings of exhilaration which had so gripped the rest of our party. Perhaps we should have asked 'Him', whoever 'Him' was, for something more exciting after all, I thought as we made our way back down the hillside.

As if he could sense our dissatisfaction, every few steps the witch insisted on stopping so that he could issue us with some new, and strange, directive.

'For the next few weeks you must wear your underwear inside out,' he instructed. 'It is a simple but effective remedy against the effects of witchcraft and, as you know, this is one of the best months of the year for all types of black magic.'

A few paces later he stopped again.

'And another thing: you must not eat meat, nor cut flowers.' He thought for a moment. 'And you should abstain from sex on Fridays. Lead a pure life, that's what He likes us to do.'

He walked on a little way, but then something else occurred to him. I saw him slow down until he and Tom were walking alongside each other.

'The spirit gave me a very good report of you, you know.' Ahead of me I could see Tom's bulky silhouette towering over the little man. 'In fact, He particularly mentioned you.'

'Oh really?'

I smiled to myself in the darkness.

'Yes, indeed,' the witch went on. 'You are going to have very good luck in your work.' I saw him half turn his head towards me. '. . . In fact both of you are.'

'Really.' Unimpressed, Tom increased his pace.

'Yes, yes.' The witch scampered on beside him, his sack bouncing over one shoulder. 'I have a picture of Him here. Wouldn't you like to see it?'

I had been so nervous on the way up the Mono Blanco that now that it was all over, I felt light-headed with relief. There had been nothing to worry about, nothing at all. My feet fairly floated over the pitted ground.

The witch trotted on after Tom. 'Are you sure you wouldn't like to see Him?'

'No, thank you.'

'You can take a picture of him if you like.'

Fatal words. Immediately, I saw Tom's pace slow down.

'You are a photographer, aren't you?' They were facing each other in the moonlight. 'Aren't you, Señor?'

'Yes.'

Amongst all his other paraphernalia, the witch was apparently carrying a picture of the 'spirit' in his sack.

'I sketched the Spirit as He appears to me and then I took my drawings to a friend who is an artist,' he explained, 'and he recreated my impressions in a proper painting. I feel sure you will like it.'

The unveiling of the picture was clearly something of an event.

By now we were nearly back to the group of farm buildings where we had parked our cars. In the distance I could just make out their outlines, reassuringly normal and human after our strange night on the mountain. The witch and his assistant, a little old man in rubber boots who had taken turns carrying the sack, struggled with a large square object carefully concealed beneath a swaddling of black cloth.

As before, the rest of us waited in one spot while the two of them carried the canvas off to a piece of flat, raised ground just above the path. There they spent some time arranging it to their satisfaction. In the moonlight I could watch their movements quite clearly. They propped the picture up and, kneeling down in front of it, one at either side, they lit some candles which they arranged before it on the ground. Then, one by one, they called us up.

As we waited our turn, I was aware that the atmosphere had become frighteningly charged. The others were jittery; excited but nervous too, as though some terrible marvel was about to be revealed to them. One by one they were called, until only the two of us were left waiting. Even with Tom there, quite close to me, I felt terribly alone in the darkness.

I watched the group gathered reverently around the painting, some standing, some kneeling. With the candles spitting and the cluster of half-illuminated faces, the scene reminded me, oddly, of a nativity scene by some old Dutch master. Then suddenly I knew what had been going on here all along, right under our noses. I knew what we had witnessed, what we had done. Rosalinda had been right all along. I felt a contraction of pure fear.

The painting was a portrait of a face, if you could call it that. The face was split down the middle, one side painted differently to the other. It had a monkey-like mouth and fanged teeth. Two horns sprouted from the centre of its forehead, eliding upwards and outwards, sharpened at the ends into savage points. One of its eyes was blue; the other cracked and red, and filled with blood.

'Who is it?' was all I could think of to say. I felt completely bewildered. 'Quién es?'

'Adonai! Adonai!' Still kneeling, but with one foot raised up like a herald of darkness, the witch was watching us with a triumphant expression on his face, 'El Señor de las Tinieblas. Adonai, the Lord of the Shadows.'

'Sí, sí, El Señor de las Tinieblas.' Behind me I could feel the fat woman breathing into my ear. 'Satanas, Señor de las Tinieblas.'

'*Satanas!*' Elena whispered on my other side. 'Didn't you realize? Didn't you know? Satan, of course.' Her voice was hoarse. 'Satan himself. Isn't he beautiful?'

I did not know what to do, so I remained where I was, staring at the picture. The others spoke amongst themselves in low, reverent voices.

'This is how He always appears to me,' the witch was saying knowledgeably. 'Sometimes He is small, like a tiny sprite. Other times He is ten foot tall.' He turned to Tom. 'You can take pictures now, if you like.'

In silence Tom took out the camera he had brought with him and got to work.

'Our grandfather too had many pictures of the Spirit,' Elena was saying. 'The artist did well. It is a good likeness.'

'Bonito, tan bonito,' Lupe sighed.

Fernando squatted a little way off. He too was staring at the picture in silence. I could not see the expression on his face. It occurred to me that, apart from the two of us, Fernando was probably the only other outsider here. We were surrounded by witches.

'There is a cave near San Andrés[1] where the spirit can also be invoked,' I heard Lupe say. 'With my grandfather I often spoke to him there and heard his voice.' She sighed again. 'It was so pretty, wasn't it, *hermana*?'

'Yes, I heard it too. *Muy ronco*, very hoarse. "Vamos a brindar por su espiritu".' Elena put on a deep bronchial voice and raised her hand in a mock salute. 'Now we are going to toast your spirit.'

The two sisters subsided in a fit of girlish giggles. A lock of Lupe's hair had fallen, bright red and snake-like, over her eyes, and her clothes were dishevelled from the walk through the woods. The effect gave her a strangely depraved look.

---

[1] The neighbouring town; like Catemaco, also known for its witchcraft.

'Once I went up to that cave with a spiritist,[1] a white witch,' she went on conversationally. With one hand she was stroking Fernando's head, much as you would stroke a domestic cat or dog. Fernando did not move; he seemed frightened to look at her. 'But the white witch could not help me. She said I had malign spirits around me and they were too strong for her. My grandfather had cured me of an illness once with black magic and ever since then I have had a black protector. That's what she told me anyway. Don't you think that's pretty?'

'Oh yes, very pretty.'

They went on like this for some time. They might have been talking about doing the shopping. I felt a wave of revulsion against them. When she was not being dreamy, Lupe spoke too much and too quickly. There was something dead in the expression in her eyes. When we came to say goodbye I gazed into her face and thought that she had the look of someone who had sold her soul.

---

[1] In Mexican witchcraft there are both *espiritualistas* and *espiritistas*, spiritualists and spiritists. Both cure sickness, but spiritists specialize in curing those who have been bewitched. According to Francis Toor, in *A Treasury of Mexican Folkways* (Crown Publishers, New York, 1947), 'Spirits of light are supposed to help the spiritist curer in his efforts to combat dark spirits, who work for Satanic witches.'

> ... you begin to realize why, when you ask Ameri-
> can residents ... for information, their replies are
> usually so vague, so contradictory, so unin-
> forming. It is not as a rule because they know too
> little, but because they know too much ... 'No
> hay reglas fijas, Señor.'[1] In just this, I feel sure, lies
> much of the undisputed charm of Mexico.
>
> CHARLES MACOMB FLANDRAU, *Viva Mexico!*

For a long time after we left Catemaco I was haunted by the
thought of what we had done. Or more to the point, I was haunted
by the fact that *I did not know* what we had done.

Back at the hotel that night I lay on my bed, ridiculously, with
my underwear on inside out, trying to make sense of it. I could
not get the thought of that devil face out of my mind. I was not
frightened, not exactly. I felt stained: not physically, but with
something which I can only describe as a terrible moral darkness,
as if I had just killed somebody, or eaten human flesh.

Tom, who does not believe in God, far less in the devil, tried
to comfort me.

'You didn't realize what you were doing. Neither of us did. The
witch told us categorically that his ceremony had nothing to do
with the devil – he tricked us. I don't see how your God, if he
exists, can possibly mind.'

'We took part in a Black Mass,' I said dully. 'We even wrote a
letter, put money into it and everything.'

Cool night air was blowing in through the curtains, but my skin
still felt hot, covered in a satiny sheen of sweat.

'Look, you are not responsible. It is your intent which matters,
and you did not intend to do anything wrong.' Tom was firm.

[1] There are no fixed rules, Señor.

'Kate, you mustn't allow yourself to start believing in all this. That's what they want, these people. Because once you start believing in it, that's when they really start to get a hold on you. Control, that's what this is really all about. Control and power.'

He was right, of course. And yet something inside me nagged away. I had known at the time that I had reached my limit, the limit beyond which I knew I should not go. Make no mistake, at the time it had been absolutely clear to me. Why then had I so wilfully disregarded Rosalinda? Why had I allowed Lupe to tempt me into changing my mind, when all my instincts had told me that it was Rosalinda I could trust, and not her? Had a part of me not in fact known, all along, what the outcome would be?

The next day Tom went back to the witch's house to take more photographs and to consult him, on my behalf, as to what exactly we had witnessed.

'He admitted that the spirit, or Adonai as he calls him, is Satan,' he reported back, 'but that since Satan is a fallen angel what he is doing in his ceremonies is merely appealing to the good side.'

Tom was cheerful after a morning's photography. He sat down and started to sort out bits of photographic equipment, ordering rolls of film, cleaning lenses with a soft blow-brush.

'You ought to go back there, it's not nearly so spooky in the day.'

I lay back on the bed and closed my eyes.

'No, thanks.'

Tom took my hand.

'Let it go, Kate. Really, you must. It is not worth worrying about it any more.'

'You're right, of course. I know you're right.'

But it was no good. The questions spun on and on through my mind. What was it that we had invoked on the mountain – some woodland spirit, Adonai, Satan, a fallen angel? I was no nearer the truth. Never has the absence of black and white in Mexico been so tormenting. For if even absolute blackness could contain a spark of light, then could there ever be such a thing as absolute good? Or was it true, as the Indian mind has always believed, that the two are in fact inseparable, two sides of the same coin? *El bueno contra el malo, y el malo contra el bueno.*[1]

Magic is not tricks; magic is what you believe. I knew that if I did not believe what had happened on the mountain, then it could not touch me, so I worked hard at believing that what I had done was not important. But if I could not believe in the devil, an insistent voice inside me continued to ask, how could I go on believing in God?

I am not a church-going Christian, but until now I had always had faith. In Mexico things were different. I became enmeshed in Gnostic doubts. Even if I allowed that there was still a God, how could he hear me from here? My God, I thought as I lay in my inside-out underwear, was an Englishman's god, a god made in our own image: gentle, white, middle-class, the comfortable God who presided over the Sunday school and the church fête. My God was a pale god: safe, a little smug, perhaps, knowing how to turn a blind eye. My God would be blown to smithereens by a single lapidary puff of the Mexican wind.

To survive in Mexico a god would have to be a god of the old order. An Old Testament deity, the kind of red-blooded, snarling god who was not afraid to show his hand, who still knew how to fight and curse, who would as soon strike us down with clapping thunderbolts and flashes of lightning, as suffer little children to go to him. Could I believe in such a god?

I had come to Mexico to find magic and I had found it in many guises. I had seen it in the illusory power of the circus, and on the walls of the monastery of Actopán; I had heard it in the poetry of a Lacandón's thoughts. Magic was in the hallucinogenic power of the land, in story-telling, in myth, and in the accidents and spillages of history. And in Catemaco I had found it yet again.

Today Mexicans might worship beneficent gods such as the Virgin of Guadalupe, but their souls still contain something of the steely, blood and death-obsessed spark of their ancestors; a spark which, however subliminal, still craves satisfaction. This is what I had seen in Catemaco. In Catemaco I learnt that magic – what

[1] For the Indians of pre-Conquest Mexico there was no division between a 'good' god or a 'bad' god; instead every deity had their good and bad aspects which could be invoked at will.

is conventionally thought of as 'real' magic this time – was not only about light and air and beauty, but also the expression of the blackest corners of the human psyche.

I had always known that in order to understand Mexico I had to make myself vulnerable to it, I had to learn to look into the dark. But in Catemaco I had found that there were more things under heaven and earth than I had ever dreamed. Was it possible that this richness of experience was now becoming too much, was actually dangerous? I had not known that I could be so changed by it. Sometimes I felt that I hardly knew myself anymore, let alone any god.

The circus was leaving Mexico City at last. We were not going far, just to Toluca, Omar's hometown, but it was a start. As Mara remarked, the Centro Commercial las Alamedas in Atizapán de Zaragoza had brought us nothing but bad luck. Audience levels, which had never been high, dwindled by the day in this poor, anonymous suburb. Sometimes Mundo was forced to cancel a whole show altogether.

And yet despite this my life at the circus had assumed a pattern and a familiarity which it is hard, writing as I do nearly two years later, to recapture. Did I ever think of England in those days? I think not. Yvonne had been right when she had warned me that the circus was not just a lifestyle, but a whole new life.

There were bad days, of course. Days when I felt suffocated by the lack of privacy, the capriciousness of that little dictatorship; days when I was frustrated by the circus's aggression, their ignorance, their complete lack of curiosity about anyone or anything who was not part of the circus world. But when I think back to those months I remember them as a time of intense happiness; a time filled with that warmth, that peculiar headiness, golden and tingling and airy, of first love.

But all was not well with Circo Bell's. Mara was convinced that the whole circus had been bewitched and certainly something was giving us a run of bad luck. First of all, Ilish injured himself when he fell off the roof of one of the circus trucks one night when he and some of the other *chamacos* were unloading some newly arrived equipment. Only a few days later Yvonne, too, had an accident.

It was during the second performance of the evening, when the metal apparatus, known as the *tijeras* or scissors, across which her tightrope was suspended suddenly slipped from under her. Yvonne's was a low-wire act, so she did not have far to fall; but she had landed on her head and, if the wooden boards had not been placed under her on the *pista* that night, as they very often were not, and she had landed on bare concrete, she would almost certainly have killed herself. As it was, she knocked herself out for a few moments and escaped with just a short trip to the outpatients at the local hospital.

In the circus it was generally reckoned that Yvonne had had a lucky escape. Severe spinal injuries, paralysis, mental as well as physical, and sometimes even death were often the fate of the circus performer's precarious artistry. Yvonne had suffered none of these, but nonetheless when I went to see her the next day I could see that she was not at all well.

I found her standing at the entrance of her caravan, slowly stirring something in one of the old cooking pots which cluttered the surface of her tiny stove. She was dressed in jeans and an old jersey. Without her make-up her face looked pale and fragile. Her curly, strawberry-gold-coloured hair was lank, pulled back in a ponytail, and there were dark rings under her eyes. The baby, Taynarí, was asleep in his hammock and once again I was struck by the neatness and order of the tiny space she lived in. Her whole caravan was really not much bigger than a walk-in cupboard.

'I'm all right. I was lucky, they say there's nothing wrong with me.' She stirred the pot with numb fingers. 'I'll be fine.'

'How do you feel?'

'OK.' She shrugged. 'A bit sick and pretty dizzy when I stand up. I can't seem to keep any food down at the moment, but it'll pass.'

'You're concussed, Yvonne. You should rest.'

'Concussed? They never said anything about that in the hospital.' She shrugged again. 'They just said to rest up for a while.' Glancing round at the baby, she smiled her ironic, lop-sided smile.

'Of course you should rest. She should be in bed, shouldn't she, Oly?'

I appealed to Olinda, who had also come to visit.

'*Claro*, of course.' Oly, for once, looked serious. 'I'll help you with Taynarí if you like.'

'We'll all help you.'

You must rest, we said. You mustn't move, mustn't do anything until you are well again, but of course, as she knew better than anyone, this was easier said than done. In the end she found a young girl, the daughter of an Indian woman who used to come round to the circus camp selling rice pudding out of a bucket, to help her with Taynarí, but even then, living on her own with a tiny baby to care for, it was impossible for her to rest properly.

Yvonne was strong, I knew. Hers was more than merely physical resilience; she also possessed that extraordinary mental strength, that gift for survival which was the legacy of so many of the circus women I knew. When Taynarí was born she had been through such a long and complicated labour that the doctor said it would end by killing both her and the baby if she did not agree to a Caesarean. She duly agreed, but the anaesthetic they gave her had no effect and she had screamed in agony the whole way through the operation. Even so, just two weeks after the birth she was back walking her tightrope again.

Yvonne was strong, but even she had her limits.

The night the circus set out for Toluca, our Pop-up was one of the last caravans to leave. I looked out of my window and saw Yvonne's caravan, its lights still blazing, on the far side of the now deserted parking lot. The door was open and I could see her coloured feather boas, like carnival streamers, hanging down the sides of the old cupboard. She had made no attempt to pack up her caravan. Her water butts were still in their usual place and the little striped canopy strung from the roof. A figure appeared in the doorway, a man I had not seen before. There was something proprietorial about the way he was standing, the way his forearm was propped against the lintel, the angle of his hips, as if the space there was already familiar.

'Who's that?' I asked Vicky.

'Yvonne's husband,' she told me. 'Didn't you know?'

'Know what?'

'They're getting back together.'

'No!' I said. And then, collecting myself, 'I mean, no, I didn't know.'

'We all knew she would. Eventually. That's where her place is, at her husband's side.' Vicky carefully rinsed the *bulgaros* in her yoghurt pot, added in some new milk, and then wedged it firmly into place next to the buckled refrigerator, making ready for the journey. 'She's leaving for the other circus tomorrow.'

'Yvonne!' As we drew up alongside her caravan, I called out to her from our truck window. Yvonne came to the door. 'Aren't you coming with us? Aren't you coming to Toluca?'

'No,' she said.

She met my eyes steadily, but offered no explanations. Behind her I could see a dark man sitting on the bed. He was holding Taynarí on his lap and smoking a cigarette. I could feel his presence, black and dusty, like a bird of ill omen. I hope he is good to you this time, I wanted to say, I hope he gives you your space. I wanted to tell her how brave she was, and how strong. But I said none of these things.

'Goodbye, then,' I said, knowing this was the circus way.

'Goodbye.'

We left her caravan, all alone in the deserted parking lot, its little lights shining through the night.

Yvonne's accident was one thing. The fire in the *carpa chica* — the little travelling tent — was quite another; in fact, there was considerable doubt as to whether the fire was an accident at all. It was one of those nights when Mundo had cancelled the eight o'clock performance and we had all ended up going to the cinema instead, Mara and Omar, Jorge Morales, Ramón, Gallo, Karina and myself. As we set off a police car came cruising slowly down the slip road which led towards the circus camp. They passed us and I saw Ramón, who was walking just in front of me, nudge Jorge in the ribs.

'*Oye*, aren't those the two rats who stopped us the other day?'

'Sí, hombre.' Jorge glanced after them. 'I didn't know this place was on their beat.'

One way or another the circus boys were always coming into contact with the police, so at the time I didn't think any more about it. It was not until much later, after we had returned from the cinema, that we realized something was wrong.

I was in Vicky's kitchen camper with Mara and Omar. Mara was heating up some supper on the stove and I had just gone to get some *refrescos* from the crate outside when Jorge came running up.

'Quick, there's been a fire . . . a fire, hurry!'

Jorge's bandana had slipped up over his forehead and his hair was wild and dishevelled. Omar and Mara came to the door.

'What's this . . . a fire? Where?'

'In one of the trucks parked on the other *terreno*.'

Jorge stopped to catch his breath. If there was not enough room on the circus site, Rolando sometimes hired another nearby piece of land on which to park some of the bigger vehicles.

'That's where the *carpa chica* is, and where Luis keeps the elephants' hay,' I heard Mara say. 'Does my uncle know?'

'Yes, he's there already.' Jorge retied his bandana hastily. 'There are fire engines and everything. Come on, quick!' He ran off down the road.

The other *terreno*, although it was not far away, was not visible from the main camp, but news had travelled fast. By the time we got there so had most of the rest of the circus. They were grouped in a subdued semi-circle around one of the trucks which was being hosed down by two firemen with water pumps. Gordo and Ricky were there talking to Antonino, his pale face grave. Next to them stood Martinelli and Rosalinda, the Professora, with her husband Juan. The next thing I noticed was the smell: the overpowering, sick-making stench of burning rubber.

'The *carpa chica*!' Mara put her hands to her face. 'The *carpa chica* has been burnt!'

In the back of the truck were the charred remains of half a dozen tarpaulin bundles. Some bales of hay, extra feed for the elephants which had been stored on the same truck, had been kicked on to the ground. They lay scattered beside the road, smoking gently.

Neither Rolando nor Jorge were at the circus that night, but I saw Mundo, still in his dressing gown, talking to Ramón. His thinning hair had been hastily plastered down over his forehead;

his barrel arms folded grimly across his chest. A police car drew up, its lights flashing. In Mexico, especially amongst the poorer classes, the police mean trouble: no one made a move towards them.

'Well, tents don't just burst into flames of their own accord,' Mundo was shaking his head, 'but I don't know, Ramón. I don't know.'

Ramón was about to argue with him, when one of the policemen sauntered up, thumbs hooked into his holster belt. Instead he moved over to where we were standing.

'It was those rats that did it, I'll bet you anything,' he jerked his chin over towards Mundo and the policeman. 'Jorge and me saw them, we actually saw them come down here, just as we were leaving for the cinema.'

'You think they set fire to the tent?' Mara was sceptical. 'Why would they do a thing like that?'

'To get their revenge of course, because we reported them.' Ramón explained. 'It was those same two police who stopped Jorge and Micky[1] and me in the supermarket the other day. Didn't you hear about it? It was quite late, and we had just gone in to buy some *refrescos* when these two policemen came up and started accusing us of stealing something off the shelves. It was so stupid; we'd done no such thing and we all knew it. They were just looking for an excuse to pick on us. They asked us where we lived and when we told them we were from the circus that's when they really got mean. They pushed us around a bit, to frighten us, you know how they do. *Híjole!* One of them even held his gun to my head.' Ramón described this all casually, as if this kind of thing happened every day. 'But of course all they wanted was our money. They took our wallets and just emptied them of everything we had.'

'Just like they did to Tom the other day,' I said, 'you remember, on the road to Puebla. How much did you lose?'

'*Na! No fue nada*, it was nothing. Only about one hundred and twenty thousand pesos.'

---

[1] Micky's brother Hector was married to one of Jorge Morales's sisters, Sonia Morales. They lived quite near where the circus was camped at this time and in those days often hung out at Circo Bell's.

Baby-faced Ramón shrugged it off with his usual bravura, but I knew this was just for show. The money was nearly half his weekly wage.

'Anyway, we thought, hell, they're not going to get away with it this time, hell no. Why should we let the rats shit on us all the time? So we went back to Micky's house, to talk to his mother. Of course, as you know Micky's mother is kind of a senior lady, some distant cousin of Salinas Gotari (the Mexican president). The police would never dare mess with her, that was how we figured it anyway. And can you imagine how pissed off she was when she heard how the police had roughed up her precious son?'

I could see the whites of Ramón's eyes glistening with satisfaction. Everyone liked Micky, who had a shy smile and a sleepy way of talking out of one corner of his mouth, but among the circus boys he was considered a bit of a *fresa*.

'Right there and then we all went down to the police station to lodge a complaint,' Ramón went on. 'We felt safe because we knew that the police would never dare mess with Micky's old lady.' He pulled a face. 'It's a pity we never stopped to think that they might come after us instead.'

Of course, no one ever managed to prove that the two policemen we had seen that evening had anything to do with the arson attack on the *carpa chica*. And despite the fact that almost everyone subscribed to Ramón's theory, it did not occur to any of them that there was anything they could do about it. The tent was a write-off.

As my friend the impresario, Rolando Bell's used to say, the story of the circus is a tragic one. 'You must write about the sad things; it is important that you do. No one can understand the circus without them,' I can remember him saying, waving his perfumed hands at me. Accidents, fires, rapes and fights, even just the daily struggle to survive. Oh, yes, I knew all about the sad things.

In the old days, I can remember Doña Elena the matriarch telling me, in the days when priests ruled the villages and men would go to the show just to see a girl's legs, the circus used to travel the country by mule. Sometimes I would think about things as they had been then, imagine them dragging themselves, step by step, across mountains and burning plains. The animals' leather halters would creak and jangle, and the women's skirts would be hemmed with dust. For days on end there would be nothing to eat but dried tortillas and beans but, in my mind, the raggle-taggle cavalcade was always marching steadily, onwards and upwards, their eyes trained to the horizon.

Doña Elena was the memory of the circus. In her were preserved all the stories that existed about Circo Bell's, all the myths that had ever been told, held for safekeeping inside her head.

'Of course in '54 we had nothing.' Fastidiously she re-arranged herself amongst the broken feathers and *bastonera* outfits in Karina's caravan. 'We had nothing, nothing at all. Then one day my son Yanko – that was my eldest son who died, may he rest in paradise – came to me. "What shall we do?" he said. "We can't go on like this, Mamá. I've been thinking," he said. "I have a friend who says that he would be willing to lend us a tent. What we should do is to start up on our own, just hire some other artistes and start travelling. As soon as we start to make some money we can begin to pay back the loan of the tent, in instalments."

'He was only seventeen, you know, my son, my beautiful Yanko, when he decided that we should found a new circus. He went to my husband – a man for whom, as you know, I had nothing but contempt and bitter hatred' – Doña Elena's rings flashed with green and bitter fire – 'he went to my husband and he said to him: "I have made an important decision. I am making my mother the new circus administrator. From our proceeds we will give you a salary each week, but only as long as you promise never to interfere with the circus's running."

'He knew, as well as I did, that the moment my husband had anything to do with the enterprise, everything would be squandered in gambling and cabarets.'

Doña Elena's red lips puckered slightly, as if she had taken a bite of some piece of fruit and discovered half a worm in the remainder.

'And so it was. From that day on I was the one who sat in the *taquilla* every night and sold the tickets. I was the one who paid all the employees, who kept the accounts. No tickets were given away and no books were fiddled, everything was kept as it should have been. And do you know what? We were full every night. Lleno, lleno.' Doña Elena leant forwards, the fingers of each hand bunched together for emphasis. '*Lleno*, like this. We paid for that tent within four days. Increíble! But that is how it was.

'Even though we paid for the borrowed tent almost immediately, I decided that I was going to make my own tent. It was only a small tent, not like these big Italian *carpas* that you have now, just small tent, but *muy bonito. Ay*, I remember making that tent.' She sat back silkily amongst the bank of pink feathers. 'I used to sit up long into the night stitching until my very fingers bled.

And it was just as well that I did. Only a few months after we were in Celaya, in the north, a sandy, windy place buffeted by desert storms. The Big Top was full that night, full to bursting point, just like it had been all the other nights since we opened. The performance had only just started when the winds began to blow. At first the only thing I noticed was a whispering through the bars in the *taquilla*, so low that I thought it was just a singing in my ears. But the whispering grew steadily louder, until eventually we could all hear it, a clear glassy sound like desert mermaids calling across the sands.

'The sound grew louder and louder, until not only the *taquilla*, but the whole of the circus camp was humming with it. The guy ropes started to groan and strain, and the tarpaulin to snap like the wings of a boat on the high seas.' She put her old woman's hands to her ears. 'Ay, I still hear that sound in my dreams sometimes, the sound of the wind tearing with its sharp claws at our beautiful tent.

'My son Yanko realized at once that sooner or later the whole thing was going to blow. There was nothing any of us could do about it. He went inside, stopped the performance, and ordered everybody out. Ten minutes later a great puff of wind carried the whole tent away. Away, away, up, up . . . and a-way!'

Doña Elena turned her kohl-darkened eyes skyward, as if watching the tent spiralling out of sight, the ropes dragging behind it like the tentacles of some billowing sea monster, getting smaller and smaller, until it was lost for ever, her tent, her beautiful new tent, disappearing over the horizon.

In Mexico I lost my faith in God, but in all my time there I never had cause to doubt the resilience of the human spirit. The history of the circus is a tragic one, as Rolando was fond of saying; but when I came to write Doña Elena's stories down I found that for every story of hurricanes and lost tents and the circus disbanding, was another about how they had come together again, and started out afresh. Her stories were stories of regeneration and living proof of the circus's infinite capacity to survive.

We had left Mexico City at last.

Along with most of the other circus vehicles, the Pop-up had travelled to Toluca during the night so when we woke up on that first morning it was to find almost all the other caravans already arranged around us in their usual semi-circle. Rolando's family caravan and the kitchen camper were on one side of us, while on the other was Brissel's parents' trailer and Jovita's wardrobe.

I sat down on the Pop-up steps, breathing in the early morning air, and looked around me. The new *terreno* was a grassy, litter-strewn space in the middle of a large piece of urban wasteland. To my left, beyond the other caravans, were some government offices and a large Aurera supermarket; facing ahead of me (and soon to be obscured by the Big Top) was a small road lined with pepper trees and a length of crumbling wall scrawled with political graffiti, mostly green and red PRI propaganda. Behind the camp, in the centre of the wasteland, were the beginnings (or the remains, it was hard to tell which) of a half-constructed building, a concrete skeleton bristling with metal rods like exposed bones.

Rosalinda, the telepathic Professora, still in her curlers, with a pair of jeans on under her dressing gown, appeared in the doorway of the next-door caravan.

'Buenos días.'

'Buenos días.'

'What do you think of the new *terreno* then?'

Looking round, Rosalinda wrinkled her nose.

'Feo, bien feo,' she shook her head. 'Ugly, really ugly. Trust that brother of mine.' Her hair, like her daughter Brissel's, was reddish, the colour of ripe buckwheat. 'And it's going to be cold, too. You mark my words.' The morning was brilliantly sunny, but with a chill in the air. Rosalinda pulled her dressing gown more closely around her shoulders. 'So close to Christmas, I don't know what he could be thinking of. Toluca must be one of the coldest places in *Mexico*,' she grumbled.

'Is the electricity connected yet?'

'No, but I've got some hot water in a thermos, Juan got it for me from that *comedor* over the road. I was just making coffee, Katty. You want some?'

'Thanks.'

'Hey, Antonino,' Rosalinda called over to one of the other caravans, 'coffee – you want some?'

'Sure.'

Antonino came over and sat down next to me on Rosalinda's step.

'How was your journey?'

'Long.' Antonino stirred three sugars into his cup. '*La Chuchina* wasn't supposed to circulate yesterday[1], so we got stopped by the police three times. Twice by the same guys and all.' He smiled sleepily and took a mouthful of coffee. 'And then Ramón got lost on the *periferico*, but we got here all right in the end.'

'Nonsense! I bet you were asleep the whole way. Antonino could sleep through an earthquake, couldn't you, my love?' Rosalinda topped up his cup from her thermos. 'Unlike that Gallo, mooning about with Karina till all hours of the night like a couple of lovesick cats,' Rosalinda pronounced sourly. 'You should have a word with her, Katty.'

It was assumed, erroneously I always thought, that I had some kind of influence with Karina.

'No wonder she scowls so during the performances.' Rosalinda started to unpin her curlers. 'Oh, good.' She looked up. 'Look, here comes Chivo with the water tanks. Go and get your buckets, you two, we're in business.'

The first day at a new *terreno* was always like this. People wandered around the camp discussing the move and the new position of the caravans; finding out about supplies of water and

---

[1] To stop traffic congestion in Mexico City, every vehicle has one day of the week when it is forbidden for it to be driven.

electricity, and where the nearest market was to be found. At the far end of the semi-circle I could see Güera with her two children, Gabriella and Alejandro, talking to Jovita, and Carmen hanging out some damp clothes to dry. Some of the *chamacos*, including Ilish and Chillón, were cleaning up the ground with rakes and brooms. Beyond them, positioned at the far side of the circular space where the Big Top would eventually go, was the solitary box-office trailer. Leaning up against its white, wrought-iron gates, I saw Olga sitting on one of the steps, her eyes closed and her face turned towards the sun. Without the familiar red and white striped carousel to shield us from public view, the *terreno* felt oddly naked and exposed.

The elephants' tarpaulin had been put up next door to the box-office trailer and so later on I wandered over with my supply of scraps. As usual, Luis's tiny bubble caravan was parked nearby. There was no sign of Luis; instead, Maria-Magdalena beckoned to me from her doorway.

Luis's wife, Maria-Magdalena, was as tiny, dumpy and vivacious as Luis was large and lugubrious. Together they had two daughters, Lupita, an exquisite child of six with creamy skin and the pale green eyes of a changeling; and Jacaira, aged four, who was dark and mischievous like her mother.

Maria-Magdalena was Luis's third wife.

'Luis has had many *golpes*, many blows in his life,' she told me once. 'When I first met him there was something very sad inside him. It was as if a hungry ghost had become trapped inside him, chewing and gnawing away at his insides. He used to sit with his head down, like this' – she dropped her chin to her chest – 'not speaking to anyone. Often he would not even bother to go to bed, but just fall asleep wherever he happened to be sitting.'

Luis's first wife had been a northerner like himself. He had a clutch of children by her and all was well until he had begun his first job with the circus. Unlike her husband, Luis's wife did not take to the travelling life, preferring to stay behind on the *rancho* with the children, spending the long evenings alone watching the rolling tumbleweed. Or so she said. Luis was away touring for six months before he was able to get away to visit his family. When he came back he found his wife pregnant again, by another man. He did not stop at home long enough to find out who.

His second wife, a Colombian, had been killed in a road accident while the circus was on tour in South America. Maria-Magdalena had met him back in Mexico when he was on tour with the circus in Zacatecas.

'That is where I am from, from a little village there, *muy escondido*, very remote, you would not know it. No one believed that I would stay with him. They thought I would only be with him for a day or two, that I would soon come back. But something about this big sad man, this man who said so little and slept so much, made me decide to stay with him. That was seven years ago now, and as you can see I am still here.'

On that first morning in Toluca I found Maria-Magdalena chopping vegetables in her caravan. In one tiny fat fist she wielded the kitchen knife, while with the other she swept the vegetable peelings dextrously on to the floor beside her. They joined a growing pile of debris which had collected in one corner of the caravan. From the inside the caravan seemed even smaller, if that was possible, than it looked from the outside, a contraption made for gnomes. At one end was a tiny bed boxed in on either side with shelves. At the other end a table and chairs, a rickety home-made cupboard regurgitating clothes, and a rusting cooker. Except for the inevitable pictures of the Virgin of Guadalupe, the chipboard walls were undecorated.

I was consumed with desire to see Luis inside his own caravan. How did the poor man manage? I could barely stand up inside it myself. I glanced at the tiny bed. He would have to concertina himself down by several sizes before he could conceivably fit into that. Perhaps that was why he spent so much time each evening sitting on the bales of hay outside. I imagined him, arms and legs spilling out through the windows and the door, wearing the caravan like a snail's shell across his back. And yet lie somewhere they undoubtedly did, for Magdalena had recently discovered that she was expecting another baby.

The smell of the goat — Magdalena wrinkled her diminutive nose — was making her feel sick.

'I'll have to get Luis to move him away a little. Normally the smell never bothers me, but in the last few weeks, *ay*, I just can't stand it.'

She shuddered at the thought. Outside I watched the milk-white goat, its eyes like two yellow crescent moons, cropping rhythmically.

Luis's dogs, both his own and those which he had either adopted or rescued, roamed around the caravan or slept in the sun. There was Reina (in English, Queenie) an old dog paralysed in her back legs, whom Luis had rescued, screaming with pain, from the side of the road one night. Someone had run her over in their car and left her to die there. Luis had heard her cries and had taken her back to the generator truck where he kept the other dogs. He bandaged her up and brought her food and water every day, but she would not eat, growing thinner and sicker until eventually, on the fifth day, he decided that she was not going to recover. He took out his gun, determined that the kindest thing to do was to shoot her, but when he looked at her lying there in the straw, looking up at him with her patient, tortured eyes, for some reason he found he could not. He left her there. The next day she started to eat again.

After Reina there was Lobo, an excitable Alsatian who was usually kept chained up to Luis's caravan so that he would not be tempted to stray; and Terri, a little shaggy thing like a Shih-tzu. As a puppy Terri had been given to Karina who had loved him and played with him, cosseting him like one of her favourite dolls, until he made the mistake of growing into a full-sized dog, after which she callously lost interest and would not even have him in her caravan. Luis took her over. Then there were the two Negras, or Blackies: one was the poodle which had once been part of some long-forgotten troupe of performing dogs and who would still occasionally show off by walking along on her hind legs; the other, a meek mongrel which in theory belonged to Brissel, but had suffered the same fate as Terri. Lastly there were two bigger black and tan mongrels, and another poodle, the one which in a spate of hot weather Luis had once decided to clip, but had been interrupted in the middle, leaving the dog with three smooth thin legs and one disproportionate, fat, fluffy one. No one could remember the genesis of these last three and I never knew anything much about them except that whenever we travelled they shared a truck with the generator and were subsequently always covered in thick layers of soot.

Outside, Magdalena's daughters, Jacaira and Lupita, played in the dust. Magdalena saw me watching them.

'They're growing up so fast,' she smiled. 'It will be time to send them to school soon.'

'Where will you do that?'

Schooling for the circus children was a perennial problem, I knew. Magdalena reached for a cabbage and started to shred it with her knife.

'We talk of leaving the circus sometimes, going back to Zacatecas maybe, somewhere where we can be near a good school.'

'Luis talks of leaving the circus?'

'You know what he's like. He says he's tired of it, that the circus is not the same as it used to be, with the younger generation growing up so fast now, and starting to take things into their own hands. "Those boys," he says to me sometimes. "Ellos no saben nada, nada! They know nothing, nothing!" As a punishment Ricky once stuck his *domador*'s spiked pole into Hannibal's ear, making her trumpet with pain – and all the audience scream. And Gordo hit Julie so hard during the act that she had an infected sore on her head for weeks afterwards. He hates to see them treat his animals like that, but they're the bosses' sons, so there's nothing he can do.'

'They are young boys, that's all. They don't mean to be cruel.'

'He's had enough, that's what he's always saying to me. He says he's going to take us back north, to his *rancho*. It's the only other life he knows, *ves*, apart from the circus.'

'Do you think he means it?'

'Are you crazy?' She smiled again, showing her gold front teeth. 'That may be what he says, but I know better than that. He'll never leave,' she said. 'He'll never leave his animals, his elephants. Never. Don't you know how it is? If they don't have enough to eat, he won't eat. He would not know what to do without them.'

I thought back to our first night at the circus. I remembered how I had seen Luis then, sitting silently as he always did, on the bales of hay outside his caravan in his old green coat and his baseball hat, his countryman's feet, fissured like ancient stones, thrust into a pair of rotting sandals. As I fell asleep I could hear the soft whiskery breath of the elephants as they swayed together and I wondered even then if it was true what they said and that Luis could understand their silent pachyderm song.

Doña Elena was the keeper of the circus stories, but others too had their own tales to tell, their own variations and eye-witness accounts, subplots which ran like brilliant hybrids through the authorized garden of the matriarch. Big Luis, a keeper of another kind, had been with the circus so long – longer even than Jovita, and it was impossible for anyone to imagine Circo Bell's without her – that no one, not even Luis himself, could remember exactly how many years it was. Perhaps it was in Celaya, or somewhere thereabouts, round about the time that Circo Bell's lost their tent in the great desert winds, that Luis Velasquez García joined the circus. Certainly he came from up north, from a little ranch near Ciudad Anáhuac in Nuevo Leon, that lonely land of lawlessness and dust, where the endlessly rolling tumbleweed can be the only sign of life a man might see for weeks on end.

On Luis's father's tiny *rancho* they grew cotton to sell at market, maize and frijoles for their own consumption. They were a large family and there were always animals around, dogs and horses, and mules to help with the ploughing, and so Luis grew used to their ways from an early age. For all his years travelling with the circus Big Luis never lost the feel of the soil beneath his feet, never learnt to wear his shoes like a city man. Instead, no matter what the inclemency of the weather, his huge cracked feet thrust out like fossils from a pair of ancient *guaraches*, the home-made leather sandals of the countryside.

Despite his imposing size, Luis was only ever Big Luis privately to Tom and me. To everyone else he was *Don* Luis, a title of respect earned by only one other person that I knew, Doña Elena herself. In the circus, Luis's temper was legendary. A man of few words, on his family *rancho* he had learnt early on in life that bullets speak louder than the human voice, and although slow to be riled he was known always to keep a loaded gun in his caravan for any eventuality — a fact which everyone, even Gordo and Ricky, knew how to respect. (And just in case they should be tempted to forget, on high days and holidays, such as his daughters' birthdays, he would make a point of bringing out his gun and firing it into the air in salute.)

Like Doña Elena herself, Luis could remember back over several decades of circus history, not only to the bad times, but to the good times too, those marvellous years when Circo Bell's had been the nonpareil amongst circuses, when the three brothers, the most handsome men the circus world had ever beheld, dominated the flying trapeze; those heady years of the *Chica Maravilla*, of the Living Sculptures, and of *Los Invencibles*.

Luis's greatest memories are of his animals. In those days it was not, as Doña Elena once put it, three mingy elephants, but an entire bestiary: leopards, lions, panthers and tigers, rhinoceros and hippopotami, horses, ponies, dogs and sleek Siberian wolves. As Doña Elena thinks back to the conquests of her handsome sons, to the rows of starlets, the platoons of feathered *bastoneras* and the massed ranks of jewelled dancing girls, so Luis thinks back to the glories of his former menagerie: to those fleets of trucks, their bellies full of snarling cages, those snorting, barking, snuffling, roaring cages, steaming with hot dung, bright with spotted and striped pelts; to the smell, overpowering to all but the initiated, of the rank and angry breath which sang out between the bars like a maleficent wind.

Now, reduced to just three elephants, I sometimes used to think that they were more like his children than his charges. He knew them with an intuitive intimacy, more like a mother than a father, which told him of their most invisible ailments, and of their subtlest moods. If Hannibal was feeling irritable, if Penny had a stomach-ache from eating plastic bags (for which she had a secret addiction), Luis would always know.

It had not always been this way.

'When I first came to the circus it was as a *velador*, a night-watchman,' Luis told me once as we waited together in the wings with the elephants for the parade to begin, 'but I didn't like that so much. So I left and went to another circus. But that job didn't last long either, and so because I needed the money I came back here. My job as a *velador* had already been filled by someone else, so instead I was taken on as one of the animal keepers.

'My first job was as a butcher. I had to slaughter the old donkeys which were bought to feed to the big cats, the lions, leopards and tigers. After that I spent two years with the wolves, and another two with the horses. Then I came over to the elephants. That was more than twenty years ago, and I have been with them ever since.'

Luis was with the circus when it went on its fateful three-year tour of South America. He remembers how they left with everything and came back with nothing, the famous menagerie squandered and spent – a leopard given away here, a panther gambled there – until the splendid convoy of animals was reduced to just one truck.

'Out of the entire menagerie we were left with just five elephants and one hippopotamus,[1] that's all. By that time the circus was disbanded, finished. Apart from the animals they had been forced to sell all the tents, see, the vehicles, the lorries, everything was all washed up. Most of the artistes had already flown back to Mexico, but of course you can't put a hippopotamus in an aeroplane, not so far as I know, so it was decided that one of the drivers and me should drive this last truck back overland.'

Luis straightened Hannibal's headdress, gave a twitch to Julie's crimson draperies.

'All was well until we got to Panama when our truck, which was very old, broke down. There was nothing for it but for one of us to travel back to the capital to find a new part that was needed. So the driver goes off, while I stayed behind with the animals and the truck. It was only after he had gone that I realized he had taken all our money with him. I was stranded there, miles from anywhere, without a peso to my name, not even enough to buy a packet of cigarettes. I didn't know how long he was going to be away – it turned out to be six days that I was there waiting for him, all alone with nothing.

[1] Back in Mexico it was decided that the hippopotamus, Miss Tequila, had grown too old for the circus and she was eventually retired to Guadalajara zoo; one of the five elephants died, and when the circus was started up again another was swapped in exchange for a new tent, leaving just the three that are there today, Penny, Julie and Hannibal.

'Well, I sat down at the side of the road thinking to myself, what am I going to do? But there was nothing to do. So I sat there all day, doing nothing. When evening came and I had fed the animals – luckily we had plenty of feed for them – I climbed back into the truck, thinking that if nothing else at least I could sleep for a while. I was just dropping off when I heard this little sound at the door. And it was this girl, see, a child of about six years old, and her brother.

'"Oye, Señor," they called up to me. "Are you hungry?"

I had not eaten anything all day so I said that I was.

"Yes, little daughter, I certainly am," I said.

'"Here, take this then, Señor," said the girl, handing me a bowl wrapped up in a cloth. "My mother says that you can eat this."

'So that night, at least, I did not go hungry. But, of course, when I woke up the next morning I was in the same way as before: all alone, with no money and nothing to eat. I was just wondering what I was going to do, when there was this little sound at the door, just like the last time. I looked out and this time I saw a young boy looking up at me.

'"Oye, Señor," he says to me. "Are you hungry?"

'"Yes, little son, I certainly am," I told him, just like the last time.

'"Take this then," the boy says, handing me some fruit. "My father says you are to eat this for your breakfast."

'And so it went on. Every morning and evening a different child came to my truck bringing me food. The people from thereabouts were poor and so of course the things they brought me were simple enough, fruit from their orchards, beans and maize, but all the same I knew that they were the best things they had to give. I did not know what to do. How could I ever repay these kind people? I thought and thought, and eventually I walked down into the village to see what could be done. "I have no money," I said to them, "but I am strong, a farming man like yourselves. I can dig and plough and wield an axe. Maybe there is something I can do for you, to repay you for your kindness?"

'But they just laughed and said there was no need for me to trouble myself.' Luis put his hand on Hannibal's flank. Inside the tip of her enquiring trunk the skin was tender and pink. 'I was sad when I heard this because I wanted to do something for them. There was this woman and she must have realized that I was feeling badly because she pipes up suddenly,

'"Oye, Señor," she says to me. "You are Mexican, aren't you?"

'I said that I was.

'"And if you are Mexican," she says, "you must be able to sing. Can you sing?"

"Sure, I can sing," I told her. "I would not be a true Mexican if I could not sing."

"Well then," this woman says, "sing for us. That is all the payment that we require. You can repay us with your songs."

'And so I sang for them. I have a good voice (once I used to sing with a mariachi band) and I know many songs, both mariachi songs and folk songs of many kinds, and so every evening I went to the village to sing my songs, my payment to these good people who had taken pity on me in my hour of need.'

FOURTEEN

> Those who do not believe in saints, will not be
> cured by the miracles of saints.
> ALEJO CARPENTIER, *El Reino de este Mundo*

Tom was learning to be a clown. Not just a walk-on, walk-off
clown in the parades and processions, a role which he had often
been roped into in the past in order to pad out the numbers, but
the real thing this time. As Clown Fatty-Fatty, Tom became a
payaso with a purpose. A *payaso* with an act.

Despite its initially depressing aspect, Toluca had effected one
of those inexplicable sea-changes in the fortunes of the circus
which Doña Elena's stories so frequently presaged. Suddenly, for
no particular reason that I could discover, we were playing to
fuller audiences than I had ever seen at Circo Bell's. In Atizapán
de Zaragoza, much as I enjoyed the long hours squashed into the
wardrobe devising new and daring combinations of eyeshadow
with Karina or reading Mara's *Book of Spells* or watching *telenovelas* on Jovita's old black and white TV, I had become disillu-
sioned with the idea of spending so much of my time preparing
for such tiny audiences and, if it had not been for Hannibal, my
enthusiasm for the parades might well have started to dwindle.

But in Toluca the circus's new lease of life inspired everyone.
Mara hardly mentioned her *limpias*; Maria-Magdalena stopped
feeling sick every time she stood downwind of the goat; Doña
Elena appeared to become reconciled to the idea of her lascivious
younger granddaughters showing off their tummy buttons in
public. Even Mundo, ever the most taciturn of the three brothers,
lost something of his usual worried air.

It was Mundo who started Tom off on his circus career. As

well as being the catcher in the trapeze act, resplendent in silver lamé, sequins and puffs of white chalk, Mundo also played the part of Mr Bell's, the circus's principal clown. As Mr Bell's, Mundo was the mainstay of the show's three comic acts; in addition, he also took part in the parades at the beginning and at the end of each performance, as well as being the circus's 'artistic director'. No wonder poor Mundo so often looked harassed.

Of the three brothers, it was with Mundo that the main responsibility of the circus (with all its dramas and its shaky finances, all the snap-crackle-pop of youthful hormones flying about) rested. At the beginning I had thought of them as a kind of entity. The Three Brothers, rather like the Three Bears, or the three Hear-no-evil, See-no-evil, Speak-no-evil monkeys; nominally independent, but in fact only having meaning in relation to each other, a trio of barrel-chested, sawdust-coated, eau-de-cologne-scented, Russian dolls.[1]

The truth was that it was Mundo, the least flamboyant of the three, who held the show together. It was Mundo alone who was at Circo Bell's on a day-to-day basis, with Rolando and Jorge, rather in the manner of their mother, both putting in the occasional royal appearance, wafting about in a haze of aftershave as if they owned the place,[2] which livened things up no end for all of us, but must often have been very trying for poor Mundo.

Despite living in such close proximity, the adults in Mundo's and Rolando's families had little contact with one another. It was a notorious fact of circus life that Señora Vicky and Señora Carmen, as Rolando and Mundo's wives were respectfully known, did not get on. As for Mundo and Rolando themselves, well, perhaps because I saw them together so infrequently, I found it hard really to fathom the true extent of their brother love.

One afternoon I came across Mundo standing outside his

[1] This was not entirely fanciful. They really did all look so similar, particularly Rolando and Jorge, whose appearances at the circus coincided so infrequently that for a long time I would regularly find myself in conversation with Jorge, believing him to be Rolando, and vice versa, and had some extremely puzzling conversations as a result.
[2] This was true in Rolando's case, but not in fact in Jorge's. It was Doña Elena who owned the third share of the Circo Bell's business.

caravan, half dressed for the first performance, gazing after his brother through beetle brows.

'Ay, este simpatico . . .' He gestured after him. His arms, the muscles of which were pneumatically swelled, like a medium-sized sumo wrestler's, hung down helplessly by his sides. 'Este simpatico . . .' His fingers twitched. 'That brother of mine, he's a complete joker you know.' He turned to me in exasperation. 'No sooner has he arrived, than he's off again. Skiving as usual!'

Mundo had his Mr Bell's face-paint on and part of his Mr Bell's costume, a stripy granddad's shirt tucked into a pair of boxer shorts. Compared to his extraordinary torso, the legs which poked out from beneath the boxers were pitifully weedy and thin. On his feet he wore a pair of old trainers. I watched Rolando, immaculately dressed in his hoodlum's suit and a crisp pink Dior shirt, walking smartly over towards the main road, tell-tale overnight bag in hand. From the back of his neck I could tell that he felt uncomfortable: perhaps he could feel Mundo's eyes still following him in fury.

'Women and cabarets . . .' I mused, watching Rolando let himself out through the box-office gates.

'What was that?'

'Oh, nothing. Nada.'

No matter what Doña Elena always said about her sons, I somehow doubted that Mundo knew anything about women and cabarets. Mundo was different from the other two brothers. Mundo was serious. Like Rolando and Jorge, Mundo might have the body of a trapeze artist, but his soul was that of a clown. Even if his heart was breaking, you felt he would still be laughing and tripping over and spurting water at you from a paper flower in his button hole.

'I remember the night my father died,' he told me. 'I was standing behind stage, ready for the performance as usual. We all knew how sick my father was, of course, but what could we do about it? The show must go on, as we say. The music signalling the clown act began, but just as I was about to step out through the curtains I caught sight of Yanko, my eldest brother, at the door of my father's caravan. Just from the way he was standing I knew that something was wrong. He caught my eye and nodded at me,

without saying anything: just tilted his head slightly forwards.'
Mundo motioned with his head. 'And I knew then that my father
had died.

'I was grief-stricken. Even though I was a grown man I wanted
to cry; I wanted to lie on the floor and shout and scream and sob.
I was overwhelmed – I had loved my father so much. But stronger
than any of these things was the sound of the music playing. It is
something so deep inside you . . . But, ah! If you are not *del circo*
it is almost impossible to explain it. Perhaps I should not even try.
Even at that moment, surely one of the saddest moments in my
life, all I could think about was that act. I knew it could not be
done without me; I knew the others depended on me to make it
work. My father was dead, but I did not hesitate. I *could* not. Even
though the tears were running down my face, the next moment I
was out there, out in the ring as usual.'

Mundo knew everything there was to know about clowns. The
clown acts used by most circuses are traditional ones, but Mundo
knew exactly where each one had originated – Italy, Germany,
Russia or America – and how they had been adapted for the
Mexican audience. He knew all the different stage make-ups of
all the famous clowns from all over the world, and could apply
them without hesitation, using a set of special greasepaints made
up for him to Doña Elena's own exacting recipe.

'This one was the Great Chupin's,' he would say as he made
Tom up before a performance, rubbing white stuff all over his
face and then adding a little black brush moustache with black
starry circles around his eyes. Or, 'This one was invented by my
father-in-law, who was a very famous Mexican clown, *el payaso*
Betonini, "Rey de las Carcajadas", the King of Guffaws.'

Unlike the girls, who always used Jovita's Wardrobe to change
in, Mundo and the boys generally used their own caravans. So
whenever Tom was back from his photographing expeditions, he
would collect his Fatty-Fatty clown suit from Jovita, change in
our caravan, and then go over to Mundo's to get made-up. He
always called Mundo 'Maestro', Teacher, which pleased them
both.

During these make-up sessions they would have long conversations, Tom sitting on one of their water butts, clutching the

rubber tubing in his billowing clown suit; Mundo in his usual pre-performance *déshabille* – grandpa shirt and boxers, or an old blue *bata* which he sometimes wore, stained down the front with splashes of greasepaint, glistening and brown now, like ancient gravy stains. As he worked, Mundo would expound his theories about clowning and clown lore, and sometimes even a trick or two of the trade. Which is how Tom's new career began.

'You see, the thing is, Tommy' – for some reason all three brothers had taken to calling Tom by this name – 'the thing is, everyone has another person inside of them, see. Everyone: men, women, children, even *los abuelitos*, the grannys and the grand-dads. Everyone has this clown person inside them, a silly, childlike being who likes to laugh and joke – literally clown around. Even the most timid people, the ones who never dare to behave like that in real life, need that kind of release.'

Like his brothers, Mundo's voice was deep and gravelly, as if he had smoked too many Gauloises. Compared to Rolando, whose dialogue resembled something between a gangster movie and one of Jovita's more salacious *telenovelas*, Mundo's conversation was measured and gentlemanly. Whereas Rolando delighted to teach us new and exotic manipulations of his favourite insults, there was something almost puritanical about Mundo, who would have blushed to think that I even knew such words existed.

Never as worldly as either of his brothers, Mundo had the toughness but also the curious innocence of someone born and bred within the purdah of the circus world. He spoke of the circus, and everything to do with the circus, with an intense and consuming passion. In fact, I rarely heard him talk of anything else. The circus was his life.

'That is what the circus – but particularly the clown acts – are all about, see. Release. Release from the everyday.' Warming to his subject, Mundo slapped more greasepaint on to Tom's forehead, rubbing it in briskly with his huge hands. 'In some ways the circus is like a fiesta.' He paused to think about this, his painted face with its smiling red and white watermelon mouth poised thoughtfully to one side.

'Yes, a fiesta! That's what. Why do you think the carnival in Rio is always such a success? Why do you think our own carnivals have always been so important in Mexican life? Did you know that every single day of the year, somewhere in Mexico, there is a fiesta, a carnival, or a saint's day being celebrated? Every single day. Increíble, no?'

From time to time Mundo would stop, as if gauging Tom's response, but a *sí* or a *no* was usually enough to satisfy him, and then he would be off again.

'You see, Tommy, the fiesta gives people the opportunity to escape from *lo cotidiano*, the boring drudgery of everyday life.' Mundo took out a stick of red colouring and, after some consideration, started to draw in star shapes around Tom's eyes. He worked neatly and with delicacy. In his hands the stick of paint looked no bigger than a child's crayon. 'Boring jobs, boring housework, all the boring, tedious aspects of bringing up children.' He dabbed away expertly. 'It gives people the chance to escape from this everyday life, to become that other person; to give vent to that gay, extrovert, wild heart which beats inside every bank clerk. Well, it is the same with the circus, with my clown act. Everyone loves a clown because secretly they have always identified with him. They long to become a clown themselves. He is their fiesta self.'

For many weeks Tom was content, as I was, just to go out in the parades. Mundo had taught him a special walk in which he was supposed to trot along waving at the crowd while at the same time, by bending at the knees, lowering himself gradually down to the floor. When he had got as low as possible, he was supposed to look down at himself in mock horror and, taking a lock of his hair, pretend to pull himself up again to his full height. Like all these things, it was much more difficult than it looked, and Tom practised endlessly.

One of the gags in Mundo's clown act involved playing a trumpet. It was a real trumpet which, being a natural musician, we would often hear him playing in his caravan. During the gag he was supposed to play it badly, whereupon one of the other clowns came up behind him and kicked him in the bottom.

'Go on, you've seen it done,' he said as we stood around waiting for Antonino's equilibrium act to finish, 'now you give me a kick.'

'Really?' Tom looked surprised. 'OK, then.'

He aimed a good kick at Mundo's proffered bum, stopping just short of actually touching him, as he had seen the others do.

'That's it, nice one.'

'What's all this, Uncle?' Mara came up, wrapped up tightly in her *bata* and teetering on her tiny silver shoes. 'Are you trying to get one of these two into a real act at last?'

'Who knows, who knows.' Mundo was concentrating. '*Vamos*, Tommy. Now I'm going to show you how to land a punch.'

He showed Tom how to simulate a punch or a slap in the face: by turning his face sharply to one side, and at the same time making a dramatic sound effect by clapping his hands together.

'That's it, good. But slower this time. No one will see you clap your hands if you keep your arms down low enough. It happens too quickly, see. And again. That's it, better. Now, wait until my hand has nearly reached your face before you turn. Everything's in the timing. And again. Good.'

I heard the sound of the audience applauding, and the introduction to Mundo's clown act strike up.

'OK. Let's go.' Mundo said, giving one last trumpet blast. 'Are you ready?'

'Ready?'

'To go on in the act of course.'

'What? *Now*?' Tom looked as if someone had offered to boil his head in oil. This was the man who is embarrassed by people singing 'Happy Birthday to you', just in case too many people should look at him all at the same time. 'But I couldn't, not possibly.'

In the back of the truck I could see Tintin jumping up and down to try to catch his father's attention. Beside him, holding his hand, was three-year-old Lely, in her little clown romper suit and bubble-toed shoes. They were on.

'Of course you could.' Mundo stood his ground. 'You watch the act every day, don't you. Don't worry, Ramón and Charlie will help you.'

'That's right, you must know that act by heart by now.'

Mara put her hands on her hips.

'If you don't go now you never will,' I said.

Between us, before he had a chance to protest, we grasped Tom by the arms and pushed him through the stage curtains and out into the spotlights. I heard applause and then a burst of laughter. It was a heartening sound. Then I remembered something: the audience weren't supposed to laugh just yet. Trying not to trip up over the electrical cables which lead into Gato's sound gallery, Mara and I raced round to the curtain edge and peered round. I saw Karina and Brissel sitting by themselves on one of the top-tier seats. They too were laughing. Karina's eyes goggled. We slipped through, unnoticed, and climbed up to join them.

'What happened?'

'Ramón and Charlie were just warming up when Tom just came sort of bursting in through the curtains.'

'Yes, I know. We pushed him through,' Mara said.

'You *pushed* him . . . ?'

'No wonder then.'

In the ring, Tom was waving and skipping about. The crowd waved back.

'He was just coming down the ramp when he tripped up . . .'

'One of his shoe laces was undone . . .'

'And so the first thing he did was to fall flat on his face.'

Karina shook her head.

'It didn't matter though,' Brissel said. 'That's the great thing about clowns. When things go wrong the audience just thinks it's all part of the act.'

In the ring Tom was warming to his part. I watched him skip about some more, jiggling his balloon-sized tummy at the crowd. The crowd roared. I could hear some of the smaller children cry out, '*payaso, payasito*'. Those in the front rows reached out their hands towards him. On the other side of the ring I could see Charlie and Ramón grinning at him. Tintin and little Lely came on now, followed by Mr Bell's, and the act began for real, with all the usual mayhem of bottoms to be kicked, faces to be slapped, all the slips, trips and farting trumpets that Mundo could devise.

Ramón and Charlie knew exactly what had to be done. Gently they rolled Tom round the ring between them; nudging him into place, easing him into the right position from which to be kicked, slapped, punched, pummelled or farted at, as required. Everything was happening very fast now. In his battered sequined hat, his suit with the rubber tubing inside it billowing out around him, Tom rebounded merrily round the ring like a vast Humpty Dumpty.

News travelled fast. Before the act was even half-way through I saw the space around Carmen's sweet stall and Sylvia's pop-corn stand at the entrance of the Big Top filling up. First Antonino, a plum-coloured velvet dressing gown over his sequined suit, then Gallo with Oly and Pamela, Gordo and Jorge Morales, Ilish, dressed in his blue *chamaco*'s boiler suit, even Vanessa, who was known hardly ever to stir from her caravan during the performances. Everyone was there. The applause (with wolf whistles and cat-calls from the boys) when the act was finished, was louder than I had heard it for weeks.

The circus's appreciation of its own art was a phenomenon which never ceased to amaze me. After a week or so living with Circo Bell's, but still with my outsider's imperfect knowledge, I had begun to think that every performance consisted of just the same tired old acts, performed year in, year out. No one appeared to practise much. Even Mara, probably the most meticulous person in the entire circus – possibly the only one, I sometimes used to think – waxed and waned in her enthusiasms for working up a new act. Most of the kids had assimilated their circus acts in their earliest childhood (as Mundo used sometimes to joke, he was surprised that his children had not popped out at birth in full clown greasepaint) and had never troubled themselves much about them since. It was nature, not art, which had fashioned their skills.

When I had been there a little longer, though, when I knew them all better, I came to realize that this apparently cavalier attitude was but another of the circus's many illusions. For a start, I had been wrong to think that I was seeing the same acts every night. No act was ever the same twice running. There were always variations, subtleties of form and exuberance which would always be invisible to any audience off the street, and even to my half-tutored eye, but which were glaringly obvious to anyone who had grown up around them.

When I had been there longer I came to realize that their insouciance masked an intense, almost obsessive, interest in these tiny nuances. After we had been with the circus for about a month Tom took a series of black and white photographs of each of the acts, copies of which he then distributed as presents. No one liked them.

'Look at Mara, her legs are in completely the wrong position,' Vicky sniffed. 'And this arm here' – she tapped the photograph disapprovingly with her fingernail – 'wrong, quite wrong.'

'Ay-ay, ay,' Mundo tutted when he saw the picture of the *bastoneras*.

'Look at this then. Pamela's headdress at completely the wrong angle. And Karina – I despair of her. Look!' He pointed to Karina's scowling face. 'So serious. Smile! I tell her, smile! But will she ever listen to me?'

Only the trapeze boys mulled over the photographs of themselves lovingly, not only the ones Tom had had printed up, but also the contact sheets. In these tiny little pictures the three flyers were so small – three fragile white specks flitting across the roof of the Big Top – that Tom and I could not tell them apart, but they recognized themselves at a glance, just by looking at the line of their bodies.

'That's Jorge, you can tell because he's got his feet apart as usual, the idiot,' Gordo explained. 'And that's Ricky – he's got a good line, but he always flies lower than either of us two.' He squinted at another of the photographs. 'That's me, of course. Lo mejor! The best!' He glanced at me slyly. 'Just look at that line. Beautiful, no? Tom caught it just right.'

'It's a great photo,' I said.

'It was a great jump.' Gordo was looking at the contact sheet reverently.

I laughed.

'How many triples is it now, Gordo?'

'So many I've stopped counting. It's getting boring. We've started practising something new already, something really difficult this time. The triple is just kids' stuff.' Squeezing his fists Gordo started to crack the bones in his fingers. He knew it made me wince. Like his father and his uncles, his hands were the hands of a trapeze artist, disproportionately large and worn compared to his slim adolescent's body, his palms scarred over with iodine-stained sores. 'That blister on my hand has opened up again,' he said, a little too casually. 'Shall I show you?'

For a while after I had received Gordo's message, via Karina, I had been very careful with him. Of all the people in the circus his family, particularly Mara, were the ones I was closest to. Our caravans were always parked next door to each other. I saw him every day and I always watched his trapeze act. He had the same wit, the same anarchic humour as his father and his two sisters whom I loved so much. I liked him, but I knew that for the time being, for both our sakes, I should keep my distance.

My position in the circus had always been a curious one. I was known to be married and was therefore, to a certain extent, protected by this status. Nonetheless, most of the time I was living there on my own. I was aware, too, that I did not conform to the way in which most Mexicans might have expected a thirty-year-old married woman to have behaved. I was too independent, and I looked too young. I had no children. I did not iron my husband's shirts. My best friends in the circus, Mara and Karina, most of the people I hung out with in fact, were still only teenagers.

Strangely, though, instead of making me more vulnerable by his absences, the longer Tom stayed away from the circus, the more I found myself protected by them, watched over like one of their own. Even if I had been tempted to find myself a *novio*, an *amiguito* to match the by now legendary quantities of girlfriends which Tom, as *Super-vago*, was widely believed to have, it would have been impossible. The girls rarely left the circus on their own. When we went out, whether it was to the movies or a funfair or even just to the shops, the boys circled round us, snapping proprietorially.

Once, on one of the rare occasions when we were all invited to a party one Friday night, I came out of the loo to find Ramón standing guard outside the door.

'That man over there,' he said with sinister emphasis, 'was *looking* at you.' I saw him eyeballing an inoffensive young man in a suit who had been standing by himself in a corner. 'Don't you worry about a thing, Katty.' Ramón cracked his finger knuckles, a trick Gordo had recently taught him. They made a menacing grinding sound, gristle on bone. 'No one will mess with you while we're around. They wouldn't dare.'

'No. I don't expect they would.'

I watched as beneath Ramón's razor gaze the man in the suit slunk off into the garden.

'We look after our own. And while Tom's away, well ... let's just say I've got my eye on you,' he twinkled at me. 'We all have.' He patted my arm affectionately. 'Nuff said.'

'Why, thank you, Ramón. That's very kind.'

I knew he meant well, but all the same I found Ramón's warning chilling, as if I had suddenly found myself under the protection of the Mafia, or under house arrest or something.

It was a terrible party. No one dared speak to me. This would not have been so bad if I had been able at least to have a drink. But Ramón did not approve of drink either. When the tequila bottle came round he was shocked that I should even consider such strong liquor.

'A beer would be all right, that wouldn't hurt you,' he kept saying solicitously, 'or even just half a beer, mixed with lemonade.'

Clearly I was not going to discover the secrets of the world that night.

The girl who was giving the party put on some music, salsas and mambos, which would have been atmospheric if only the room had not been so brightly lit. We were in a suburban house, full of teenagers, in some anonymous *barrio* of Mexico City, I had no idea where. Omar, who because of his father the politician, was worldlier than the others and knew about alcohol, purloined the tequila bottle and after a few drinks pulled Mara into the centre of the room and started to dance. Mara looked shy. No one else was dancing, but Omar moved flamboyantly, aware that all eyes were on him. He wore black patent leather shoes and white socks; his hips rippled bonelessly.

No one else danced. No one else even spoke much. The circus kids sat at one end of the room, eyeing up the rest of the guests who stood around drinking at the other. Just like the Jets and the Sharks, I thought. The Jets looked like nervous sheep. The boys wore thick-soled American trainers and the girls had lacquered fringes, teased into stiff quiffs as brittle as spun sugar. Some of the boys were already quite drunk.

At our end Vanessa sat with Charlie, and Karina with Gallo, as if they had been skin-grafted to their sides. They did not appear to be enjoying themselves: perhaps they didn't dare. Gordo and Ricky were drinking Coca-Cola and showing off, throwing handstands and doing balancing acts with cushions from the sofa. The girl who had invited us to the party and two of her friends looked on admiringly.

Ramón came and sat down next to me. I asked him if Marisa, his girlfriend, was coming, but he said no. The thought of her even speaking to another man, he said, made him feel ill with rage.

Mara came up and perched next to me on the arm of her chair. She and Omar seemed to be the only ones who knew how to behave at an ordinary party.

'Why don't you dance, Katty? Omar will dance with you if you like.'

'No, thanks.'

Somehow, under the unforgiving lights, even with Omar as a partner, it was a dismal prospect.

'You're not enjoying yourself, Katty?'

Ramón's baby-face looked down at me innocently.

I smiled.

'Too much testosterone,' I said to him, in English.

'Please?'

'Never mind.' I took a sip of my watery beer. 'Are you always this . . . protective, Ramón?'

Immediately Ramón looked cheerful again.

'With my friends, always.'

He took a swig of Coca-Cola from his glass. His features were so soft and fresh, almost pre-pubescent, I thought looking at him, and yet there were times when I would catch an expression in his eyes – cold, ruthless almost – and I knew that inside that *squinkle* skin was someone far, far older than he appeared on the outside.

'Did you have many friends, back in Monterrey, I mean?'

'*Claro*, of course. When I was on the streets, I used to hang out with the gangs there, even when I was just a young kid. First I was with the *Cholos*, and then later with the *Casaphantasmas*. There were many gangs in Monterrey, and so there was always fighting. You learnt to look after one another, watch each other's backs, otherwise you'd be finished, washed up' – he made a gesture, pulling his finger across his throat – 'it was the only way.'

'They were all men, I suppose? In the gangs, I mean.'

'Of course.' Ramón took another sip from his glass. 'Although I did look after two girls once, two prostitutes.' The Coca-Cola left a soft brown rim, a fizzy half-moon moustache on his adolescent upper lip. 'They were not from Monterrey and so they needed someone who knew the ropes. They asked me to help them, to be their *padrote*, you know, their pimp, for a few months.'

'How old were you?'

'Not so old,' Ramón shrugged, 'but old enough. Ten or so, I guess, although the girls were older than me, sixteen or seventeen. I used to stand on the street corner with them – we had a patch just a block or so from Sandbornes – and when the punters pulled up, I was the one who went over to speak to them. They were *puras fresas*, most of them, young rich kids looking for a quick screw. I used to settle the price – forty thousand pesos per girl – and take the money in advance. There was always a danger that when they got to the hotel the men would either refuse to pay, or simply take the money back by force.'

'Where did you live?'

'We all lived together, in hotels, you know, ten-thousand-peso-a-night rooms, the same kind of places where they went to turn their tricks. The girls paid. After the streets, I thought it was such a luxury. We all used to sleep in the same bed, all three of us together.' Ramón smiled. 'It was better for them to have me rather than a man as their *padrote*. They had my protection, but they were still in control that way. We lived together like that for nearly five months. The girls were grateful to me. They used to bring me presents every day; buy my food, and clothes sometimes too.'

'Good times, ha?'

'Claro pues.' Ramón's eyes were veiled. 'After that I went to work at the *feria*, the big fair in Monterrey. First I worked in the snake pit, and then in the zoological. They were famous for their freak animals there, you know, the cow with six legs, the bull with three horns, all that kind of thing. After I went to the *feria* I didn't see the girls so much. Besides, my brother worked there too, and I was scared he would find out what I had been doing.'

'What happened to them?'

'Quién sabe? Who knows? Maybe they found someone else to look after them.'

'And maybe not.'

'Maybe not.' Ramón shrugged. 'You must understand. I was one of the lucky ones, *ves*. Mostly no one knows what happens to kids like that.'

Technical hitches in putting up the Big Top in Toluca had meant that the circus had an unprecedented two nights free before the show could get going in earnest. Those 'lost days' between *terrenos* always had a very particular flavour of their own, something between a school half-day holiday and a kind of morning-after feeling, but I remember that time in Toluca especially. With so much time on their hands, the circus was able to indulge in what it enjoyed doing best – going to the circus.

I had been to other circuses before. To the Circo Hermanos Vasquez several times with Gordo and Jorge Morales, and to the Circo Americano one Sunday with Doña Elena, who invited us to go there with her to visit her eldest daughter, Amapola. But this was different. This time the whole circus was going to the circus.

The circus in question, Circo Atayde, was well known to Circo Bell's. They were tented in a small village about half an hour from Toluca. As we arrived a long line of villagers was already queuing up outside the box-office waiting for the doors to open for the eight-thirty performance. Of course there was no question of any of us queuing, let alone paying for our tickets. We walked past them all and were ushered straight into the best seats, the front-row boxes. We had left late and so most of the others from Circo Bell's were already there by the time we arrived, dressed in their Sunday finery, either settled into their seats, or making the rounds of the Big Top, talking to their friends. Everyone was there: Mundo and Carmen with their two smallest children, Lely and Augustin; Chillón and Güera and their family; Brissel with her mother and father, Rosalinda and Juan; even old Jovita, smartly dressed in a skirt and blouse, her head a resplendent orb of perfect, curlerless curls.

Tom and I shared a box with Mara, Omar, Oly and Antonino. The Big Top was filling up. Although it had turned into a cold evening, inside the tent it was warm, and smelt familiarly of saw-dust and animal dung. There was a buzz of chatter all around us, and the sound of children's voices, shrieking and laughing as they ran up and down the aisles. A man in clown *pintura* came round selling marionettes and fairy wands filled with coloured water and sequins; another was selling from a tray filled with bags of popcorn and chocolate bars; a third hired out cushions to anyone wanting insulation from the cold pinch of the flimsy steel chairs – all the extra money-making ruses employed in the circus world which by now I knew so well.

I had never been here before in my life and yet everything about it, from the shape and construction of the Big Top to the rusty music playing over the loudspeaker, was familiar. That electric charge, the build-up to the performance itself, was in the air and I felt all over again that tiny shiver of anticipation, that catch in the back of the throat, I had felt the very first time I had watched Circo Bell's perform.

Some of the artistes had seen our party arrive and came out from backstage to talk to us. They were fully made-up, their spangled costumes concealed beneath stained old *batas*. Antonino intro-duced us to some acrobats he used to work with in another circus. Oly and Mara presented us to an aunt and two cousins who performed a high-wire act. To my surprise, some of the people I even recognized myself as occasional visitors to Circo Bell's. Every-one seemed to know everyone else.

'This is Lely, my youngest,' I could hear Mundo saying to a man dressed as a clown.

'Well, hello, young lady.' The clown squatted down beside her, taking her hand in his ruffled glove.

'She's just three but she's performing already, with her brother, Tintin. You know him, my son Augustin.'

Mundo was looking spruce in a suit, his hair well watered and combed down carefully over the bald patch at the back of his head.

'Is that so?'

Shyly, Lely smiled up at him through her pink ribbons.

'I hear that Gustavo and Carlos Bell's are coming back from Germany soon,' I heard the clown say.

'That's right, they're with Circo Kröne now, you know. The stars of the show and all that ... Increíble, no?' Mundo was in his element. 'Taught my trapeze boys everything they know ...'

And so it went on.

I saw Ramón come in with his girlfriend Marisa, a charming, Abyssinian-haired dancer who used briefly to work at Circo Bell's before we arrived, and I thought how different the atmosphere here was to the party we had been to just a few nights ago. I watched Marisa greet the others – I even saw her be kissed on the cheek by two of the Circo Atayde boys – but Ramón, as far as I could see, was still behaving quite normally. He had neither gouged out their eyes with his fingers, nor ripped their heads off with his bare hands. He was even smiling.

Within the circus, apparently, the rules were different. This was the known world. This was safety. This was the extended family into which, from his violent, pimping, street-kid days, he had been adopted; the circus was his caste now, his clan. 'I can go to any circus, anywhere in this country,' he had boasted to me once, 'and I know there will always be a job for me, a hot meal, somewhere to lay my head. It will be the same for you, too, now that you can say you were once with Circo Bell's.'

It was not only in Mexico City, or big towns like Toluca, that this sense of clanship existed. Like an invisible construct of veins and arteries, a network of circuses existed throughout the whole of Mexico, joined together not only by families, friendships and old rivalries, but also by some intangible quality, something at once tender and steely which I can only describe as the very heart-beat of the circus itself.

We watched all the acts that night. There were elephants and performing dogs and clowns, an Argentinian *gaucho* with his spin-ning balls, a knife-thrower, and even a strongman.

The strongman was a burly figure with pale, almost sandy colouring and a slightly silly look about the mouth; his partner was a tiny platinum-blonde, a contortionist who tied her rubbery limbs up into knots and then offered herself up to be tossed and lifted and spun about as if she was no heavier than a fallen petal. Next to me, Mara and Oly looked on intensely.

'Look at her *traje*, I ask you!' Oly giggled. The girl's costume was slashed up her legs to an almost indecent level. '*Abuela* would have a fit.'

'She doesn't get her back nearly arched enough when she goes over into that crab. Even you could do better than that, Oly.'

They watched each act with critical eyes, whispering between them.

The next act involved what were known as *pulseras*, literally 'bracelets', in which a girl walked up and down a staircase on her hands, spinning coloured rings around her arms and wrists. It was quite amazing, I thought, the feats people had dreamt up to do with their bodies. 'She's good,' Mara admitted, as the girl hopped down the stairs on just one hand, spinning six different coloured rings up and down her free arm. Meditatively she passed me her bag of popcorn on to which she had poured a liberal sprinkling of her favourite red chilli sauce. (Mara could eat nothing without chillies on it – even her favourite sweet had a chilli flavouring, a repellent yellow lollipop coated with spicy red powder).

At the end even Oly, for whom it was a point of honour never to be overly impressed by anything, applauded the *pulseras* girl.

Although I knew perfectly well that they had seen all these acts before, in any number of different circuses, Circo Bell's enjoyed the evening with a passion which I had never seen in any audience before. Their enjoyment was different from mine. It lay not in the exoticism of the acts, nor in some crude overall flavour of the thing, but in its detail; in those tiny nuances, those minute fluctuations of light and shadow which only they, like true aficionados, were capable of appreciating.

I remembered what Mundo had said about the circus being like a fiesta and I wondered if, despite the familiarity of it all, they too could experience that release from the everyday which Mundo had talked about. But again, as I watched them, as I watched those faces which I had come to love so much, I realized that the quality of their release was different from mine. It was not so much a catharsis as an act of profound recognition; as though, in being confronted by themselves, by their mirror images in the ring, they had tasted the truth, were free, in some way, to become most truly themselves.

FIFTEEN

> Considering another aspect of the question, it is
> clear that whereas in Western Europe folk dance,
> for instance, has lost all magical or invocatory
> character, rare is the collective dance in America
> that does not incorporate a deep ritualistic
> meaning.
>
> ALEJO CARPENTIER, *El Reino de este Mundo*

Much later, after we had left the circus finally, I often used to
think of Mundo's theories about clowns and how the circus func-
tioned as a kind of fiesta, releasing people from their everyday
selves.

Of all the countries I have travelled through, I have never been
anywhere where the fiesta is taken as seriously as it is in Mexico.
We came across fiestas everywhere, in all the forms and disguises
which the Mexican exuberance could devise: saints' days and village feasts, pilgrimages and processions, bullfights, flower and
music festivals, beauty pageants, parades and candle-lit vigils; even
the circus itself. It was as if the Mexican's need to escape from
behind the mask of their machismo, from their Indian fatalism,
and from all the violence and fear and corruption of their lives,
built up to such a pitch that finally it was torn from them, like
a rocket or a burst of silver stars, transformed into a thousand
celebrations.

And the poorer and more disenfranchized the community, particularly among the Indian peoples, the greater the detail, the intensity – to the point of *ekstasis* sometimes – with which their fiestas
were conducted.

The first time I saw the demon army we were sitting in the corner
cafeteria in Jesús-María. At first they were no more than a rever-
beration, a distant rumble coming from far off, from the very belly
of the earth. On our table, glasses and bottles shook, and the

tables around us rattled – a demonic presence felt long before it came into sight.

Apart from a loincloth at their waists, the men were naked. The entire surface of their bodies, their limbs, their smooth naked chests and backs, were striped over with black and white paint. I guessed that they were mostly young men, aged between about fifteen and twenty, although it was impossible to tell with any particular accuracy. Each man wore an animal mask over his face, a white mask to match the white body paint. I saw coyotes, deer, bulls, baboons, owls, and others impossible to identify; monstrous, snouted faces with teeth and sharpened fangs, a faint lapidary glitter just visible behind the eye-slits.

At their approach there was an involuntary movement. Everyone in the cafeteria drew back from the porch and we stood pressed together, as though for protection, just inside the door.

In silence the army marched past us at a steady trot into the dirt plaza beyond the café. Four captains, recognizable by their white képis, marched at their head, while the rest were arranged into two parallel phalanxes behind them. Because of the press of people I could not see down the road in the direction from which the army were coming, and so at first I could not tell how many of them there were. As they passed us I counted ten, twenty, fifty rows of men, but still they kept coming at that same inexorable slow run.

In their hands the demon army carried flat-edged swords, their tips painted white. Seventy, a hundred rows went by. Outside in the silent street the sun burnt down on to baked adobe roofs. Ninety degrees in the shade, but the army never altered their pace. Everyone was indoors: doors slammed, shutters scraped across windows. Little whirlpools of dust, like avenging spirits, eddied through the deserted streets. I was still counting. A hundred and twenty, a hundred and fifty rows at least. They ran and ran, and there was no end to them.

In their dazzling white masks, the army looked neither to left nor to right. At their waists they each wore a river tortoise shell, filled with seeds which rattled as they ran. Fine white dust licked at their naked ankles and the ground trembled beneath their feet.

Two hundred rows went past us in all. Four hundred men. They crossed the little plaza in front of the church, turned up a street behind the *ayuntamiento*, and were gone.

'The demon army,' Juan said, when the last of the dust had died down. 'The *Judea*, as they are known here. The Jews. From now on, all civil authority is suspended and the town is under their control. Even if we wanted to, we cannot leave here now.'

I knew then that we had passed into a time which is known among the Cora people as the *días prohibidos*, or forbidden days: a sacred time which seeks to recreate the beginning of the world, the time before the creation of Tayan, the deity known to the Cora as Our Father the Sun. The infernal army which we had just seen represented the inhabitants of this pre-Creation world, all the deer, the owls, the iguanas and other monsters who inhabited the dark caves and caverns before Our Father the Sun came into being.

We sat down at our table again and the owner of the café, a stout mestizo woman in a flowered pinny, brought us some more *refrescos*.

'Haven't you got any beer?' Victor looked glum.

'Plenty of beer, but not until Saturday. Not until all this is over.' The woman gestured into the somnolent street, to where the dust had been churned by the demon feet. 'It's one of the forbidden things. No alcohol, no music, no cars circulating, not even any washing in the river is allowed by the *Judea* while they control the town.'

'And definitely no photography.' Pancho grinned at Tom through a mouthful of crooked gold-capped teeth.

'Photography! Ni hablar!' The woman rolled her eyes heavenward. 'If they even see you holding a camera they'll confiscate it, or worse. If you want to take pictures, Señor, you've come to the wrong place. Take it from me, I'm a Mexican but I'm married to a Cora. I know their ways.'

Behind her on the wall of the café hung a picture of the Virgin of Guadalupe. Beneath it a tiny revolving fan whirred a thin stream of hot air into our faces.

'At least we've been allowed to stay in Jesús María, Señora.' Juan passed a handkerchief over his face. 'We were already late when we picked these two up on the road,' he indicated Tom and myself. 'Their truck had broken down. We wanted to stay in Mesa del Nayar for the night, the village just before here, but they wouldn't have us.'

'It was already nearly dark.' Victor rubbed a hand over his heavy jowls. 'But no sooner had we driven in when we were surrounded by all these men carrying sticks. Their bodies were all painted over with black, so that only the whites of their eyes were showing.'

'They made us pay a fine – 100,000 pesos – just for the privilege of being able to pass through their village at all. "*Co-operación*" they called it,' Pancho said.

'And they said that if we stayed they would shut us up in the church for three whole days, until the forbidden days were over . . .'

'They were going to keep us there and not let us sleep or anything, but prod us with sticks all night long to make sure that we had no rest . . .'

'It was only because we had been giving a lift to some other Cora that they let us get away so lightly.'

'It was an assault, Señora.' Even Juan, the most senior of our three companions, sounded aggrieved. 'An assault, nothing less. I wouldn't have minded giving them something, but 100,000 pesos! I am a Mexican, am I not? I should be able to go anywhere I like in my own country without having to pay for the privilege.'

'Don't tell me about it.' The woman sighed. 'It's lucky you came on here. Jesús María is a bigger place, so things are a little more relaxed. But it didn't always used to be this way, I can tell you. The *Judea* used to be much stricter. *Ay*, they were terrible. No dejaron a la gente reir . . . they wouldn't even let people laugh, I tell you. Nothing. If you had a child who was sick and you needed to fetch water for him, you had to go out in the middle of the night to get it and hope that no one saw. And woe betide you if they did.'

Juan, Victor and Pancho, from the Boneteria Britannia, Mexico City, had picked us up, as Juan said, the day before on the dirt road where we had broken down in our truck exactly four hours up the eight-hour track which led into the desiccated hills of the north-western Mexican state of Nayarit.

With his gold chains and his baseball cap, his smooth-skinned belly just beginning to spill over his waistband, Juan, at forty-ish, was the oldest of the three. He had an avuncular, slightly bullying relationship with the two other boys, who fetched his cigarettes, queued up to buy his *refrescos*, pulled and pushed our car, and carried out as many other small errands as he, in the kindest possible way, could devise for them.

The two boys, it has to be said, were not prepossessing. In his early twenties, Victor was large and stolid-looking, with a pale, unhealthy complexion; while Pancho, his friend, was tiny, wiry and dark.

As a travelling salesman, the sock, knicker and pantyhose business had sent Juan to many parts of Mexico, where he had conceived – for a Mexican, at least – an unusual passion for all things which were both native and Indian. He had been to the Tzotzile and Tzeltal villages of Chiapas at Carnival, he had visited the Otomies, the Tarahumaras, the Tarascans, and even been as far as the great Maya ceremonial sites of the Yucatán. Now, like us, he was trying to reach the Cora, who at this time of year were the least hospitable of the Mexican indigenous tribes, for their 'Easter' celebrations.

This part of the Nayarit sierra is one of the remotest places in Mexico. We had arrived in Jesús-María, an impoverished settlement of single-storeyed adobe houses, late the night before and had been invited to stay in the house of Melesio Valentín, a Cora Indian, to whose family the good-natured Juan had also given a lift the day before.

Melesio's house was very simple. There were only two rooms and no windows. We slept in a row on sacking on the floor, with the door open to the moon and the stars to let in the breeze. Very early the next morning, before there was a danger of the *Judea* being about, I went down with the women to the river to wash.

The river had all the beauty of the early morning. In the midday heat these hills have the disturbing energy of mirages; now the slopes above us were desiccated and barren still, but somehow quieter, sapped of their usual strength. Their colours were quieter too, alternately pink and mouse-coloured, except for the banks of the river itself which were stitched along with reeds and with cactus and with the spiny, acid-green trees known as guamuchils.

Boys brought their animals down to drink. Women in little groups were washing, their clothes spread out to dry on the rocks like the petals of tropical plants, lime green and ochre and turquoise. The water was cold against my skin, and afterwards I sat alone on a rock in the pale sun, with my skin smelling of river water, watching the women and the boys downstream and wondering what it would be like to stay here for a time, as we had done with the circus, to seek out the rhythms and textures of ordinary life, and how long it would take me to find out their true patterns.

But this was not ordinary life. For the Cora, the *días prohibidos* are a magical time, a time when the rules of ordinary life are suspended. Already there was a fever in the air, and the *Judea*, as yet unseen, were on the move.

My second sighting of the *Judea* was from Melesio's house. I was sitting with his daughter-in-law, Paula, a beautiful Cora girl with high cheek bones and skin like spun silk, eating the pods of the guamuchil tree, a sweet white fruit with a shiny black pip, about the size of a pea. It was still early, but already the sun was too hot to sit in. As we sat there, there came a thundering sound and all at once the baking street, with its dust and picking chickens and sleepy brown adobe houses, was full of noise and confusion.

The demon army had metamorphosed during the night.

Instead of black and white body paint they had daubed themselves in every conceivable colour: legs and torsos and chests were daubed with psychedelic swirls of fluorescent oranges, purples and yellows; bright pink tiger stripes were offset with startling green leopard spots, navy blue zebra dashes against crimson hyena crescents, bars of cerulean boa criss-crossed with deep-sea amethyst scales and fins. The masks, pure white the day before, were now painted spring greens, scarlets, vermilions, ochres and lilacs.

When she saw the *Judea*, Paula's lapful of guamuchil pods fell to the floor. Plucking at my arm for me to do likewise, she shrank back out of sight into the shadows. For these were no longer the silent and organized army they had been the day before, running in perfect formation behind the four captains. Down the dusty street they came, whirling and chattering like desert ghouls. When they spoke, the noise that came from beneath their masks was incomprehensible to me, at once guttural and distant, as if they were speaking from the bottom of the sea.

Two mestizo men came walking down the street towards them. One of the *Judea* challenged them, asking for cigarettes. The first man offered him one willingly enough, but as he held the packet out the demon plucked the whole thing from his hand and ran off gibbering. I watched as he ran back to the rest of the army with his booty; a self-satisfied shriek went up as he shared the cigarettes round.

The demons were approaching Melesio's house now. Paula was still flattened to the wall in the darkest corner of the room, but I could see nothing to worry about. The doorways and windows of many of the neighbouring houses had filled up with people watching the show. They were laughing as the demons capered and skipped, licensed fools in their fantastic animal motley. So far the atmosphere was lighthearted, or so I thought. Somewhere at the back of my mind I remember registering how few women there were about, and that those who were in evidence were mostly the old grandmothers, but Indian women are almost always more retiring than men on these occasions, and so at the time I did not think much about it. Tom and Juan came out of the next-door room and were immediately rounded on by two of the demons. One wore a coyote mask painted yellow and green, the other a deer head, with real antlers fixed to the papier mâché frame. Juan surrendered the rest of his packet of Rothmans, but when Tom was discovered to have nothing on him to take, the demons growled at him angrily. The crowd laughed. As a *gringo*, the only one in town, Tom was bound to be a particular object of the devils' buffoonery. One of them raised his sword and with the flat hit him across the arm. But this was a show, and it was only a jesting blow – or was it? I saw Tom hesitate. Beneath the mask, the glint of the man's eyes gave nothing away.

Now three of the demons appeared in Melesio's doorway. I could not understand what they were saying, but by their pointing gestures I guessed they must be making the same request – cigarettes. '*No fumo*, I don't smoke,' I explained, thinking we would have to buy a few packets, if only to have something to give away.

But the three men only shook their heads, babbling at me, louder now, in their strange gibber-language.

I thought how strange it was: not that I could not understand them but that, hidden beneath their masks, I could not read the expressions on their faces. All of a sudden I was unsure. Was this in jest or for real? It was impossible to tell. I turned to see if Juan might have a new packet of cigarettes which I could give them, and as I did so I felt one of them starting to lift up my skirt with the point of his sword. As I pulled the material away from him another made a grab for my breast, but before he could touch me I had darted back inside the house and slammed shut the door. Outside in the street I heard the sound of fingernails scratching against the wood and then the crowd laughing again; but after a few more minutes they went away and I was left alone with Paula, the frightened whites of her eyes glowing opposite me in the dark.

The process of demonization, like the process of arriving at the divine, is a slow and complicated one. During the 'forbidden days' in Jesús-María the Cora experience both. Neither is arrived at easily.

The demon army, the *Judea*, make their first appearance on the Tuesday of Holy Week, but they do not become infernal beings immediately. In order to pass without danger from ordinary time into sacred time, from the real world into the magical world of their mythic origins, in their first metamorphosis the *Judea* are merely ghosts. They march the streets silently, their bodies painted over in pure white, powerless to do anything but survey the streets where, much later, when they are fully awakened, their great battle will take place.

But as the week progresses so does the metamorphosis of the *Judea*, who gain in both strength and colour, as though gradually being pulled into focus. By the Thursday, the day we arrived, they are strident and bold in black and white; by Friday they have erupted into fantastic colour. It is then that their strength is at its most terrifying.

Having made their magical transition, the *Judea* are now compelled to carry out the consequences of their metamorphosis to their ultimate conclusion. They have won their first battle, which is for control over the community of Jesús-María itself. During the *días prohibidos* all civil authority is suspended, and the *Judea* alone rule. All the rules of the real world are turned on their heads. Everything which symbolizes real life is forbidden; everything which is forbidden in real life is courted, magnified, driven to its most extreme limits. *Novios* may not walk hand in hand; women may not knit nor sew nor chastise their children; there is to be no bathing in the river; nor are beasts of burden to work in the fields. There is no music, no alcohol, no driving of vehicles. The *Judea* themselves must speak backwards and, despite the intense heat and the physical demands of their task, may not eat or drink until the afternoon. To give them energy under these gruelling conditions many take peyote, the hallucinogenic cactus bulb which grows in the northern deserts and is sacred to many of its Indian tribes.

All day the demon army cavorted through the town, appearing and disappearing out of the dust like a fantastic mirage from the hills. Sometimes they marched in strict formation under the discipline of their captains; at other times they roamed in small bands, mischievous and free as they had been outside Melesio's house. They ran in and out of the crowd at will, nicking cigarettes, *refrescos* and lighters, knocking off the men's sombreros; doing anything, in fact, which took their pixie-like fancy. They threw water and urine and burning straw; they ran races and staged mock fights with their swords. Their movements were gleeful, Puck-like; and they made strange little crowing sounds as they pounced.

It was not dangerous to be around them but it was never exactly safe, either. Everything they did was apparently playful, but their playfulness had a wild, bacchanalian quality which was only ever a whisper away from real menace.

With Juan, Pancho and Victor, we went back to the cafeteria from which we had first seen the *Judea* marching the day before. It was on the plaza – if that was what the empty, beaten mud space in front of the church could be termed – and therefore had the best view. I also hoped that we might be less visible there among other mestizos than in a purely Cora district.

As well as the animal-demons and their captains, other figures now came drifting into the plaza to join them, men with masked faces and outsized Mexican sombreros carrying drums and flutes. With them were their 'women', young boys cross-dressed in frocks or skirts, with well-padded breasts and long, blonde wigs.

'They are dancing troupes' – Juan adjusted his baseball cap so that his eyes were shaded from the glare – 'but comic ones. Sort of like clowns. We saw some last night, Pancho and me, after you had gone to bed.'

With his luxuriant handlebar moustache, the gold chains jangling at his neck and the buttons of his shirt straining over his nascent paunch, ever since he had rescued us on the road the day before, Juan had seemed to me like the archetypal Mexican. And yet now, amongst these Cora, I was struck by how foreign, almost European, he seemed in comparison.

'How do you see yourself amongst all this?' The three of them seemed so out of place here, almost as much so as we were ourselves. 'Don't you ever feel Spanish at all?'

'*Spanish!* Ni hablar!' I knew I had uttered a terrible heresy by even suggesting it. 'No, *hombre*,' Juan shrugged his shoulders with feeling, 'the Spanish were the oppressors of our people, the destroyers of our civilization.'

The conventional response, just as I had expected.

'Indian then?'

Juan looked over into the packed and dusty plaza.

'You mean, am I proud to be descended from Moctezuma and all that shit?' He shook his head. 'No, *hombre*, not that either. People say we're a mixture of Spanish and Indian, but quite frankly I don't feel part of either. Us Mexicans, you could call us a *pueblo huérfano*, an orphan nation. And as for me . . .' he shrugged again, 'well, I'm just *me*, I guess.' He laughed, scratched at his spilling belly. 'Just your average son-of-a-bitch Mexican.'

We watched as the dancing troupes capered beneath the three-foot brims of their hats, piping reedily.

'But look at these Cora, though, they're something else, aren't they?' Juan spoke indulgently, in the manner that more enlightened mestizos often use to talk about the indigenous population. 'They like to – how do you say? – take the piss out of us Mexicans . . .' The smile froze on his face. 'Dios mío!'

One of the musicians had grabbed the 'woman' in the long

blonde wig, pulled down his trousers, and was proceeding to mount her from behind. I could see his penis, brown and flaccid, rubbing between his partner's proffered buttocks. They fell to the floor, writhing in the dust in simulated ecstasy.

'Ah!' The crowd lining the street outside, in the ironmonger's shop opposite us, and beneath the café porch, drew in their breath. 'Oh!'

Some people were laughing; others had turned away, too shocked to watch. A group of young mestizo girls, their hair braided into neat schoolgirl plaits, hid their faces, giggling helplessly into each other's shoulders.

Two other members of the dancing troupe came up. Unlike the others these were not wearing outsized Mexican sombreros; instead one had on a plastic mask of the Mexican president, Salinas Gotari, and the other a strange headpiece which I saw now was in the shape of an erect penis. Two swollen balls hung down on either side of his cheeks. When the man in the hat had finished, Salinas Gotari and the Penis took over, falling over themselves in their efforts.

'Ay!' The crowd sighed again, horrified, titillated. Pancho and Victor's mouths hung slightly open. Juan had sunk down into his seat and pulled his baseball cap down still further over his eyes until I could not see his expression at all.

I felt a tap on my shoulder. It was Carmen, the proprietor, the one who was married to a Cora Indian. She was beckoning to me.

'I have a better place for you.' She glanced towards the thrashing bodies, and then back at me. 'Come with me, all of you, up to my roof.' She put her hand on my shoulder. 'No one will see you there.'

I did not have to ask why she was doing this. I had found these scenes more disturbing than I would ever have imagined. Not because of the sex, which was pure burlesque, so much as the sight of its main recipient: a blonde, and therefore foreign, woman. I was used to the idea that in almost all parts of Mexico blonde hair is extremely rare; but in Jesús-María that day, amongst a predominantly dark-skinned Indian crowd, even to me that wig, peroxide white and hanging to the boy's waist, was shocking in its impact. It sung out like a clarion call, like a roll of drums. A clap of thunder. I looked at that blonde figure, fucking so merrily now with the president of Mexico – and I saw myself.

For the audience, most of whom would never have been to a theatre or any other kind of live performance, here was the greatest spectacle of their lives. This was the circus, I realized, carried to its wildest excess. Here was both release and recognition. The Cora had come together – many such as Melesio and his family travelling many days to be here – not just to celebrate their version of the Resurrection, but also to celebrate the fact that they were Cora. During the rest of the year they might be reviled and humiliated as one of the poorest and most diminished of Mexico's indigenous peoples, but for this brief, magical space, this reign of the demon army, they were restored to their truest and purest selves.

But there was something else, too. Even at its crudest and most burlesque, I was struck by the seriousness of this spectacle. Even at its most basic level, that of pure entertainment, every part of this elaborate masque was imbued with meaning. The Cora's idea of the sacred was not limited to our narrow Sunday School perspective. For them the sacred encompassed not only the forces for good, but also – in the shape of the demon army – their dark face, and the seeds of their destruction. Everything else, the clowning and buffoonery, the orgiastic ritual and self-parody, were simply extensions of this mystical vision.

That afternoon was never-ending, stretched out on elastic. On Carmencita's roof the sun glanced down on us with ferocious multiple slanting blows. From our hiding place the five of us watched as the demon army began to reassemble itself under the direction of the captains, forming up into two parallel lines in front of the church. Up until now Christian Easter rites and Cora ritual had remained separate, but now the two were beginning to come closer, encircling one another until finally they would merge. The *Judea*'s last and greatest battle was about to begin.

As we watched, a child dressed in a yellow robe with a crown of leaves about his head was brought running out of the church. He was led by the hand by one man, while two others ran in front of him, lashing at him with cords. At the rear came two more young boys, their bodies painted all over in black.

At the sight of the child a great howl went up among the demon army. They did not move, even when the child was led running between their ranks, but beneath their masks their strange subterranean backwards-language reached fever pitch. Some bayed and gibbered, while others crouched down on their haunches, pawing and sniffing at the ground as if any minute they would spring forwards and devour him.

Led by his entourage the Jesus-child vanished into the dusty back streets. The demon army waited for about five minutes and then started to run after them. Jesus would not be crucified that day, but hunted down, like the Deer God of the ancient Cora legends. All through the baking adobe streets of Jesús-María the demon army gave chase to the Jesus-child. It was hotter than ever that afternoon, but sustained by the peyote their pace never faltered. In their two parallel flanks, the coyotes and the deer, the owls, the iguanas and the baboons moved with that same remorseless tread that we had seen on our first day. As they ran tiny whirlpools of dust kicked up from beneath their feet, mingling with their daubed and smeared and chequered bodies, until, like a hallucination, the streets were running with rivers of pure colour.

On and on they went, tracking the child from house to house. At their head was a *marakame*, a witch doctor with turkey feathers in his hat. At each cross-roads he knelt down like a hunter to examine the dust for signs of the child's footprints. Each time the demons came to a house where he was hiding they would try to break in, beating the door with their fists, digging in the ground around it with their bare hands, scratching, snuffling, howling for blood. And each time the doors were thrust open, and the child was dragged running past them and out on to the next stage of his weary run, they would crouch down on their haunches, spitting with wordless fury.

In the extraordinary heat of that afternoon, with all the colour and the dust and the glancing light, and with the taste of the sacred peyote still on their lips, I wondered how the world looked to them just then. How, exactly, was it altered?

Watching the demon army as they crouched down on their haunches, hissing and hooping and sniffing the ground, it seemed to me that their metamorphosis was complete. This was not a masque after all. This was real. These were no longer just men in papier mâché masks, but real coyotes, real wolves, real demons from the mythological past. This was the circus *reductio ad absurdum*. After nearly a week of this existence they had finally crossed the point at which fantasy and reality meet, passed over into some magic realm that the rest of us would only ever dimly guess at.

We had only been a week or so in Toluca when the weather turned suddenly and uncompromisingly cold. It was the beginning of December. Christmas decorations were appearing in the shops and already there was thick snow on the peak of the Nevado de Toluca. In the evenings, waiting in the wings for the performance, I huddled with the other girls, shivering in my tiny red spangled costume, watching my skin turn blue and goosefleshed. Audiences dwindled again. Those who came brought rugs to put over their knees and woolly hats. In the parades sometimes I could see Hannibal's breath condensing in the icy air.

Tom had gone off again for a week on one of his trips, to photograph the famous Quetzales dancers at the festival in Quetzalan. I hoped it was warmer where he was than it was here. We had no heating, and the fabric walls of our caravan meant that even during the day, as Mara had predicted, its heat retention was non-existent. In bed, without Tom's extra body heat, the cold was unbearable. Instead, most nights I took to sleeping with Mara in Vicky's kitchen camper.

Mara's bed was in a narrow space like a kind of shelf which protruded forwards over the cab of the truck. Although once you were up there there was not enough headroom even to sit up in, the walls were lined with faded floral wallpaper. We slept with no sheets, only a pile of blankets topped with an ancient sheepskin, as heavy as if it was lined with lead. There was no privacy at all, but then there was rarely any privacy anywhere in the circus. We climbed up to sleep there when we were tired, and sometimes fell asleep with Oly or Gordo or Antonino – whoever happened to be visiting – still sitting around at the table beneath us chatting, or heating up frijoles and tortillas for a late-night snack. We were glad when they did, for Vicky's gas stove was the closest thing there was to any kind of heating.

Other times, when everyone else was sleeping, we would talk for hours long into the night wrapped up inside the heavy sheepskin. Sometimes it was just circus gossip, but most often we told each other about our lives. I would tell her about Tom and how we had met at Oxford when we were students, and about our travelling lives together; and Mara would tell me about Omar, about how she hoped to marry him, and her plans for them in the future.

'If only we could get married,' she would often say, 'everything would be different. Who knows, perhaps we could even go and work in another circus for a time.'

'You mean leave Circo Bell's?' I could not imagine the circus without Mara.

'I would miss it of course. Miss my family – Papá and Gordo and Oly. But with this circus, you know, Katty, it's really impossible to save money.' How to save money was one of Mara's most enduring worries. She sighed heavily.

'Because we are family, when the audiences are low my uncle simply doesn't pay us,' she explained. 'He has to pay the other artistes first, and sometimes there just isn't enough to go round. What can we do? Omar always gets paid of course, but we have so many expenses – we have to buy all our own costumes, you know, and all our props too.

'So you see,' she went on, 'if we went and worked for another circus, then they'd have to pay us, and a proper wage too. Maybe we'd even find work with a circus abroad. There was a man here the other day, an agent from a Japanese circus looking for new acts. He really liked our box act and said that we should make up a video of it for him to send out to them. We haven't heard anything back yet, but you never know. If he liked the act that much, then maybe there are other people out there who would too.'

Mara rolled over, pulling the sheepskin more tightly round her. In the darkness I could see her black eyes gleaming.

'Katty, do you think he'll *ever* marry me?'

'Don't be silly, Mara, of course he will – he wouldn't dare not to.' I teased her.

'Ay Chihuahua!' I heard her giggle into her pillow. 'But seriously, Katty, you know what men are like, so many objections always. We're too young, he says. Not enough money saved up. Where would we live? All that stuff.'

'Yes, I know. But it's true, you are both still very young. Maybe not you so much, but Omar – how old is he now?'

'Eighteen.'

'Eighteen is very young for a man to take on all that responsibility.'

But Mara, who has always had an old head on a young body, knew her own mind.

'I know I am ready,' she said simply. 'I love Omar, and he's my best friend, too. In fact, he is my only real friend in the circus.' She had turned away from me on to her side. 'At least he was until I met you.'

It was warm beneath the sheepskin. I moved closer to her until our bodies fitted together like two spoons.

'Your mother is always saying that I am like an older sister to you. It's true. I've always wanted an *hermanita*, you know, a little sister – and now I have you.'

'Mmm.' Mara's voice was sleepy now. 'You know, Katty, everything is going so well now, between Omar and me, that I can't help thinking . . .'

'Hmm?'

'Well, I know you'll laugh, but I keep on thinking that something terrible is going to happen . . . Don't you ever get like that?'

'Shhh. Nothing terrible is going to happen, I promise, *hermanita*. Go to sleep now.'

It was hard to believe that my time with the circus was almost up now. I had come so far, and seen so much, that I could hardly imagine any other kind of life any more. And yet just a few more weeks and I would be leaving them, going down south to the Yucatán for Christmas. I closed my eyes. Tried not to think about it. But already people were saying to me, '*Ay*, Katty, how you are going to miss us when you go'.

By the next morning I had forgotten all about Mara's premonition. Thinking back on it, there was no real reason why I should have remembered. There was certainly nothing unusual about her behaviour. She may have been a little paler than normal, perhaps, a little quieter even, but at the time I probably put this down to the cold, or to the fact that she had been working too hard. Despite her intensely practical nature, Mara's mind was always so full of spells and superstitions and arcane magical beliefs of one form or another that it never even occurred to me to take any of it too seriously.

Besides, at the time there was too much else to be thinking about. Carlos and Gustavo, the famous trapeze cousins, were due to be arriving any day now, and the whole circus was itching with anticipation. Gustavo and Carlos were the sons of Doña Elena's eldest son, the beloved and brilliant Yanko who had founded Circo Bell's but had later died in mysterious circumstances, by falling out of a hotel window in Mexico City. Although, like the rest of the family, they had learnt their craft at Circo Bell's, at an early age Carlos and Gustavo's trapeze act had been contracted by the famous German circus Kröne.

Amongst the younger cousins, Ricky and Gordo particularly, Gustavo and Carlos were legendary figures. Gordo had spoken to me of them often.

'They were the most brilliant trapeze artists in the world,' he told me once, flicking through an old copy of *Maromas*, the circus magazine which he had brought along in order to show me their photograph. It was after lunch and I was in my caravan trying to mend a hole in my *mayas* before the evening performance.

'Theirs was the most famous act in the most famous circus in the world. Imagine it! Mexicans, see. Isn't that what I have always told you?'

In a fit of enthusiasm Gordo cracked all five knuckles in his right fist simultaneously. 'They used to work together, although now Carlos is retired it is just Gustavo who still flies. He'll fly here too, at Circo Bell's, if we can persuade him. You must see it, Katty. *Vas a ver*, you'll see, you won't have lived until you see what he can do in the air. The height he can get, and the *line* . . .' Lyrically Gordo waved his damaged hands in the air, outlining an imaginary silhouette. 'He says that when I'm ready he's going to take me back to Kröne with him.' A note of pride crept, uncon-cealed, into his voice. 'To join his act, you see,' he added, just to make sure I got the picture. 'You'll have to come to Germany to see us then. You will come, won't you?'

'Claro que sí. Of course.' I put a final stitch into my *mayas*. 'But it's a big step. Are you really sure you'll be ready?'

'Sure. Everyone knows I'm the best.'

'How many triples are you on now?'

'Quién sabe?' Gordo said, full of nonchalance. 'Too many to count. The triple's just for kids. I'm working on something else now – something that's really difficult this time.'

'What's that?'

'It's called the "double full". My uncle Mundo invented it, although it's never been done before, not by him, not even Gustavo or Carlos, so if either Ricky or I ever get it ... *Caray!* Can you imagine? That'd really be something. That'd be circus history in the making.'

'What do you have to do?'

'It is a backwards somersault, at the full stretch, like this' – he held out his hand out in a straight line – 'but at the same time that you're turning backwards, you've also got to get your body to spin sideways, in a double twist like this.' He made a kind of corkscrew motion with his finger. 'Very tricky, I can tell you. You feel like you're careering about all over the place.'

He saw the look on my face. 'OK, here's another way of thinking of it. The other phrase we use to describe it is the '*triple combinado*', the combined triple. It's a triple because there are three full somersaults in it, see. One backwards, and two sideways. But we say it is 'combined' because they're not successive, like in an ordinary triple. You're doing the two sideways twists simultaneously with the backwards somersault. Get it?'

'Yes, I think so.' I tried to imagine it, but all I could see was Gordo, a white and silver blur, spinning formlessly through the dark. 'Any luck?'

'Nah, not yet,' he shook his head. 'I've got the three triples worked out, that part was relatively easy. It's holding the catch at the other end that's the problem. I keep falling into the net. But I will, don't you worry.' Smiling, he cracked his finger joints at me. 'I promise you, one day I will.'

Gustavo Bell's was slim and dark like his cousins. He had the classic trapeze flyer's physique, broad shouldered but slight, and was about my height, just five feet two inches. I guessed him to be about my age, too, or perhaps just a year or two older, in his early thirties. Gustavo said little, and smiled much. He brought presents with him for his little cousins, thoughtful but unostentatious. He sat around until late in Vicky's kitchen camper; obediently ate the *pollo en mole* which she had prepared in celebration for him; listened gracefully to Rolando's stories. He wore a leather jacket, kid-brown and shiny, of the finest and most expensive European leather, but apart from this one garment, anyone newly arrived at the circus would have found nothing to distinguish him particularly from anyone else.

And yet Gustavo bore about him an aura of almost unbearable glamour. Its quality was quite unlike anything else that I have ever come across, since it lay in nothing that he either did, or said, or possessed – but in something completely external. It lay in what he *knew*, and in the things he had seen, with Kröne and other circuses; in all the famous artistes he had worked with, in all the great acts he had seen, in all the fair cities and capitals he had ever passed through. He arrived in our little circus, with its shabby caravans, rat-infested *terrenos* and dwindling audiences, like a meteorite, so glowing and other-worldly that his very success, while invisible, seemed imprinted into his skin, his hands, his hair, incandescent as fairy dust.

The weather grew worse. Not only was it cold, but the rains had started now too. What would begin as a brilliant morning, with bright sun and blue skies, would turn in a matter of minutes into a deluge. On one particularly cold day the rain turned to hail, which sprang and clattered off the sloping red and white tarpaulin roof of the Big Top like frozen moth-balls, piling up in snowy drifts on the ground beneath. Inside, the Big Top was a shambles. Despite the extra layers of sawdust Chillón put down to soak up the worst of it, streams of water trickled everywhere, growing into puddles too big even to jump across. Everyone slipped and skidded in the mud, and for the first time that night I saw Martinelli drop one of his juggling balls. He told me later that even the ring had got wet and had put him off balance.

The only person who was immune to all this was Gustavo. He walked around the circus camp, a leather-jacketed demi-god, his boots still spotless. The boys followed him everywhere with adoring eyes.

Gustavo often went to sit in with them, to watch while they practised, and it was here that I found him one day. He was sitting in one of the back rows, one boot over his knee, his arms resting languidly over the backs of the chairs on either side of him. Above us Mundo was coaching Ricky and Gordo. In the empty Big Top the ropes of the trapeze squeaked rhythmically; their voices sounded above us, thin and far-away.

I sat down on the seat next to Gustavo.

'It must be quite a change to see them like this, no?'

He smiled.

'When I went away they were just little boys.' He shook his head. 'They used to watch me and my brother practising. I can see them now, sitting here and looking up at us with these big, wide-open eyes.' He made a movement with his hands. 'And now I get back and find that they are throwing the triple without even blinking.'

We watched as Ricky put some fresh chalk on his hands. He swung out on the trapeze, once, twice, before spinning outwards, his body curling through the air towards Mundo's waiting hands. He connected, but clumsily, and Mundo couldn't hold him. Ricky fell, bouncing but unhurt, into the net below.

'What do you think?'

'He's good, actually.' He nodded. 'They both are.'

'In different ways though?'

'Yes. Ricky's the stronger, I think.'

'And Gordo?'

'Oh yes, Gordo.' Gustavo looked up contemplatively. 'Let's watch this, shall we?'

Now it was Gordo's turn to fly. I admired both Ricky and Jorge Morales's work on the trapezes, but it had always seemed to me that Gordo brought an effortlessness to his art which by comparison made everyone else look laboured, clumsy even. We watched as he launched himself into the space between the two trapezes, slim as a will-o-the-wisp and twice as fast. He spun neatly, one-two-three times, head and ankles tucked into his body, before stretching out again with perfect timing to catch Mundo's hands. They swung together, once, twice, before Gordo twisted back, catching his own trapeze again and landing noiselessly, feet neatly together, on the tiny perspex platform opposite. The whole movement was fluid, elegant; perfect in its symmetry and grace.

'And Gordo?' I was anxious to hear Gustavo's opinion. 'I've always thought Gordo has something extra . . . I don't know how to describe it.'

'Oh yes,' Gustavo nodded thoughtfully, 'he has something, definitely. That extra something, as you call it. He is beautiful to watch, no?'

'Yes. Every time.' I nodded. 'He says you're going to take him back to Kröne with you?'

'He does, does he?' Gustavo looked amused. 'Well, one day, maybe.'

'He says he's ready.'

'He probably is, professionally. But he's so young. He can have no idea of what it means to leave his country, his family. It's a big step. Here he is – how shall I say it? – the king pin. Over there – *nada*!' he shrugged, 'He is nothing. No one. And that's tough.'

If he said anything more I don't remember what it was, because at that moment an unusual movement caught my eye through the raised tarpaulin walls of the Big Top. It was Omar. He had his back to me and was running towards Rolando's caravan. From the awkward way that he was moving it looked as if he was carrying something heavy, although I could not see what it was. As he manoeuvred his way in through the door he turned just fractionally towards me. I saw then that he was holding a body in his arms.

It was Mara.

SIXTEEN

Everything has a second or third face, and our
poetic task is to find the hidden dimensions of
things and events.

ISABEL ALLENDE, *Latin America: The Writer's
Journey* (edited by Gregory Price)

'It's her lungs.' Omar looked grave. 'Pneumonia, the doctor says.
That's what he told me, anyway.'

'Pneumonia?' I have always associated pneumonia with tem-
peratures and fevers and aching limbs, but Mara had none of these
things. 'It's rather sudden, isn't it?'

'That's what comes of not wrapping up properly after your
shower.' Vicky looked down sourly at her daughter, wiping her
oniony hands on her apron. She had no time for illness. Mara lay
in the big bed at the end of the caravan in which Rolando and
Vicky and Belén usually slept, her face, looking pinched and white,
peering out over the black and white zebra stripes of the coverlet.
At first I wondered why she did not speak, then I realized – she
was in too much pain. She closed her eyes; a single tear drifted
slowly down her cheek.

I went outside with Omar.

'What happened exactly?'

'This morning she started to get this pain in her chest, for no
reason particularly. It got worse and worse, until eventually she
was in so much pain . . .' Omar looked pale '. . . that it became
unbearable. It all happened so quickly. I decided to take her to
the doctor, but she couldn't even walk. I had to carry her into the
taxi. When I picked her up she fainted,' he said bluntly. 'I've never
seen anyone faint with pain before.'

'Pneumonia. Are you sure that's all the doctor said?'

'The x-rays showed that there was some kind of shadow on her lung. He said he thought it was a bubble of blood. Something like that.' He shook his head. 'Whatever it is, it's giving her a *lot* of pain.'

'A bubble of blood?'

It didn't seem very likely somehow. Omar shrugged.

'Whatever it is, if you ask me it's these *terrenos* which are doing her in.' He looked around the desolate piece of wasteland beyond the circus camp, with its graffiti-etched walls and the abandoned building, iron girders sprouting forlornly from the upper stories like the antennae of some monstrous urban insect. There's so much shit around in these places. Not just here, but in every *terreno* that we have been in. Remember Lomas Verdes? And when I say shit . . .' he shook his head again, '*hombre*, I don't mean just any old rubbish, although there's plenty of that too, I really mean *shit*. It dries up in the sun, and then the wind comes along and blows it right back in your face again, *comprendes*? That's what we're breathing in every day, most like. You, me, Mara. Even the kids.'

Behind him I could see Lely, Tintin and Alejandro racing through the tall grasses behind their caravan, chasing butterflies in the sun. It was a pretty scene, there were even some flowers, yellow and white ones shivering delicately against a navy sky. But I knew better now. I did not need Omar to tell me the thousand and one uses of a piece of prime open scrub land such as this one. Rats the size of cats roamed the undergrowth – I had seen them – and there was a rumour going round lately that a few nights ago a girl from the town had been raped here by some local boys, only a few yards from our caravans.

'Have they given her something for the pain?'

'The doctor gave me a prescription.' Omar pulled out a piece of paper from his jacket. 'I'd better go and get this right now.'

'You do that. I'll sit with her until you get back.'

I have never seen anyone in real pain before, far less someone I love, and I wish never to, ever again. I sat by Mara's bed that afternoon and held her hand while she screamed, literally screamed, in agony. The painkillers which Omar brought back from the chemist had some effect; the pain came on in spasms now. One minute she would be speaking quite normally, the next she would be doubled up again, tears running down her cheeks, howling for it to end. Once or twice I wondered if she would survive it. For some reason I did not trust the doctor's diagnosis; which meant, if I was right, that none of us really knew what was wrong with her.

She looked so very frail lying there. I smoothed her hair away from her face, I let her squeeze my hands until my bones cracked, and yet I knew she could not see me. As the pain consumed her I saw her eyes cloud over and her face take on the dazzled look of a person shipwrecked, out of reach of any of us now, but still clinging precariously to some small piece of herself, as though her very survival depended on it.

We had been in Toluca over two weeks now and it was time to leave. Rolando had found another *terreno* no more than half an hour's drive away, in a small town called Santiago Tianguistenco. It would be an easy move, but I still worried about Mara. Even though she had been so much better over the last few days, I wondered if she was really fit to travel just yet.

Rolando was reassuring. 'It will be good to get her out of Toluca. It's very high here, higher than Mexico City, and very cold.'

'Don't I know it.'

The nights had continued to be freezing.

'We thought of taking her back to Mexico City, you know, Vicky and me. To my mother's house.' Rolando had been beside himself with worry about Mara, whom he adored. 'But she's strong, my daughter. She'll be fine now. You mustn't worry.'

'If you say so.'

'You wanted to go *en gira*, go on tour with the circus, right, Katty? And you see' he waved his arms expansively – 'I have arranged it for you.' He made it sound like a personal compliment. Luckily (perhaps unluckily) I knew Rolando too well by now to be wholly taken in. His business arrangements, I knew from long experience, were conducted like some ancient Greek mystery in which Rolando was ever the sole initiate.

'Small towns and villages from here to Acapulco, just like I always said,' his silky voice rasped at me seductively. 'We'll be at the beach by Christmas, what do you say? White beaches. Sea air. Coconuts. And there are some great cabarets in Acapulco,' he winked. 'Girls and stuff. You know. Dancers.' He traced a licentious figure in the air. 'I'll take you both there, you and Tommy. How about it?'

'Sounds good to me,' I smiled.

Rolando, *pinche* Rolando, always knew how to cheer me up. He knew as well as I did that by Christmas we would be gone, but neither of us had the heart to mention it.

By Christmas we would be gone. The words had a hollow, faraway cadence, like listening to the sound of the sea through a shell. It was an idea which I understood in my mind, but not in my heart. It was months now since I had had any kind of life outside the circus; the outside world seemed a remote place, all shadows and forgotten etiquette. What should I talk about? How should I behave? I would no longer be Katty, the exotic *Inglesa*, the friend of Mara and Karina, riding on Hannibal in the parades, bedecked in spangles and a red feather boa; but just plain old Kate again, another dusty traveller in a T-shirt and jeans. The same old daughter, same old sister, same old friend.

And yet would I really be the same? I thought not. I had not changed in any conventional sense. I still looked the same, acted the same, spoke the same languages (with a few of Rolando and Güera's embellishments). And yet I knew that somewhere, in some hidden part of myself, I had undergone my own metamorphosis.

In Mexico there was a time when I believed that I had lost my faith in God. Later I realized that it was not so much a loss of faith, as the fact that I had been looking for Him in the wrong places. In Mexico I discovered a God who was infinitely vaster and more mysterious than I had ever believed possible; a God who transcended all of man's beliefs.

For the Indians of the northern Mexican desert, the peyote cactus is worshipped as a god: its hallucinogenic properties have the power to transport a man from the real world into the realm of the divine. This sense of the divine was part of Mexico's hidden language, the magical language I had spent so long trying to understand. It encompassed all things, both good and evil, light and dark. In Mexico, God was the Cora's sacred cactus bulb, the Virgin of Guadalupe, even the dark angel of the Mono Blanco,

Adonai. But God was also in ordinary things. God was in ordinary men and women – capricious, cruel, generous to a fault – in their community and in their daily struggle for survival. In their lives.

The day we left Toluca was one of those cloudless days which sometimes follow particularly bitter nights in high places, with that thick, translucent light, clear and rich as honey, and navy blue skies. I sat a little way off from the circus camp on one of the concrete blocks near the abandoned building site, writing up my diary and warming myself in the sun. It was market day. An Indian woman in a cotton sunhat picked her way through the scrub carrying a bundle of flowers, white dahlias, flowers for the dead; then one of Toluca's bird men, a *pajarero*, balancing a tower of singing cages strapped to his back.

The *chamacos* were loading up the last of the Big Top, the bundles of red and white tarpaulin, guy ropes and wooden benches, on to the trucks. Under Chillón's supervision they heaved and sweated, lowering the two white towers with ropes. Later, they too sat in the sun beside the empty circle, smoking cigarettes and talking: Ilish, with a pink paisley handkerchief tied over his head like a pirate; Chivo, one of the drivers; Gato, the soundman; Junian, a new *chamaco*, with his woolly, half-grown moustache and a wife (or so he claimed) so pitifully shy and young I guessed her to be no more than about thirteen.

Once the tent was down I knew that most of them had nowhere to go until it was erected again at the next *terreno*. Most of them had no caravan, and probably could not afford to rent rooms in town, and so for the most part they slept in the Big Top itself, or in the box-office, or even in the back of one of the empty trucks, wrapping themselves up against the bitter nights in any spare lengths of tarpaulin or circus matting which they could find.

For once I knew exactly how they felt, for I had no place of my own now. The day before, Tom had left the circus to drive back up to Texas with our caravan (Mexico had proved unexpectedly expensive and we needed the money from its sale to finance the next six months of our travels.) Even so, I was luckier than they. Vicky had offered to have me to stay for the extra week that I would be here by myself. 'Estás en tu casa,' was all she had said.

'You are in your own home.' The phrase is well-known Mexican *plaisanterie*, but I knew that she would not have made an offer she didn't mean.

Dismantling the Pop-up had been a sad business. In just a few months we had acquired an extraordinary collection of stuff. Crockery, saucepans, buckets, a drinking-water *garafon*, the chemical loo so despised by Mara; a squashy pink dog (I still have it) won at a fair one afternoon and bequeathed to me by Antonino; various small presents, cards and half a vast, iced cake left over from the surprise party which Mara had organized in the Big Top on my birthday the week before; and last of all a collection of circus memorabilia by now nearly as extensive as Gordo's – books, magazines, posters, programmes, old ticket stubs, even some wonderful 1950s Circo Bell's writing paper left over from more affluent days which, amidst a frieze of clowns and elephants and a battalion of red and white striped tents marching heroically into the horizon, still bore the wistful logo 'El Espectáculo Más Famoso de América'.

Jovita eyed our packing-up with interest. When she wasn't peering out at us from her hidey-hole in the wardrobe, she was making unaccountable trips to and from Vicky's kitchen camper past our front door, lingering to exchange weather forecasts and the latest *telenovela* gossip with Rosalinda, Güera, Antonino, whoever happened to be nearest our doorstep at the time, her hooded eyes flickering over their shoulders all the while trying to decipher the movements within.

'For God's sake,' Tom said after a while, 'ask her in. I can't stand it another minute.'

So Jovita came in for coffee. Our things were already stacked in piles: Tom's gear, my gear, bits and pieces to be thrown or given away. We did not have much to dispose of, really, but what little there was I had already earmarked: the *garafon* was to go to Vicky; the rest of the cake to the children; my Advent calendar to Luis's daughters, Lupita and Jacaira; my spare blanket to eleven-year-old Ernesto, the latest runaway to join the circus *chamacos*; the crockery and kitchen utensils, including the chemical loo should they want it, to Olga and Ilish to help them on their way to setting up a proper home of their own.

Jovita spotted the crockery immediately.

'You'll be taking that with you, I suppose?' She made a vague gesture with her hand towards the pile on the bed.

'No. We won't be needing any of that anymore, Jova,' I said sadly.

When I looked at the little pile of cups and plates I almost felt like crying. Tom and I had bought them together in the Aurera supermarket on our very first day with the circus.

'Really?' Jovita's unconcern was magnificent. She gave a tremendous sniff. 'Pretty . . .' picking up one of the cups and holding it to her ear, she flicked at it ruminatively with her fingernail; the blue and white china pinged dully, '. . . if you like that kind of thing.' She sniffed again, a little louder this time, and made a jerking motion with her chin. 'You selling, then?'

'No.' I laughed. 'Actually I was going to give most of it away. The kitchen stuff, that is. To Olga and Ilish.'

'You're going to *give* it away?' Jovita sounded startled. 'Well, if you're going to *give* it away . . . To Olga and Ilish?' She brought herself up sharply. 'What do they want with it? They haven't even got a caravan.' Her tone was accusing. The perennial chaplet of curlers, round and plump as sausage rolls, framed her monkeyish old woman's face.

'Well, no, they haven't.' I was beginning to feel embarrassed. 'That's the point. They're a young couple, you know, just starting out. Look, Jovita, if there's anything you like the look of, please . . .' I motioned towards the bed.

'You mean it?' She brightened immediately. 'You mean I can have these cups?' Her fingers closed over the blue and white flowers.

'Claro que sí. Of course you can.'

I watched as she tucked them away into her jacket. 'And these plates, too? Part of the set, aren't they?'

I thought of them joining her little clutch of possessions in the wardrobe, the old black and white TV set, the one smart suit and blouse, the gaudy image of the Virgin of Guadalupe, swaddled in ribbons and plastic lace.

'Please, we'd like you to have them.'

Her pockets clanking, Jovita scuttled off, well pleased with her morning's work.

Although it was hardly great riches that we were distributing (a second-hand port-a-potty is one of the less glamorous gifts it has ever been in my power to dispense) more than anyone else I was glad to be able to help Olga and Ilish.

On a daily basis I did not see very much of either of them. Olga was naturally retiring and of a serious turn of mind, more interested in her books than in talking bawdy in the wardrobe with the rest of us. And yet, ever since she had confided her story to me, of her unhappy life and how she had run away to the circus for love, I had felt a particular affection for her . . . and no small curiosity for the demon lover who had enticed Snow White out of the school playground and into the circus *demi-monde*, from the innocence of gym-slip and knee socks into a spangled bikini, false eye-lashes and ostrich plumes.

On the face of it, it seemed impossible that these two should ever have come together. Olga, so respectable, so prim, with her modestly downcast eyes and her pale and frothy clothes, more suited to some Southern belle debutante than to the harsh life of the circus *chamacos*. And then Ilish. Wild Ilish, with his drugs and his booze and his extravagant good looks. The *güero loco*, the mad *güero*, they used to call him.

I often watched them together. I believe that everyone has a secret life, but this was beyond anything I have ever known. For who could ever know what passion, what erotic delirium he must have stirred in her? Who would ever know what exquisite derangement of the senses could have persuaded a girl of Olga's sensibilities to parade, semi-naked, in all the vulgarity of a cabaret costume, around a circus *pista* every night? Of all the improbable details in little Olga's bizarrely improbable life, this always seemed to me the strangest.

The facts about Ilish were few. When I first came to the circus no one knew much about him, except that he came from the north, from Tamaulipas, and had been working the circus circuit more or less continuously since, as a young boy, he had run away from home. Later, odd details began to filter through. Like Olga's, his life was full of the kind of baroque misfortunes normally only found in Mexican soap operas. Perhaps it was one of the bonds between them. His mother had died when he was a baby. Then, when he was just seven the rest of his family – his father and eight brothers – were all killed in a car accident. Ilish's father was a man of property, leaving him two houses and several plots of land, and Ilish should have grown up to a considerable inheritance, but like the poor boy in the fairy tale his entire fortune was stolen by scheming relatives. By the age of eight he was out on the streets, penniless and alone.

I sometimes used to think that Ilish must have been a changeling, so un-Mexican were his looks. He had a pale angular face, and slanting eyes like something from a Greek icon. The effect was both hungry and aristocratic, a composition more fitted to an Eastern European, a Slav or a Cossack, than a Latin. He was rather taller than the other *chamacos*, and bore himself differently. As a sign of his otherness he was given to wearing talismanic items of clothing. The latest was a wide-brimmed black hat, austere and Spanish in design, which he wore about the place with an air of enigmatic *élan*.

Despite Olga's efforts, I knew that Ilish still did drugs. According to Antonino, who smoked the occasional joint with him, their effects on him were always unpredictable. Marijuana, which normally has a calming effect, sent him into a state of wild frenzy. If he got his hands on any pills, he would always pop the lot, regardless of their strength, often mixing them at random with booze, coke, crack, whatever he could get his hands on. Late at night I had seen him sometimes, disorderly and glassy-eyed, trying to find his way back to Olga's bed. They said that when he was younger he had done time. Had killed a man. No one knew the details.

Although on a day-to-day basis I knew Ilish quite well by now (he would often help us with practical details, like connecting our electricity supply and so forth) I was also aware of his reputation, and had always hesitated to approach him on any more intimate basis. Now, the holiday feeling induced by the dismantling of the Big Top, the sun, the sense of time running out, made me bold. When the other *chamacos* drifted off to their various jobs, I went and sat next to him. After a while we got talking.

'When I was just eighteen,' Ilish told me, 'I was sent to prison for a crime I did not commit: a kidnapping. The police had to find a culprit. They could not find the real one, so they found me instead and I was sent to the *penal*, which is for really serious crimes. Things had been rough before, but it was there that the *güero loco*, the mad güero, was born, the *güero loco* who is known in every circus from Chihuahua to Chiapas. That place was the nearest thing to hell that I have ever known.'

Sitting beside the deserted camp, I remember the sound of his voice, surprisingly gentle, and the way the sun warmed our faces like a summer's afternoon.

'It was in the *penal* that I first started the drinking, the drugs. I was not like that before, you know, but inside – well, inside that shit is the only thing you've got. I did everything, every pill, every powder, every weed you can imagine. I was heading down, down into perdition. I had been sentenced to five years of hell for something I did not do and, even though I was still so young, I felt that my life was already over. Do you know how that feels?' Ilish turned to me. His voice was light and sweet, but there was a shadow in his face which I had never seen before. 'Do you know how that feels? To be not yet twenty – and to be dead already?'

He lit a new cigarette.

'Then one day after I had been inside a few weeks, I remembered something, a strange thing which had happened to me the year before. I was still living up in the north at the time, in one of those small towns up by the border, and I was walking down the street one day when I saw these guys trying to steal this gringo's car. To this day I don't know why I did it. I just rushed in there. There were three of them' – he paused – 'but I was a good fighter, right? I'd learnt to fight when I was just a kid living rough on the streets. Or maybe I was just feeling a little crazy that day, who knows? Anyway, before I knew it I'd laid two of these guys out, with my bare fists. The third was so scared he just legged it.

'This gringo was pretty impressed. So impressed, in fact, that he asked if he could buy me dinner that night. So he takes me to this fancy place – all white tablecloths and shit. I'd never been anywhere like that in my life. Over dinner the gringo tells me that he's a business man, from *el otro lado*, from the other side, of course, from Chicago, if I remember right. A rich son-of-a-bitch. His name was Julian, but apart from that he didn't tell me a whole lot about himself. He was too busy asking me questions about myself.

'He wanted to know everything. About me, about my family, about my whole life. And so I told him – about my mother dying, and then the car accident which killed my father and brothers. I even told him about my father's sisters taking everything, and about my life on the streets. But what interested him most – after the fact that I had no relatives, or none who cared about me anyway – was about the fighting. He asked me all these questions, like where did I learn to fight? Had I ever had any formal training? Was I the kind of person who provoked fights, or did I just do it to protect myself? What kind of things made me aggressive? A lot of weird stuff.

'Then he asked me – very casual, like – if I had ever thought of fighting for money? I said, "No way." I was a little crazy sometimes, maybe, but not that crazy. I don't know if he was going to make me some kind of offer then or not, but suddenly he stopped. He seemed satisfied with my story, and that was it. When he came to leave he gave me his card, and said that he owed me one – you know, because of the car. If ever I was in trouble, he said, whatever it was, I was not to hesitate to call him. And that was the last I saw of him.

'Anyway, when I remembered this I thought, what the hell. I sat down and I wrote him this letter telling him what had happened to me. I don't think I ever really expected to hear anything from him, but about a week after I sent the letter, for Christ's sake, this guy, Julian, actually *turns up* at the prison. What's more, he didn't come to see me, not straightaway anyway. Instead, he goes straight to see the prison governor and they made a deal.

'The deal was this: the governor agreed to reduce my sentence from five years to three years. He also agreed to a training programme, to take place on the premises, and as many leaves of absence as were necessary. In return I was to become one of Julian's prizefighters.

'That was his game, see. Fighting. I suppose I should have guessed, but I had no idea that a scene like that even existed. Anyway, according to Julian, I was a natural. All I needed was a little encouragement, a little refining in my methods and, according to him, we'd all be rich. The governor, of course, was on a percentage. Easy money, or that's what it looked like to them. Each night there was a fight Julian came to fetch me from the *penal* and we'd cross over to the other side . . .'

'You mean they actually let you cross the border?'

'Sure.' Ilish shrugged. He lit a second cigarette from the butt of his first. 'The guy, Julian, he was rich like I said. And in this country' – he made a gesture, rubbing his fingers back and forth over his thumb – 'with money, anything's possible.'

Smoke from his cigarette trickled up between his fingers. He had long fingers, an artist's hands. I could not imagine him as a fighter at all.

'And so what about the fights? What were they? Like boxing matches or something?'

'*Boxing* matches?' Ilish gave a hard little smile. 'Na. In boxing there are *rules*, aren't there? A referee. Someone to pull the other guy off if things get a little rough. When I say I could fight, I mean, I could *fight*.'

I don't know how often he talked about this strange episode in his life, but a change came over him as he reminisced. This was no longer the Ilish that I knew, carefree, a little crazy sometimes. This was another, darker Ilish.

'The fights that Julian got me into were illegal, even in Mexico. No gloves, no rules. That's why there was so much money in them. The one to win was the man who left the other guy unconscious on the floor. Or dead.' Ilish's eyes narrowed. 'I never killed a man in those fights myself, but I saw others do it. Enough to know that it was just a matter of time.' He shivered. 'Sometimes, even now, it still scares me to get into a fight. In the *penal* it was different because I knew the guys in there could *aguantar*; they were like me and I knew they could hack it. But outside' – he jerked his head towards the little semi-circle of caravans – 'Gordo and Ricky, know what I mean? All these little boys who think they're so tough.' He held his palms up to his face and regarded them dispassionately. 'I could tear them apart with my bare hands.'

For a while Ilish sat just smoking. He was silent for so long that I thought he had finished, but after a few minutes he went on with his story.

'You wouldn't believe the sums of money that used to change hands. No wonder the governor agreed to Julian's deal. But it wasn't only him; at the prison they all used to bet on me, and I didn't used to do so badly out of it myself. Julian used to pay me eight hundred dollars a fight – and that was whether I won or lost. But I always won, didn't I? Like I said, it was what I was good at. It was the *only* thing I was good at,' he added with a trace of bitterness. 'In three years I only ever lost three fights. I was famous for it. Everyone knew me: the *güero loco*.

'From the moment I started fighting my life changed. I was well looked after. No one could touch me. No one could lay a finger on me, there was too much at stake. One guy tried it on once – a *marica*, a homosexual, know what I'm saying? So I opened the window on the third floor where my cell was, and I just threw him out.' He drew on his cigarette. 'That's right,' he exhaled again, slowly. 'I just threw him out. It killed him, of course.' He stared, musing, into the middle distance. 'You probably heard that I killed a man?'

I nodded. 'Something like that, yes.'

'Well, now you know. I killed a man, but still no one could touch me. There was too much at stake. So. I had power now, and money, too, lots of money. I had everything I could possibly want. My cell was well decorated. I could have as many drugs as I knew how to take. Before a fight Julian would ask me what I wanted – women, drink, drugs . . .' He snapped his fingers suddenly, making me jump. 'Whatever would make me fight better. Once there was this English girl who I liked. Real classy. I often used to see her at the fights. Julian got her for me too – I never asked how.'

'And having a woman made you fight better?'

'Sometimes,' he shrugged. 'Sometimes it was drugs. Or drink. Whatever.'

'But how could you fight someone just for the sake of it, when you'd never even set eyes on them before?'

It was a woman's question, I knew, but I had to ask it all the same. Ilish was silent for a long time, thinking.

'I guess I'm just naturally aggressive,' he said eventually.

'Yes, but to beat someone unconscious just for the hell of it, surely it needs something more than that?' I floundered in these unknown waters. 'Doesn't it?'

'No *comprendes* – you don't understand, do you? I never thought of the person. I just thought of winning.' The cigarette had burnt right down to his fingertips, and a yellowish stain was spreading around his knuckles. 'Like I said, I *had* to win. I was programmed to win.'

'What do you mean, programmed?'

'It's like I told you. They had a lot invested in me. Julian, the governor, everyone.'

'It was the money, then?'

He made an impatient gesture with his hand.

'I was always paid. Eight hundred dollars whether I won or lost. But if I lost I got something extra. Ha!' Ilish laughed. It was a tired sound. 'If I lost, they used to beat me. The guards, I mean, Julian instructed them to do it. Not that they needed much instructing, they were laying their bets just like everyone else. They used to strap me down and then beat me with sticks, across my legs, my head, stomach . . .' He blinked. 'Sometimes I could not stand up for days afterwards. And you ask why I only lost three fights in three years. Well, that's why. I didn't dare not to win.'

Santiago Tianguistenco, a small town of churches and ragged children and telegraph wires, was the last *terreno* I visited with Circo Bell's. *Tianguis* is an Indian word meaning market, and the *terreno* hired by Rolando turned out to be on a piece of ground usually used by the travelling salesmen who came into town once a week with their pots and pans, their crates of oranges, their incense and bundles of herbs. The usual debris which always had to be cleared up and burnt before the Big Top could be put up contained within it a sweet-smelling humus of fruit peelings, rotting avocados and the blackened husks of over-ripe bananas.

Those last few days had a strange, dislocated quality to them. I was still staying with Rolando's family, but our numbers were sadly depleted. Mara was no longer with us. Just when everyone had thought she was getting better she had given a tremendous cough, and was instantly in such crippling pain that she could hardly breathe. Her body temperature dropped alarmingly. Vicky and Omar, who were with her at the time, wrapped her up in a blanket and took her straight to the doctor in Toluca, but when he could not be found they decided not to take any chances. They returned to the circus, commandeered Mundo's car and drove her at once to Mexico City, where a hospital consultant diagnosed not pneumonia at all, but a lung infection.

As Rolando had assured me, Mara was strong. With the right medication she showed signs of recovery almost immediately, but it was decided that for the time being it would be better for her not to come back to the circus. I spoke to her once or twice at Doña Elena's house from a pay phone in town. She sounded a little wan, but cheerful.

'We miss you. Things aren't the same here without you.'

'I miss you all too.'

Her voice sounded faint. The pay phone was in a haberdashery shop, and I had to struggle to hear her over the sound of three women arguing over the price of a delivery of new wool.

'Oly's going crazy. Without you here, she's having to do everything on her own.'

Vicky had also stayed on at Doña Elena's to look after Mara, and had kept Belén with her.

'Tell her not to fight with Gordo.'

'Estás loca? Are you mad? What else would they do all day?'

'What about my acts?'

'Oly's been roped into that too. She and Brissel are sharing. One night on, one night off. They're not bad, actually.'

'Where's my father?'

'Quién sabe?' That circus refrain again. 'Who knows? I thought he was with you.' I smiled into the hand-piece. 'What do you think? Acapulco maybe?'

Mara laughed. 'Of course. Acapulco by Christmas, wasn't it?'

'That's what he always tells me.'

I heard her laugh again.

'Mara?'

'Yes?'

'I'm leaving for the Yucatán in four days.'

'Yes. I know.'

'I won't be seeing you then?'

'It doesn't look like it, Katty.'

'Well . . .' Suddenly I found that I could not go on with this conversation. 'Look, I'll ring you, OK? I'll write.'

'Sí.' At the other end of the line Mara's voice crackled lightly. 'No te vayas a perder, Katty.'

What she had said was, don't go and lose yourself, Katty. I knew what she meant. Don't be a stranger. Don't lose touch. I realized then how unlikely it was that I would ever see her again.

'I won't.'

How could I? Mi hermana. My sister. I hung up.

Strangely, it was Oly who made the next few days bearable.

'Are you going to cry when you leave us on Sunday, Katty?' she would say, stretching her Cabbage Patch doll eyes at me. Behind the veneer of innocence, I could see them glittering with suppressed naughtiness.

'Of course not.'

'Oh, yes you will, you know.'

'No, I won't.'

'Oh yes, you will. You're the blubbing type. I can tell.'

'I am not!'

'It's quite all right, you know. Jacqueline always cries.' Jacqueline was Rolando's eldest daughter from his first marriage who had recently been to visit the circus with her husband, Tony. 'I can see you now, just the same, *boo-hoo-hoo*.'

Sometimes she would try another tack. We were eating lunch together one day in Vicky's kitchen camper when I looked up to find her staring at me with a stricken expression over her plate of frijoles.

'Only three more days to go,' she said with a voice of doom. 'I don't know how I can bear it . . .' her voice cracked.

'Piss off, Oly.'

'You think I'm joking, don't you?' Her voice rose histrionically. 'Well, I'm not, I'm not. Look! A real tear . . .' She pointed to one of her saucer eyes, and there, sure enough, was a single, trembling droplet.

'Only one mingy tear?' I helped myself to more beans. 'Better not squeeze any harder or your eyeball might fall out.'

'Damn.' Oly shovelled more beans into a tortilla, biting into her taco hungrily. 'Really thought I had you that time.'

Rolando, Scarlet Pimpernel-like, came and went, his movements known only to himself. Sometimes he would turn up in the caravan in the middle of the night, snatch a few hours' sleep and then be up, dressed and gone again the next morning before the rest of us had even stirred. With Mara, Vicky and Belén still with Doña Elena in Mexico City, for the most part it was just the three of us – Oly, Gordo and myself – living in the caravan.

The nights continued to be clear and extremely cold. One morning we found Belén's goldfish frozen solid in its bowl; Gordo discovered it stiff and floating beneath a sheet of ice. I took to sleeping with Oly in Rolando and Vicky's bed. These days it was about the only place in the entire circus where I could get properly warm. I almost dreaded one or other of them getting back and the time when I would have to return alone to the kitchen camper which, even with Mara's sheepskin, became icy as soon as the sun went down.

Gordo and Oly fought, as they always did, but the very fact that there were now so many fewer of us cramped into the caravan's tiny spaces brought with it a new sense of calm. In the daytime Gordo was much occupied with practising his new jump, the *triple combinado*, and did not have as much time as usual to torment his sister. I enjoyed the evenings best, when a weary truce existed between them, and all three of us would huddle together on the bed, wrapped up in blankets, watching Gordo's circus videos, the film *Trapeze* and recordings of Billy Smart's and the quirky Magic Hat Circus.

My last day with the circus was a Sunday. It also turned out to be the day of the *homenaje*, or homage ceremony to the two trapeze cousins, Carlos and Gustavo Bell's. This turned out to have been organized not by the circus, as you might have expected, but by the local *ayuntamiento*, or town hall. When I asked Omar about it, he looked disdainful.

'It's just some *tonteria*, that's all. Some nonsense cooked up by Rolando.'

'Really?' I was surprised by his reaction. 'It sounds rather wonderful to me. Look at this: 'Homage to Santiago Tianguistenco's most illustrious sons . . .' I read out the flowery Spanish from an invitation that Mundo had given me that morning.

Omar grinned into his bowl of washing-up. 'Don't believe a word of it. It's just Rolando trying to get out of paying his taxes, that's all.'

Very occasionally Omar showed a refreshing impatience with the circus's obsession with itself.

'I'm not sure I see the connection.'

I picked up a tea towel and started to dry the soapy plates.

'Gustavo and Carlos's grandfather came from Santiago Tianguistenco, apparently – sort of helped found it, or that's what they're claiming anyway.' He paused, washing-up brush in hand, as if this should explain everything.

'So?'

'So Rolando goes to the *ayuntamiento* and tells them that Carlos and Gustavo are the world's most famous trapeze artists, and then persuades them to do this *homenaje* number, right?'

'Right.'

'Well, once they've fallen for the whole illustrious sons bit, and are getting to like the idea of a bit of a knees-up, Rolando quickly turns it round and makes it seem like Circo Bell's are doing them a really big favour by coming here at all. He persuades them that it was all their idea in the first place, and what's in it for him? Anyway' – Omar scrubbed at the inside of a saucepan caked with blackened beans – 'the long and short of it is a free *terreno*, and an agreement that they won't have to pay any taxes on any money which the circus makes while it's here.'

'Well, you've got to hand it to him, haven't you.' I could not help laughing. '*Pinche* Rolando.'

Perhaps he was rather better at this kind of thing than I had given him credit for.

The *homenaje* to Gustavo and Carlos Bell's took place that afternoon in the foyer of the Cine Lupita, just behind the main plaza in the centre of town. Neither Omar nor Oly expressed any interest in the proceedings, and so I left them behind and drove there with Mundo and Carmen instead.

Outside the cinema we found a straggling collection of people, most of them from the circus, standing around with the self-conscious, strangulated look of people who are unused to wearing Sunday finery. Gustavo, who had exchanged his leather jacket for a suit, was already there with his brother Carlos, a slightly older and quieter version of himself. Also there were Karina and Gallo; Rosalinda and Juan with Brissel; and Mundo's children Ricky, Pamela, Tintin and Lely. Neither Jorge nor Rolando, whose brainchild the whole thing was, managed to turn up, and Gordo, having been told by his uncle that he should wear a tie for the occasion, disgraced himself by choosing one with a topless woman emblazoned across the front – it belonged, needless to say, to his father.

In the foyer the people from the *ayuntamiento* had arranged a little exhibition, a mixture of old catalogues and press clippings, and a collection of framed photographs of the brothers which I recognized from Doña Elena's house. The *homenaje* itself was very short. There were the usual speeches, someone read out the brothers' CV, and then the two ceremoniously cut a piece of ribbon, declaring the exhibition open. Someone produced trays of sparkling cider. There were more speeches, stories, congratulations.

The highlight of the *homenaje*, though, was not at the Cine Lupita at all, but back at the circus, where Gustavo was to make a special guest appearance on the trapeze that night with Mundo and the boys. I had arranged to leave for Mexico City on the eight o'clock bus, but it left, conveniently, from the very *terreno* where the circus was tented, so as long as the performance was not delayed, I would just about catch their act before I went.

Except for Oly and Karina who had offered to come with me to the bus stop, I had said most of my goodbyes earlier on in the day. After lunch I went to see the elephants for the last time, taking them some sugar cane which I had bought specially in the market. Hannibal snatched hers from me at once, snapping the thick stems greedily with her trunk. I looked up at her little eyes, rimmed with pink, and resisted the impulse to rest my head against her whiskery, dinosaur skin. Luis was nowhere to be seen.

I had always known that the circus was never sentimental about these things, and now, more than ever, it was a relief that it should be so. That evening, with Karina and Oly, I carried my bags into the Big Top. As we sat waiting for the performance to begin I looked around me for the last time. For all Oly's teasing, I was surprised to find that I did not, as I had secretly thought I would, feel like crying at all. Instead, I remembered how I had felt before I left England, when all I had to guide me was an anonymous photograph, bought in Belgrade, of an ageing circus artiste.

'Somewhere out there,' I had said to Tom, turning the picture in my hands, 'is a circus, the circus that we will travel with when we are in Mexico. We don't know who they are, we don't even know their name, but they exist. Already, even now, although they cannot know it, our lives are linked.' And I knew then that if I was not wholly sad that day it was because part of me would never leave Circo Bell's and that, however far away I was, they were part of me now for ever.

I had come to Circo Bell's because I wanted to find out about magic, and yet the circus that I had found was no fantasy world. The circus was real, more brutally real than anything I have ever experienced. Although I knew that living with them had changed me, I have always found it hard to put my finger on exactly how or why. All I know is that there were times when I was with them when I felt that I had never lived before, and that my life was but a pale thing before I knew theirs.

What is magic? A way of thinking, poetic rather than logical. A sense of the sacred. God, even.

Magic cannot be explained or proved in any rational sense, but then again we do not laugh or love or shout or sing only through rational parameters. Magic is the pushing back, in ways which often we do not understand, of the boundaries of our understanding.

That night I watched Gustavo Bell's on the flying trapeze. And of course, just like they said, he was beautiful to watch: he had that special polish, that charisma, which transforms the acrobatics of the trapeze into art. I watched him with pleasure, pleased that I knew enough now to appreciate his skill: the line of his body, the elegance of his movements, the neatness of his tucks.

The act was nearly over now. Both Gustavo and Ricky were down, taking their bows.

'*Vamos*, Katty. It's time to go.' Beside me I felt Karina pulling at my arm. 'Come on, you'll miss the bus.'

As I stood up to go I looked up to the little perspex platform, high in the spotlit roof, to where Gordo was still standing. He caught my eye and smiled, then made a small movement with his hand as if I should stay a minute longer.

'*Vamos*, Katty.' Karina was still pulling at my arm.

'What's he up to?' I hesitated.

'The *triple combinado*,' Oly whispered into my ear. 'You remember, the new jump. Didn't you hear, he's going to try it for real tonight.'

A small crowd, including Rolando and Jorge, had appeared at the *taquilla* entrance to the tent. I saw the *chamacos*, Ilish and José Jaime and Chillón in their blue boiler suits watching him from the wings, their faces turned expectantly up towards the spotlights. The Big Top fell silent. Except for the lonely creak of Mundo's trapeze as he swung above us, there was no other sound in the world. I saw Gordo reach for the chalk and carefully dust his hands in readiness. He moved so slowly that I wondered if he was deliberately delaying the moment. Was he frightened? Nervous? Exhilarated? I could not tell.

At last I saw him reach for his trapeze and, in one fluid movement, launch himself into the void. I had watched him do this so many times, and yet it was as if I had never seen him before. His body, sheathed in white and silver, was as fine and honed as a blade. I watched him swing, once, twice, three times, steadily gaining height, until suddenly he was flying through the air, spinning and tumbling with such speed that for a moment he refracted into pure light, a white and silvery blur, as if I was seeing him through tears. Then his hands came to rest in Mundo's hands at last, and they were swinging together, up, up, up into the Big Top roof.

The circus. My circus. Circo Bell's.

In the end I did go back to Circo Bell's just one more time.

The following May, just a week before we returned to England, Tom and I travelled nearly a thousand kilometres back to the circus from Durango to stand as godparents, *padrinos del lazo*, at Mara and Omar's wedding.

The Big Top was once again tented not so very far from Toluca and Santiago Tianguistenco, my last two *terrenos* with them the previous December. On the day I helped Mara, now fully recovered, to dress, and saw her kneel to receive a blessing from Rolando, my friend and *compadre*.[1]

There were no performances that night. Instead, what felt like the entire Mexican circus world crammed into the Big Top for the wedding party. In our absence we found that there had been some additions to the Circo Bell's players, and some departures, most notably Karina who had gone back to the States to live with her mother, taking Gallo with her; and Ilish and Olga, who having bought a tent with their savings, the first step along the path to setting up their own home, had found jobs with another circus. Pamela had celebrated her fifteenth birthday – although not in Acapulco, as Rolando had once promised her – and had found her first *novio*, Jesús Vasquez, Bruno's dashing cousin from the Circo Hermanos Vasquez. Vanessa and Charlie had been married secretly in Mexico City, and Vanessa was expecting their first child in just a month's time. Antonino and Ramón were still living in La Chuchina. Gordo and Ricky were practising for the quadruple somersault on the trapeze.

Circo Bell's are currently performing somewhere in Mexico, with shows at 6.30 and 8.30 pm Monday to Friday; Saturdays 4.30, 6.30 and 8.30; and Sundays 12.30, 4.30, 6.30 and 8.30.

---

[1] In Mexico, as in other Latin countries, the relationship between a parent and the godparents of their children is formally acknowledged by the title of *compadre* or *comadre*.

Dervla Murphy

One Foot in Laos

'Devotees of Dervla Murphy's rugged style of travel will not be disappointed by this latest book . . . she has written a first class report on political, economic and social change in Laos.'

RICHARD WEST, *Spectator*

Dervla Murphy's 'inner click' – the one that tells her to abandon whatever plans she has made and follow her instinct – leads her to little-known Laos, the most heavily bombarded country in world history (during and after the Vietnam War), from which tourists were excluded until 1990.

Her attempts to trek through the high mountains, far from the motor roads, are repeatedly thwarted for various reasons, both sinister and comic, and after injuring her foot she is forced to buy a Thai manufactured bicycle. But Hare, as she names it, proves less than reliable at more than one crucial moment. Fortunately Dervla finds that the kindly, gentle and welcoming people of Laos more than make up for all her difficulties and their laid-back nature is marvellously infectious.

'A fresh picture of an enigmatic country.'

ANTHONY SATTIN, *Sunday Times*

'A passionate, angry book that chillingly describes a beautiful but benighted country.' *Sunday Tribune*

0 00 655221 8

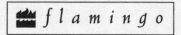

Kevin Rushby

Chasing the Mountain of Light

Across India on the Trail of the Koh-i-Noor Diamond

'One man's remarkable odyssey on the blood-spattered trail of the world's greatest moonstone . . . a story that evokes the fabulous mines of Rider Haggard and the adventures of Sindbad, following a path that at times shimmered tantalisingly in the air like stardust before disappearing into a labyrinthine underground of dealers, smugglers and petty crooks.' *Sunday Times*

Kevin Rushby follows the path of the Koh-i-Noor diamond (now part of the Crown Jewels) through many fascinating corners of India, from the allegedly extinct mines of Golconda in the south to the Mughal palaces of Agra and Delhi in the north, ending in Amritsar, fabled Holy City of the Sikhs.

Along this route he uncovers the illicit diamond trade of today and stumbles across historical characters who owned the diamond – from Babut, the first Mughal, who calmly gave the great jewel away, to Nadir Shah who waged war for it.

Through his travels Rushby finds the heart of Indian culture and discovers the religious symbolism and mysticism behind the passion for diamonds – a journey that is humorous, informative and, as it progresses, increasingly dangerous . . .

0 00 655215 3

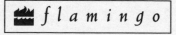 flamingo

City of Djinns

A Year in Delhi

William Dalrymple

WINNER OF THE
1994 THOMAS COOK TRAVEL BOOK AWARD AND
SUNDAY TIMES YOUNG WRITER OF THE YEAR AWARD

Alive with the mayhem of the present and sparkling with the author's ubiquitous, irrepressible wit, *City of Djinns* is the fascinating portrait of a city as has never been attempted before. Meeting an extraordinary array of characters, from the city's elusive eunuchs to the embattled descendants of the great Moguls, from the rich Punjabis to the Sufis and mystics, and investigating the resonances of these people and their modern ways with the India of the past, this is a unique and dazzling feat of research and adventure by one of the finest travel writers of his generation.

'A sympathetic and engaging portrait of this age-old city . . . It is fine, entertaining, well-written stuff, thoroughly researched but with none of the stern academic tone that so many historical profiles adopt. What sustains it, apart from his erudite knowledge of Moslem architecture, medicine, music, military architecture, and arcane religious principles, is Dalrymple's sense of historical adventure. Just open your eyes, he says. If you know how to look, even the empty tombs and abandoned ruins of the past are alive . . . '   *Financial Times*

'Unlike much of modern travel writing *City of Djinns* is informative, learned and funny . . . a lively and sometimes profound book.'
                                                              Economist

'Scholarly and marvellously entertaining . . . A considerable feat.'
                                            DERVLA MURPHY, *Spectator*

ISBN: 0 00 637595 2